William Hickling Prescott

ALSO BY PETER O. KOCH
AND FROM MCFARLAND

*John Lloyd Stephens and Frederick Catherwood:
Pioneers of Mayan Archaeology* (2013)

*Imaginary Cities of Gold: The Spanish Quest
for Treasure in North America* (2009)

The Spanish Conquest of the Inca Empire (2008)

*The Aztecs, the Conquistadors, and the
Making of Mexican Culture* (2006)

*To the Ends of the Earth: The Age of
the European Explorers* (2003)

William Hickling Prescott

The Life and Letters of America's First Scientific Historian

Peter O. Koch

McFarland & Company, Inc., Publishers
Jefferson, North Carolina

LIBRARY OF CONGRESS CATALOGUING-IN-PUBLICATION DATA

Names: Koch, Peter O., 1953– author.
Title: William Hickling Prescott : the life and letters of
America's first scientific historian / Peter O. Koch.
Description: Jefferson, North Carolina : McFarland & Company, Inc.,
Publishers, 2016. | Includes bibliographical references and index.
Identifiers: LCCN 2016015956 | ISBN 9781476665337
(softcover : acid free paper) ∞
Subjects: LCSH: Prescott, William Hickling, 1796–1859. |
Historians—United States—Biography.
Classification: LCC PS2657 .K63 2016 | DDC 907.2/02 [B]—dc23
LC record available at https://lccn.loc.gov/2016015956

BRITISH LIBRARY CATALOGUING DATA ARE AVAILABLE

ISBN (print) 978-1-4766-6533-7
ISBN (ebook) 978-1-4766-2467-9

© 2016 Peter O. Koch. All rights reserved

*No part of this book may be reproduced or transmitted in any form
or by any means, electronic or mechanical, including photocopying
or recording, or by any information storage and retrieval system,
without permission in writing from the publisher.*

On the cover William Hickling Prescott (1796-1859)
(courtesy of Historical Findings and the Library of Congress);
stack of books © 2016 LeitnerR/iStock

Printed in the United States of America

*McFarland & Company, Inc., Publishers
Box 611, Jefferson, North Carolina 28640
www.mcfarlandpub.com*

For Brandon, Jessie, Crystal, Ashley, and Angeline:
The next generation of historians and explorers.

Table of Contents

Introduction   1

1. Puritan Pedigree   13
2. Worldly Views   33
3. Scholarly Pursuits   50
4. Their Catholic Majesties   65
5. Exceeding All Expectations   89
6. Continuing with the Spanish Theme   105
7. A Sudden Interest in Mexico   122
8. The Conquest of Peru   148
9. Philip II   174
10. Growing Health Concerns   205
11. The Final Chapter   218

Chapter Notes   225
Bibliography   235
Index   237

Introduction

To those who presumed to know him well, William Hickling Prescott, following his graduation from Harvard College, appeared to be a young man who was entirely ill-suited for a career as an historian, much less a chronicler of Spain's emergence as the greatest power in the Western world. This aspiring scholar was born to a distinguished Massachusetts family of means that had played a prominent role in the settlement of the colony as well as the defense of Boston during the Revolutionary War. The Prescotts also helped pave the way for the bustling port town of Boston to become the largest city in all of New England. The historian's grandfather, Colonel William Prescott, was hailed by all as a hero of the Battle of Bunker Hill, the first major battle of the Revolutionary War. His father, who was also named William Prescott, was a savvy and highly regarded lawyer who skillfully parlayed his business acumen into a financial fortune large enough to assure that his family would want for nothing. He was endowed with qualities that seemed to ensure his future success—tall, handsome, charming, intelligent, fun-loving, and gregarious—and many were convinced that the young William Hickling Prescott would follow in the footsteps of his father and enter the respected and rewarding field of law.

Thanks to his father's professional and financial success, William H. Prescott was fortunate to attend the finest schools in Salem and Boston. Though a good student, there was little indication of any exceptional ability other than an aptitude for committing lengthy passages to memory. He was, at best, an above average student, despite a learning disability that made it hard for him to comprehend anything beyond basic math—a condition that presented an extremely difficult challenge to his required Harvard College courses in mathematics and geometry. In order to get by in these subjects, the ever-resourceful student committed complex numerical equations to memory. His impressive powers of recall was an ability that he nurtured and refined over the years and which later proved a most valuable asset for his writing career.

William made a number of friends and acquaintances at school, many of whom he would remain in touch with throughout his life. George Ticknor, Arthur Middleton, William Gardiner, Franklin Dexter, John Ware, Jonathan M. Wainwright, and Charles Folsom were among the list of classmates who were drawn to Prescott's quick wit, sense of humor, boundless curiosity, kindness toward others, and generally cheerful nature. The future historian liked to amuse himself with puns, many of which were quite atrocious, and his abrupt outbursts of laughter proved highly infectious—even when no one knew exactly what it was that he seemed to find so amusing. While he eventually learned to control his fits of laughter, William would forever remain an unapologetic punster.

Prescott frequently had trouble staying on task, and in order to compel himself to focus on work he would often make small wagers with friends, betting that a particular assignment would be completed by a specific date. William always made good on these friendly wagers but on the rare occasion when he succeeded in winning a bet he would graciously refuse to accept payment from the losing party. Unfortunately, it took Prescott a very, very long time to accept the fact that he had an aversion to imposed deadlines.

William Hickling Prescott (1796–1859) (courtesy Historical Findings and Library of Congress).

It was near the end of his junior year at Harvard that William suffered a life-altering incident; he was struck in his eye, which happened to be wide open at that precise moment, by a hard crust of bread flung with full force by an unruly student during a melee in the student commons. His left eye, for all intents and purposes, was instantly, and forever, rendered blind. Soon thereafter, Prescott's good right eye was weakened by infection and strain, which made reading a difficult and agonizing proposition. After graduation from Harvard in 1814, William studied law in his father's office but soon had to quit after a bout of acute rheumatism caused his one good eye and his lower extremities to swell to painful extremes, a condition which left him in a very weakened state. Mr. and Mrs. Prescott decided to send their ailing son abroad in the hope that he would benefit from the salubrious climate and the attention of distinguished oculists and physicians.

William sailed first to the Azores, where he rested at the home of Thomas Hickling, his maternal grandfather. Following a noticeable improvement in his health, the young and adventurous traveler felt strong enough to sail to England to consult with prominent doctors regarding his visual impairment. Disappointed to learn that there was no sure remedy for his affliction, William decided to sail across the English Channel to explore some of the well-known historical sites located in France and Italy. He would return to Boston with a newfound interest in European history and the knowledge that he would have to endure unexpected periods where his vision would shift between fair and near blindness. Though plagued by the fear that one day he might suffer permanent loss of his ability to see, Prescott tried his best to remain optimistic; he held out hope that one day his rheumatic affliction would leave his body and permit him full use of his one good eye. But as time wore on, William came to accept the fact that he would have to learn to live with both his recurring ailment and his permanently impaired vision.

Prescott had to reconsider his occupational choices once he realized that his poor eyesight and reoccurring health issues would prevent him from pursuing a career in the fast-paced and demanding fields of either law or business. While money was clearly not an issue, William did, however, concern himself with how he was going to make his own way in the world. Since his inquisitive mind would not allow him to settle for the leisurely life of an idle gentleman, and his character would not permit him to simply rest on the laurels of his accomplished father, William decided that he would devote his time and effort to becoming a man of letters. It was certainly an ambitious choice for someone with such limited eyesight, but Prescott possessed the firmness of purpose needed to achieve such a lofty goal. With great discipline, he dedicated himself to the scholarly study of English, French, Greek and Roman, and Italian classical literature. George Ticknor, a good friend and professor of Spanish languages and literature at Harvard, would encourage William to add Spanish literature to his curriculum, which, in due course, led to his passionate interest in the storied history of Spain.

The life of William Hickling Prescott is an uplifting and inspiring tale of one man's courageous struggle and indomitable will to overcome adversity. William labored under persistent physical handicaps: near blindness in one eye, limited use of his good eye, and an acute rheumatic condition that periodically ravaged his body. In spite of these disabilities, William chose to pursue a literary career. Since his poor eyesight severely restricted his ability to pore over the mountain of books and manuscripts related to his studies, the hopeful scholar often had to rely on family and friends to read them to him. Not wishing to become a burden to those who were close to him while he embarked on his chosen vocation, Prescott decided to employ the services of a private secretary who would spend numerous hours reading to him.

William's impaired vision would compel him to rely heavily on his prodigious powers of recall. At his peak, the Boston historian was able to retain some 60 pages of written material to memory, but in his later years, most noticeably while working on *History of the Reign of Philip the Second, King of Spain*, 40 pages seemed to be his limit, a decrease which he attributed to his advancing years. Prescott viewed his diminishing ability of memorization as a "sad failure," but even at its lowest point it was still a remarkable feat to commit so much writing, as well as accompanying notes and new revisions, to memory.

Thanks to the support of a wide network of friends and acquaintances, Prescott was able to make crucial contacts abroad who were in a position to provide him with materials relevant to his research, much of which were long-forgotten manuscripts buried deep in European archives beneath centuries of accumulated dust. Previously, historians relied primarily on sources readily at hand, but William was determined to collect every bit of historical evidence pertaining to his subject that his aides could possibly locate—searches that led to the discovery of materials and documents long forgotten and therefore never viewed by other historians. Prescott endeavored to obtain copies of original sources, a decided and highly successful effort that later led him to be recognized by many as America's first scientific historian. Over time, the Boston historian managed to assemble a vast library estimated at over 5000 volumes. A large number of these books were obtained from the great libraries of Europe, particularly those located in Spain.

Prescott corresponded on a fairly regular basis with a great many friends and admirers, as well as a long list of prominent authors, historians, statesmen, and scholars. His letters touched on a variety of subjects specifically tailored to the reader, communications which offer significant insight into many of the important issues of his era. William also maintained for more than 35 years a private journal that he referred to as his literary memoranda, in which he periodically posted his most pressing thoughts and concerns pertaining to his ongoing literary efforts—notations which provide a better understanding and appreciation of the weals and woes of America's celebrated historian. A thorough study of these letters and memorandums reveals the undeniable fact that William Hickling Prescott was truly at his happiest while pursuing intellectual interests.

Growing up as a respected member of Boston's polite society, William acquired a fondness for hosting and attending dinner parties and taking part in various social gatherings, leisurely affairs that offered him an opportunity to interact with people of diverse backgrounds and interests. His outgoing and pleasant nature plus an uncanny ability to converse easily with politicians, royalty, scholars, historians, publishers, businessmen, and anyone else who wished to share a moment with him, enabled Prescott to move comfortably within almost any social circle. William was also blessed with a youthful appearance and spirit that attracted the attention of others.

"If I were asked," said a lifelong friend of Prescott, "to name the man whom I have known whose coming was most sure to be hailed as a pleasant event by all whom he approached, I should not only place Prescott at the head of the list, but I could not place any other man near him.... Foremost among the qualities in his character was his universal, constant, and extreme kindness of heart, and its fitting exponent in as sweet a temper as ever man had.... All whom he came near felt, what he never seemed to feel, that there was, if not some reunification of right, at least a charming forgetfulness of self in the way in which he asserted no superiority over any, but gave himself up to the companion of the moment, with the evident desire to make him as happy as he could. And his own prompt and active sympathy awoke the sympathy of others. His gayety became theirs. He came always bringing the gift of cheerfulness, and always offered it with such genuine cordiality that it was sure to be accepted and returned with increase. No wonder that he was just as welcome everywhere as sunshine."[1]

William learned on his own to write with a noctograph, a newly-invented device specifically designed to aid the writing efforts of the blind. Prescott's completed writings on the noctograph were copied in large print by his secretary so that he would be able to proofread his work. Prescott's initial literary publications were lengthy critical essays, the first of which appeared in the *North American Review* in 1821. These innocuous critiques marked his first steps along the path to becoming an accomplished writer.

During his tireless quest to become a man of letters, it dawned on William that his interest leaned toward the history of Spain, and therefore he began to labor in secret on an account of the momentous reign of King Ferdinand and Queen Isabella.

Determined to produce an historical account of exceptional quality and lasting importance, William trudged through the many essential tasks an historian must perform before ever beginning to write: laborious research of his chosen topic, meticulous comparison of similar historical accounts, and the painstaking compilation of vital notes. Regarding his thoughts on the evolving role of the historian, Prescott wrote, "Libraries were to be ransacked; medals and monuments to be studied; obsolete manuscripts to be deciphered. Every assertion was to be fortified by an authority; and the opinions of others, instead of being admitted on easy faith, were to be carefully collated, and the balance of probability struck between them. With these qualifications of antiquarian and critic, the modern historian was to combine that of the philosopher, deducing from his mass of facts general theorems, and giving to them their most extended application."[2]

Once he had committed to memory a vast section of his organized notes, Prescott would compose and edit entire chapters during his daily horse rides or leisurely strolls. He would then retire to his dimly-lit study to compose his work with the aid of his trusty, but rather cumbersome, noctograph. After a decade of laboring in secret, Prescott's hard work paid off when his scholarly three-volume *History of the Reign of Ferdinand and Isabella, the Catholic* was published in 1838. Lauded by critics both at home and abroad, William Prescott was promptly hailed as the new literary lion of America, and in certain circles he was admiringly referred to as the American Thucydides. Many years later, Van Wyck Brooks, the renowned literary historian, commented, "The book had been planned like a battle and built as stoutly as a Salem clipper, destined to sail through many enchanted minds for generations to come."[3] The success of this book opened a great many doors for the 42-year-old historian.

"When one work is finished," William advised, "don't pause too long before another is begun—and so on till eyes, ears, and sense give way—then resignation!"[4] His next writing project dealt with the Spanish conquest of Mexico. To aid his research, Prescott obtained the services of four copyists in Madrid who managed to send him several thousand sheets of hand-copied manuscripts that had long been buried and forgotten in the Spanish archives. He also obtained similar help from friends and acquaintances in Mexico who obliged his request for material related to the history of the Aztecs and other indigenous tribes of Mexico. Since he knew little about the lay of the land, Prescott relied on Fanny Calderón de la Barca, the wife of Spain's minister to Mexico, to provide him with detailed descriptions of the flora, fauna, and topography of the region that he proposed to write about.

The Boston historian spared no expense in obtaining materials relevant to his subject; he shelled out more than $3000 for a set of tomes titled *The Antiquities of Mexico*, a rich collection of pre–Columbian works that bankrupted Lord Kingsborough and landed him in debtor's prison. *History of the Conquest of Mexico*, which was published in December of 1843, is considered by many to be Prescott's masterpiece. The timing of this release was certainly fortuitous, for it appeared just as awareness of the Aztec and Maya civilization had begun to capture the imaginations of Europeans and Americans. Hailed by critics and enthusiastically received by the public, William's second historical account was a tour-de-force that secured his place among the great scholars of history.

In his determined effort to be fair in writing about the exploits of the conquistadors, Prescott declared: "It is far from my intention to vindicate the cruel deeds of the old Conquerors. Let them lie heavy on their heads. They were an iron race, who periled life and fortune in the cause; and as they made little account of danger and suffering for themselves, they had little sympathy to spare for their unfortunate enemies. But to judge them fairly, we must not do it by the lights of our own age. We must carry ourselves back to theirs."[5]

While working on his next historical account, William Prescott decided to release a collection of his previously published reviews, which in America was titled *Biographical and Critical Miscellanies* and in England *Critical and Historical Essays*. While of interest to a select number of readers, these recycled articles did little to enhance the reputation of the Boston scholar. Shortly thereafter, the historian broke new ground with the release of *History of the Conquest of Peru*, which also was enthusiastically received by critics and readers alike. Up to this point, very little was known about the vast empire forged by the Inca until William Prescott pieced together a detailed account of their rapid ascent to power.

Prescott's accounts of the Spanish invasions of Mexico and Peru focused on the hero's quest to achieve a most challenging but seemingly attainable goal. Tension steadily builds as the central characters must overcome one apparently insurmountable obstacle only to have to confront another of equal or greater magnitude. It was a theme that both readers and critics found enchanting. Returning to his interest in Spanish history,

William went on to write *History of the Reign of Philip the Second, King of Spain* and a 200-page addendum to William Robertson's *History of the Reign of the Emperor Charles V*.

Prescott was adept at developing an interesting and flowing narrative, building anticipation, incorporating variety, and advancing a satisfying resolution—essential writing qualities that help to maintain reader interest. But what distinguishes him from other historians was his detailed attention to the development of his main characters, a concerted effort which so effectively breathed life into their persona. From the first, William understood that an historian must be more than just a compiler of facts. He taught himself to carefully sift through select historical accounts and meld them into a romantic narrative that strictly adhered to the truth, which he was able to achieve by making thorough use of the numerous records left by those who participated in these historical events.

In his 1838 essay on Sir Walter Scott, Prescott emphasized the importance of creating a compelling narrative, which he believed could be achieved by focusing on the character of the principal participants: "There is no kind of writing, which has truth and instruction for its main object, so interesting and popular, on the whole, as biography. History in its large sense, has to deal with masses, which, while they divide the attention by the dazzling variety of objects, from their very generality are scarcely capable of touching the heart. The great objects on which it is employed have little relation to the daily occupations with which the reader is most intimate. A nation, like a corporation, seems to have no soul, and its checkered vicissitudes may be contemplated rather with curiosity for the lessons they convey than with personal sympathy. How different are the feelings excited by the fortunes of an individual—one of the mighty mass, who in the page of history is swept along the current unnoticed and unknown!"[6]

In order to reveal ideas and facts that others may have failed to notice or appreciate, an historian must make every effort to seek out reputable sources that will enable them to remove any shroud of uncertainty pertaining to the topic in question. A true history must avoid the moral judgments imposed by later generations; right and wrong are often subjective terms that can radically change from one generation to the next. Prescott was determined to seek out the historical truth concerning his subject, evidence of which is displayed in his numerous and detailed notes. While some readers and reviewers complained that his notes were excessive and tended to be a distraction, many felt that such detailed footnotes helped them better understand and appreciate how the historian arrived at his conclusions.

What also set Prescott apart from other historians was his impartial treatment of events and individuals, an approach which freed him from the prejudicial views that so often tarnish the truth. Prescott made every effort to view his subject in the context of the time in which it occurred—not allowing his writing to be swayed by the moral judgment of his era. By disregarding the fabrications of the Black Legend, this self taught historian was able to compose a far more just historical account of Spain's emerging and expanding empire. He was described by the esteemed historian Samuel Eliot Morison as "the first English-speaking historian of Spanish lands whom a loyal Spaniard could read without disgust."[7]

William Prescott was the first American historian to achieve international acclaim, which he earned after being widely hailed by critics and readers abroad for the scholarly execution of his first book, *History of the Reign of Ferdinand and Isabella, the Catholic*. His elegant literary style helped to awaken interest in the works of a great many other American authors. The Boston historian was held in such high esteem amongst European and American scholars that he was the recipient of four honorary degrees and awarded membership in 27 prominent historical and philosophical societies during his lifetime. Fame, however, never spoiled Prescott, and he was certainly never one to boast of his many literary achievements. The Rev. James Walker, D. D., a classmate of the celebrated historian and president of Harvard University, wrote: "He [Prescott] never aspired to become the representative of a new movement or idea. He was content to be himself."[8]

Meticulous in his research, Prescott employed the services of qualified scholars to scour the archives of Spain, Mexico, France, England, and Germany for unpublished copies of documents and manuscripts that would shed new light on the historical topics he proposed to write about. Not content to learn just the facts, he sought to punctuate the authenticity of his stories by having aides supply him with detailed descriptions of the terrain, flora, and fauna unique to the lands where his heroes trekked.

Prescott's books instruct as well as entertain, which are two significant reasons why his historical accounts were, and continue to be, so popular. He was one of those rare historians who could effectively meld history and literature into an elegant and compelling writing style that appealed to the casual reader while still adhering to the strict criteria of the scholar. Believing that the reader should not be subjected to the prejudice of the author, Prescott avoided passing judgment whenever possible. He understood that opinions are subject to changes caused by shifts in moral, political, and religious values, and therefore felt the facts of the story should speak for themselves. Prescott was a master of narrative history; his vivid descriptions infused new life into the history and culture of Spain, the bold adventures of the Spanish conquistadors, and the extraordinary achievements of the pre–Columbian civilizations of Mexico and Peru.

William noted that it was his desire to write not only the details of the epic adventures of the conquistadors that had been told by others but made it clear that it was his objective "to exhibit this same story, in all its romantic details; not merely to portray the characteristic features of the Conquest, but to fill up the outline with the coloring of life, so as to present a minute and faithful picture of the times."[9] He sought to avoid the historian's sin of including fictitious words to the voices of his heroes, taking care to always note the source he used when quoting a speech attributed to key figures.

Not everyone, however, was enthralled with the historian's literary style. Henry David Thoreau, who knew Prescott, expressed his disdain for any historian who infused literary language into their historical accounts: "They give you one piece of nature at any rate, and that is themselves, smacking their lips like a coach-whip,—none of those emasculated modern historians, such as Prescott's, cursed with a style."[10] Additionally, there were a handful of critics who charged that the Boston historian's account of the Spanish conquest of the Americas unfairly cast the inhabitants of the New World as being vastly inferior to the invaders from the Old World, a criticism that continues to find favor in certain circles.

In his biography of William Hickling Prescott, Harry Thurston Peck stated: "Prescott never wrote a sentence that can be remembered. His strength lies in his *ensemble*, in the general effect, and in the agreeable manner in which he carries us along with him from the beginning to the end."[11] In an article about William Prescott that appeared in the November 1957 edition of the *Atlantic Monthly*, Samuel Eliot Morison wrote, "I shall not attempt to analyze his style because it has to be enjoyed and admired, not plucked apart."[12] The Boston historian had hoped that his writings would be of interest to his generation as well as future generations. In this effort, William Prescott clearly succeeded where so many others have failed.

In defense of his work, Prescott noted his meticulous attention to the proper use of primary and secondary sources for his research: "I have shown to the reader the steps of the process by which I have come to my conclusions. Instead of requiring him to take my version of the story on trust, I have endeavored to give him a reason for my faith. By copious citations from the original authorities, and by such critical notices of them as would explain to him the influences to which they are subjected, I have endeavored to put him in a position for judging for himself, and thus revising, and, if need be, reversing, the judgments of the historian."[13]

To this day, Prescott's writings continue to thrive; his is still the source that any respectable historian will turn to when conducting research into the awe inspiring accomplishments of the Mexican and Peruvian civilizations or investigating the daring exploits of the Spanish conquistadors. Evidence of the enduring popularity of William Prescott's work resides in the fact that his *History of the Conquest of Mexico* has been translated into ten languages and *History of the Conquest of Peru* into 11 dialects. Any scholar who choses to ignore Prescott's insightful and thoroughly documented historical accounts does a terrible injustice to their own work, a failure that deprives the reader of a truthful rendering of these epic events that forever altered the course of world history.

A biography of Boston's most famous historian would not be complete without acknowledging the efforts of those who have labored to keep his name alive. Prior to this work, there have been four published biographies of William Hickling Prescott. The first was written by his good friend George Ticknor and published in 1864. The next was Rollo Ogden's 1904 memoir of the historian. A third biography written by Harry Thurston Peck was published in 1905. Six decades would pass before the fourth biographical sketch of Prescott was written, a work penned by C. Harvey Gardiner and published in 1969. In 1925, Roger Wolcott, a great-grandson of the celebrated Boston historian, published *The Correspondence of William Hickling Prescott 1833–1847*. There are also a number of important books that focus on various aspects of Prescott's writing career, most of which are duly noted in this bibliography. Overall, each of these works provide a measure of insight into the historian's trials and tribulations, as well as his unshakable will to succeed in a vocation which seemed beyond his physical capabilities. The untiring efforts of the staffs at the Boston Athenaeum and the Massachusetts Historical Society to preserve the legacy of William Hickling Prescott deserve special recognition.

This brings us to the reason why I felt there was a need for another account of the life of William Hickling Prescott. While it would be impractical for a biographer, and certainly tedious for the reader, to delve into every single aspect of Prescott's life, the previous memoirs tended to gloss over various individuals and events that I believe had a very meaningful impact on the Boston historian. John Lloyd Stephens and Frederick Catherwood, the pioneers of Mayan archaeology, and the infamous murder of Dr. George Parkman by Professor John Webster, the latter a convicted murderer who had close ties to the Prescott family, are two such significant examples. Lastly, and perhaps most importantly, William Hickling Prescott has been a favorite author of mine ever since I first read his books about the Spanish conquests of the Aztec and Inca empires, two classic works that piqued my interest in Mexican, Peruvian, and Spanish history.

In his review of Washington Irving's *Conquest of Granada*, which appeared in the October 1829 edition of the *North American Review*, Prescott wrote, "The perfect historian: He must be strictly impartial; a lover of truth under all circumstances, and ready to declare it at all hazards: he must be deeply conversant with whatever may bring into relief the character of the people he is depicting, not merely with their laws, constitution, general resources, and all other more visible parts of the machinery of government, but with the nicer moral and social relations, the informing spirit which gives life to the whole, but escapes the eye of a vulgar observer. If he has to do with other ages and nations, he must transport himself into them, expatriating himself, as it were, from his own, in order to get the very form and pressure of the times he is delineating. He must be conscientious in his attention to geography, chronology, etc., an inaccuracy in which has been fatal to more than one good philosophical history; and mixed up with all these drier details, he must display the various powers of a novelist or dramatist, throwing his characters into suitable lights and shades, disposing his scenes so as to awaken and maintain an unflagging interest, and diffusing over the whole that finished style, without which his work will only become a magazine of materials—for the more elegant edifices of subsequent writers. He must be—in short, there is no end to what a perfect historian must be and do. It is hardly necessary to add that such a monster never did and never will exist."[14] In this author's modest opinion, William Hickling Prescott came as close as any historian in fulfilling these lofty requirements.

1

Puritan Pedigree

There are moments in the lives of men, which, as they are seized or neglected, decide their future destiny.[1]

The Family Tree

The Prescott family first arrived in America during the year 1640. They were Puritans from the northern county of Lancashire who, just like their brother Pilgrims who had sailed from England 20 years earlier to establish a Christian settlement in New Plymouth, simply wished to escape the religious persecution they had been subjected to in their homeland. The Prescott clan would make a home for themselves in Middle County, which was part of a vast colonial region known as New England.

John Prescott, his wife Mary, and their four children were the first of their family name to migrate to the New World. A skilled blacksmith and millwright, John Prescott was born in Standish, England in 1604, or possibly the following year. On January 21, 1629, John wed Mary Platts in a ceremony which took place in Wygan, Lancashire. As victims of religious intolerance, John and Mary decided they would follow the example of the many Puritans who sought to find a better way of life across the Atlantic. They docked at the island of Barbados in 1638, where they chose to settle for nearly two years. A fifth child, named Hannah, was born during their stay at Barbados. John and Mary Prescott were eventually the proud parents of eight healthy children.

John Prescott and his family moved to Watertown, Massachusetts in 1640. Three years later they chose to settle an untamed frontier along the Nashaway Plantation. The Prescotts were joined in this venture by Thomas King and several other Puritan families. John would soon find it necessary to petition the General Court of the Colony for the construction of a bridge across the Sudbury River. On one occasion Prescott lost his horse and nearly his own life while crossing a treacherous stretch of this river. Roughly one week later, his wife and children nearly drowned while wading across the Sudbury on horseback. Despite these serious dangers, the General Court was unwilling to honor Prescott's request.

The Prescott family cleared a plot of land that laid the foundation for the town that was to be named Lancaster. John and his fellow settlers had first petitioned the court for the right to incorporate as the township of Prescott. However, the General Court ruled that it was inappropriate to name a town for a living founder, which they felt smacked of hero-worship. A compromise was reached in May of 1653; the settlers were permitted to incorporate as the township of Lancaster, which honored John Prescott's home county in England. There were nine families living in this settlement at the time of incorporation.

Wondrous tales have been passed down from one generation to another of the numerous occasions that John Prescott had to valiantly defend his property and family from fierce attacks by natives bent on keeping white settlers off their land. A familiar family legend speaks of John having to face his enemy alone while donning a coat of mail and armor, protective covering similar to that used by the chivalrous knights of days past, which "struck terror to the savage foe by an appearance more frightful than their own."[2] John's horse was stolen during one of these native raids, a valuable animal he managed to retrieve after chasing down and confronting the thieves.

In another confrontation, the natives set fire to his barn, but John Prescott single-handedly drove them off his property, rescued the horses and cows, and extinguished the fire before it consumed the entire structure. Shortly thereafter, a band of hostile Indians returned and set fire to his saw mill, but Prescott was able to put out the fire before the damage became too great. On another occasion, the Indians launched an attack on his house. Prescott and his wife bravely stood their ground; Mary loaded the muskets that John continued firing until the natives finally retreated. John had a number of guns on hand, one of which was a favorite he had brought with him from England. A suspension of hostilities made it possible for the settlement to grow and prosper. The Indians even volunteered to help the colonists build new homes. This peace with the natives would last for nearly 20 years.

John Prescott swore an oath of allegiance in 1652, and was appointed a freeman in 1669, the latter of which accorded him important voting privileges. In addition to being a prominent member of the church, John held a number of influential town offices that helped to promote an elevated degree of wealth and status to the Prescott name. He would help defend Lancaster against two major native attacks during the Indian uprisings known as King Philip's War, the bloodthirsty campaigns that terrorized settlers throughout the New England region. The first raid on Lancaster took place on August 21, 1675, an assault which resulted in the death of eight residents of Lancaster.

The next deadly native raid occurred on February 10, 1676. Metacom, an Indian chief who was better known as King Philip, launched an early morning attack with a band of 1500 Wampanoag, Nipmuc, and Narragansett warriors. At the time of this assault, Lancaster was home to more than 50 families. The ensuing massacre claimed the lives of 50 or more settlers, a few of whom were taken prisoner. Counted among the dead was Jonas Fairbanks, John Prescott's son-in-law, and Joshua Fairbanks and Ephraim Sawyer, both of whom were grandsons of the town founder. Lancaster, which was in utter ruins, was abandoned, but many families, including the Prescotts, chose to return three years later to begin rebuilding their small town. By most accounts, John Prescott passed away in the year 1683.

John and Mary Prescott had a son named Jonas, who was born at Lancaster in the year 1648. Jonas later took up residence at the neighboring town of Groton and would serve as a captain of the militia that protected the ever-vigilant settlers from the periodic and terrifying Indian raids. Jonas Prescott met his end in 1723.

Benjamin Prescott, a son of Jonas, was born on the fourth of January, either in the year 1695 or 1696, according to varying accounts. He bravely served as a colonel in the militia of Groton and the neighboring county of Worcester. He also represented the town of Groton at the General Court of the Colony. Benjamin was chosen in 1737 to settle a boundary dispute with New Hampshire but declined after learning he would have to travel to London, where there was currently a virulent epidemic of smallpox, a disease which he had not been exposed to previously. Mr. Edmund Quincy went in his place and died shortly after he had contracted this highly infectious disease. Benjamin Prescott passed away in 1738 at his farm after having over exerted himself in a vain effort to rescue his hay before it became drenched by an approaching rainstorm.

Benjamin Prescott fathered three sons, the eldest of whom was James, a true patriot who served with great distinction in the militia and rose to the respected rank of colonel. Like his father before him, James would represent Groton at the General Court of the Colony. Later, he was a representative at the Governor's Council. At the start of the Revolutionary War, James would faithfully serve the Colonial cause as a member of the Provincial Congress and the Board of War. At the end of the war he held the office of county sheriff and later Judge of the Court of Common Pleas. James Prescott passed away in 1800 at the age of 79.

Benjamin's youngest son was born in 1731 and christened with the name Oliver. He graduated from Harvard College in 1750 and established himself as a physician to the residents of Groton and the neighboring settlements. Beginning in 1777, Oliver served for several years as a member of the Governor's Council. The following year he received a commission as major-general in the service of the Commonwealth. Oliver continued his public service with an appointment in 1781 as Judge Probate for the county of Middlesex, a position he held until his death in 1804. Oliver fathered several sons, the oldest of whom was also named Oliver. The younger Oliver is noted for his extensive research on ergot, and wrote a paper concerning the unusual qualities of this fungus. Oliver Prescott's studies and lectures on this topic gained the notice of prominent physicians in Europe. A paper he wrote on the medicinal qualities of ergot was translated into French and German and was included in the *Dictionnaire des Sciences Médicales*. Oliver Prescott passed away at the town of Newburyport in 1827.

The middle son of Benjamin Prescott was William, the famous grandfather of Boston's most celebrated historian. William Prescott was born in Groton on February 20, 1726. Like his great grandfather, William possessed an adventurous spirit and chose to settle along the wilds of Middlesex on a plot of land he had purchased from the local Indians. During his service in the militia, Prescott named the township he had founded in tribute to Sir William Pepperell, the Massachusetts commander who had recently made a name for himself with his heroic capture of the French garrison at Fort Louisbourg. The Pepperell homestead would pass from father to son. In 1755 William served briefly as a lieutenant in the Colonial army that fought against the French force stationed in Nova Scotia. He returned home and married Abigail Hale, a descendant, like himself, of the original English Puritans who had settled the region.

In August 1774, William Prescott passionately pleaded with his fellow townsfolk of Pepperell to rally around the courageous colonists of Boston who had chosen to resist the unjust rule of the British Crown. All would willingly pledge their unwavering support in a letter that Prescott had written for the benefit of the hard-pressed Bostonians. "Be not dismayed," he stated, "nor disheartened in this day of great trials. We heartily sympathize with you, and are always ready to do all in our power for your support, comfort, and relief, knowing that Providence has placed you where you must stand the first shock. We consider, we are all embarked in one bottom, and must sink or swim together."[3]

William Prescott's distinguished service as a soldier and his fervent support of the colonial cause earned him an official appointment to lead a regiment of minutemen, a select company of well-trained men who, as their name indicated, were expected to be ready at a moments notice. On April 19, 1775, Colonel William Prescott learned of the minutemen clashes with British troops at Lexington and Concord, and rushed to Groton to collect men to cut off the British soldiers who were retreating toward

Statue, Colonel William Prescott, Boston, Charlestown, Massachusetts (courtesy Historical Findings and Library of Congress).

Boston by way of Cambridge. Though unsuccessful in their effort, the spirit of revolution, however, was now in full bloom.

On the evening of June 16, 1775, General Artemis Ward dispatched 1000 soldiers under the command of William Prescott and Israel Putnam to defend two vulnerable mounds located in Charlestown, which were respectively known as Bunker and Breed's hills. Colonel Prescott chose to leave a reserve force at Bunker Hill while he took the bulk of the army to nearby Breed's Hill to await the imminent arrival of the British troops. The commander and his men spent most of the night laboring to build a redoubt at the top of the hill and strategically positioning themselves for the impending battle.

The following day marked the first true battle of the Revolutionary War. Dr. Oliver Prescott, Jr., who was a nephew of Colonel William Prescott, wrote, "On the morning of the battle, Governor Gage, the British commander, viewed the American works from an elevated position (Copp's hill), and called upon the tory refugees to see if they knew the commanding officer. Abijah Willard, a mandamus counsellor, whose wife was a sister to Colonel Prescott, having viewed the works with the glass, informed Gage that he knew the commander well. 'It is my brother-in-law, Prescott.' 'Will he fight?' asked Gage. 'Yes,' replied Willard, 'that man will fight h—l, and if his men, are like him you will have bloody work to-day.'"[4]

Colonel Prescott and his troops were steadily pounded by canons aboard British ships anchored in the harbor as well as a battery positioned across the river at Copp's Hill. The heavy bombardment provided cover for 2300 British soldiers under the command of General William Howe to come ashore and march against the colonial troops. To make sure that each shot counted, Colonel Prescott is often credited with issuing the legendary order, "Don't fire until you see the whites of their eyes." As instructed, the colonials waited until the enemy was well within range before opening fire. Their patience and excellent marksmanship helped to repulse the charge of the much larger and better equipped British army.

The British forces quickly regrouped and launched a second attack, but once again were unable to break the ranks of the entrenched colonials. A lack of ammunition and the constant blasts of British firepower forced the patriots to abandon their position during the third assault. Risking his life to provide cover for the orderly retreat of his men, Colonel Prescott stood his ground until the last possible moment. After being compelled to withdraw, Prescott immediately presented himself before General Ward to request additional troops and sufficient ammunition to proceed with an assault that very night. He pledged to retake the hill or die trying. Cooler heads prevailed and his request was summarily declined. The bloody confrontation had claimed the lives of some 400 American patriots and 1000 seasoned British soldiers. The resolve and fortitude of those who fought at the Battle of Bunker Hill had won an important psychological victory for the colonial cause, one which would encourage other colonists to take up arms against British rule. After learning of this conflict, George Washington declared, "The liberties of the country are safe," and Benjamin Franklin wrote, "England has lost her Colonies forever."[5]

Colonel William Prescott later served under the command of General George Washington, who personally praised his service to the cause and publicly referred to him as "Prescott the Brave." He resigned his commission in 1776 and returned to his 250-acre farm in Pepperell. William volunteered during the autumn of 1777 to join other patriots in the capture of Burgoyne at Saratoga, a stunning victory which helped to convince the French to ally themselves with the American colonists. William Prescott once again retired to Pepperell where he remained until his death, which occurred on October 13, 1795. While hailed as a great hero for his bold stand against the British, Colonel William Prescott was saddled with outstanding debts at the time of his death, which proved a heavy burden for the family he left behind.

William and Abigail Prescott had only one child, a son also named William, who was born at the Pepperell family farm on August 19, 1762. He was schooled by his loving mother until the age of 14, at which time he was placed in the care of Master Moody of the Dummer Academy in Essex County, who was considered the finest instructor of Latin and Greek in all of New England. Master Moody saw to young William's education for nearly three years, which was more than sufficient preparation for his admittance to Harvard College in 1779. William attended Harvard for four years, and graduated with honors. To help support his family and to pay off the mounting debts incurred by his father, William had to forgo his class commencement in order to accept a teaching post at a school in Promfret, Connecticut. One year later he moved to Beverly, Massachusetts, where he ran a private school and studied law under Nathan Dane, a noted jurist who later founded the Law Professorship in Harvard College. During this time, William was honored to receive an invitation to join the household of General Washington to serve as a tutor to a young family member. However, prior obligations compelled him to politely decline this generous offer. The vacant position was filled by one of William's college classmates.

Life in Salem

William Prescott was admitted to the bar in 1787, after which he proceeded to open his own law practice in the small community of Beverly. But after two years he chose to move to the neighboring town of Salem, where there were more opportunities to expand his practice. Nearly a century had passed since the hysteria of the infamous witchcraft trials led to the condemnation of 30 individuals, 19 of whom were hanged, for consorting with the devil—an unseemly event that had long tarnished the name of Salem. The town had since grown into a respectable community that prospered from industry and commerce. Salem could soon boast of having a number of famous native sons, a list that included Timothy Pickering, a soldier and statesman noted for his service as postmaster general and secretary of state; Nathaniel Bowditch, a pioneer in astronomy and navigation; and Nathaniel Hawthorne, author of *The Scarlett Letter* and numerous other works. The town would later brag that it was the birthplace of the celebrated historian William Hickling Prescott.

Skill and determination enabled William Prescott to grow a very suc-

House in Salem, Massachusetts, where Prescott was born (from *Complete Works of William H. Prescott* published in 1912 by DeFau & Co.).

cessful law practice. He would use some of his newfound wealth to pay off the remaining family debts, thereby removing the liens that had hung so heavily over the Pepperell estate. After his father's death, this loving son did his very best to furnish his mother with all that she ever needed or desired, provisions which continued without complaint until her passing in 1821. William Prescott was actively involved in the welfare of his adopted Salem community: He was a cofounder of the Philosophical Library Company and clerk of the Essex Bridge Company. In 1798, the young lawyer contributed $1000 toward the construction of the frigate *Essex*. Prescott also served as a director of a marine insurance company and was one of the founders of a private school headed by Jacob Knapp. A devout Christian, William Prescott was an active member of his church.

While practicing law in Salem, William met and courted Catherine Greene Hickling, the daughter of a once-prominent Boston merchant who had moved away to serve as the United States Consul at St. Michaels in the Azores. Born on August 1, 1767, Catherine was just a young girl when her mother passed away. Her father, Thomas Hickling, was in St. Michaels at the time of his wife's death. It was agreed that it would be best for Catherine to remain in Boston under the care of their loving grandfather Rufus Greene. As she neared the age of 18, Catherine decided to sail to the Azores to spend some time with the father she barely knew. During this pleasant reunion, she would pass the time learning to speak Portuguese, the language of her father's adopted homeland. After a stay of two years Catherine decided to sail to England, where for the next two years she toured London and the surrounding English sites.

William Prescott and Catherine Greene Hickling were married on December 18, 1793. Afterwards, the newlyweds moved into their large and elegant house on Essex Street. Though five years younger than her husband, Catherine had matured into a woman of extraordinary charm and excellent character. She enjoyed music, dancing, taking long walks, riding horses, and was especially fond of reading. Catherine was a devout Protestant but tolerant of other Christian faiths. She would give birth to seven children but only three would survive beyond the age of one. On May 4, 1796, Catherine gave birth to a son, William Hickling Prescott. He was their second child; the first, also a boy, had died during infancy. Catherine Elizabeth Prescott, who was affectionately referred to as Lizzie, was born on November 12, 1799. The third surviving Prescott child, Edward Goldsborough Prescott, who was also known as Ned, was born on January 2, 1804.

Catherine Prescott doted on her children, especially little William. She simply could not bring herself to correct or restrain her son's indulgences. The inquisitive and intuitive lad was encouraged to say whatever was on his mind, an allowance that occasionally led to some rather embarrassing scenarios. A benefit from such liberal child-rearing was that William never suffered from a lack of confidence. The spirited youth possessed a cheerful disposition, which he clearly inherited from his mother. Catherine made sure to find the time to instruct her son in the basic lessons he would need to know for school, and would read him books that were geared toward stimulating his fertile mind. William was always very close to his mother, a bond that endured throughout their many years together.

Once he was of suitable age, William began his formal education with Miss Mehitable Higginson, a school mistress who preferred the title of school-mother. She was a descendant of the eminent Francis Higginson, who emigrated to Salem in 1629, when there were but seven homes in the town. Miss Higginson's school for the young was a center of learning for the upper-class children of Salem. The personable little William Prescott quickly became a favored student of the school-mother.

At the beginning of 1803, the six-year-old William was enrolled in the private school of Jacob Newman Knapp, a teacher known to all in Salem as Mister Knapp, except to his students, all of whom were required to address him as Master Knapp. William's father was among a small group of Salem residents who, out of a deep and abiding concern to provide the best possible education for their children, had helped to establish this school. Young William demonstrated all the attributes of a good student: quickness of mind, inquisitive, perceptive, and a strong ability to retain what he had learned. He got along quite well with his classmates—perhaps too well, as he was inclined to neglect his studies in favor of play. A tendency to daydream kept William from becoming a truly exceptional student. He did, however, display a fondness for books, a love of reading that continued throughout his life. William often offended classmates with his outspoken manner, a trait inherited from his lawyerly father, a man who was never one to mince words.

Meanwhile, William Prescott's professional and financial affairs continued to prosper at Salem. He served as the town's representative in the state legislature and as a senator from Essex County. In 1803 the ambitious lawyer was forced to curtail some of his business activities after suffering a hemorrhage of the lungs. Prescott was asked in 1806 to serve on the bench of the Supreme Court of the Commonwealth but declined the appointment. Seven years later he would respectfully turn down a renewed request to sit on the bench. A devoted family man, William Prescott had refused these honorable appointments on the grounds that such service would interfere with the time that he cherished spending with his family. William's business acumen firmly established him as a prominent member of the community and earned him the means to provide a comfortable lifestyle for his family.

The esteemed Judge Joseph Story, Associate Justice of the Supreme Court and a Dane Professor of Law at Harvard University, wrote of his admiration for Judge William Prescott: "He was a decided federalist, and at all times one of the ablest and most accomplished of the federal leaders. A man of more chivalric honor, of more probity, sound sense and discretion I scarcely know. From the moment I came to the bar, he treated me with unhesitating kindness and respect; and when such occurrences were rare from other quarters, I constantly received from him invitations to the parties at his house, as if I belonged to the circle of his own friends." This fellow resident of Salem concludes his praise by declaring, "It is my pride to count him among those choice friends, whose regard would flatter my pride, and whose censure would infuse the most serious doubts into the estimate of my own conduct."[6]

Boston Roots

After 18 years as a resident of Salem, William Prescott decided during the autumn of 1808 to move his family and law practice to Boston. Catherine Prescott made note of their sudden change of address by recording, "September 13, 1808—We began to remove our furniture from Salem to Boston. Saturday 17 we removed our family, and took possession of the front house in Bumstead Place, at 750 dollars a year."[7] Their new residence at Tremont Street overlooked Boston Common. The Prescotts' next rented home was in Summer Street, alongside Chauncy Place. Afterwards, the family lived for a few years in a house situated at the corner of Otis Place. In 1817, Judge Prescott purchased a mansion along Pond Street, which was the family residence for the next 28 years.

Now that the elder William had a much larger pool of wealthy clients to represent, the move to Boston soon proved to be a rewarding experience for the Prescott family. Over time, these important business connections led to opportunities to invest in a number of Boston's leading manufacturing, banking, shipping, railroad, and insurance firms, many of which proved hugely profitable. The jurist was greatly admired for his integrity, legal and business acumen, kindness toward friends and acquaintances, love of family, and keen mind. William Prescott would succeed H.G. Otis on the Bench of Common Pleas in the year 1818. A steadfast Federalist, Judge William Prescott remained a member of the bar until 1828, a distinguished law career that spanned just over 40 years.

Four days after settling into their new home, the younger William Prescott was enrolled in the private school superintended by the Rev. John S. Gardiner, the rector of Trinity Church. Founded by Dr. Gardiner while he was serving as an assistant to the previous rector of this Episcopal church, the reverend viewed the school as an opportunity to pass along his extensive knowledge of classical literature, an expertise he acquired in England under the tutelage of Dr. Samuel Parr, a renowned 18th century classicist. On the 26th of September, young William Prescott entered Mr. McThean's school, and on the third day of October he began his studies at Mr. Tancon's French school.

William attended classes conducted at the Reverend Gardiner's home library in Franklin Place, where the teacher imparted his deep love of classical studies to a class of around a dozen lads. This small gathering of students was confined to young boys whom the rector felt would truly benefit from his teachings. Dr. Gardiner drilled his students in Greek, Latin, and English compositions. Most of the instructions were oral, which added much needed coloring to these antiquated themes. The students were required to memorize and recite verses of text, lessons which helped Prescott hone his proficient powers of recall. Dr. Gardiner was an engaging teacher who had a profound impact on the fertile minds of his young students, especially William, who, over a three-year period, he managed to instill a lasting appreciation of classical studies. Now that his curiosity was piqued, William willingly received instructions in French, Italian, and Spanish from private tutors, studies that awakened his interest in the great writers of Western Civilization and would prove very useful to the profession he would later choose to pursue.

Young William Prescott was affectionately labeled with the sobriquet of "the Colonel," which Dr. Gardiner bestowed upon him in tribute to the memory of his heroic grandfather, the officer who had fought with great distinction at the famous Battle of Bunker Hill. He was often called Will by his father, while Edward, his younger brother, was frequently referred to as "the Judge," a reference to the honorable position held by their father.

The future historian found a kindred spirit in William Howard Gardiner, the son of his instructor. Together, they attended private lessons in math and writing. These two lads of similar age and similar interests were constant companions, a bond of friendship that endured a lifetime. The young boys entertained themselves with fanciful games that drew heavily upon both their recent history lessons and vivid imaginations. Both youths were infatuated with the news of the Napoleonic Wars that regularly appeared in the Boston papers. These exuberant friends would reenact the European battles of their day as well as the famous battles, such as Thermopylae and Marathon, that they had learned about in school. Each liked to study and imitate the tactics of famous military commanders and utilized pieces of paper, which they cut into different shapes, to designate the battle formations of infantry, cavalry and artillery regiments. They even found some old armor at the Boston Athenaeum, which they donned to play the roles of the heroic knights of *Amadis de Gaula*, which was one of Prescott's favorite stories. William also enjoyed recreating the epic Battle of Bunker Hill, where his grandfather had fought with valor.

There were occasions when their imaginative behavior went too far; enthralled by a thrilling performance of the circus, the two boys attempted to replicate an animal act, which abruptly ended with the scorching of a family cat they had forced to participate in their impromptu show. Another incident involved the two boys managing to get their hands on a pair of loaded pistols, which they fired into the air and nearly killed a horse that belonged to the Prescott family.

These two best friends also amused themselves with creative stories, which they composed in concert. One would start the story and the other would follow, a routine which continued back and forth until the tale reached a mutually acceptable conclusion. George Ticknor noted in his biography that Prescott's stories seemed to be the more imaginative of the two, which he attributed to the numerous tales of adventure that the future historian had already read. Prescott, however, seems to have had a different recollection of his story telling days with Gardiner. A few years before his death, while entertaining a grandson on his knee who wished to hear a story, William called out, as his friend Mr. Gardiner entered the room: "Ah, there's the man that could tell you stories. You know, William," he continued addressing his friend, "I never had any inventive faculty in my life; all I have done in the way of story-telling in my later years, has been by diligent hard work."[8]

At age 12 William befriended an older student who would play an influential role in shaping his career. George Ticknor, a recent graduate of Dartmouth College who was William's senior by five years, received private instructions from Dr. Gardiner once the reverend's noon class for the younger boys had been dismissed. These two promising students of literature soon began studying Latin and Greek classics together, and quickly became fast friends at both school and home. Ticknor fondly remembered the Prescott house as always being filled with much warmth and joy. He also noticed that Catherine Prescott showered her beloved son with considerable affection. William Prescott also made friends with William Amory, eight years his junior, who was the son of Thomas C. Amory, a well-to-do merchant. This friendship led to introductions to the Amory clan, which included Susan, a young girl who would later become his wife.

William and Catherine Prescott passed on to their children their immense love of books. As an avid reader who was particularly fond of history, Judge Prescott collected books of varying interests that found a permanent home in his ever-expanding library. From an early age, the Prescott's eldest son enjoyed reading, especially thrilling tales filled with adventure and romance. One of young William's favorite stories was the chivalrous sagas of *Amadis de Gaula*, the wondrous accounts of a wandering and courageous knight, tales that served as a source of inspiration for a great many Spanish conquistadors. Unfortunately, books were not always readily accessible. At the time, there were few American authors, and those who did write could not expect to rely on this profession as a means of support. There were very few book shops in Boston, and most books had to be imported from Europe, particularly those produced in London, a factor which greatly added to their expense.

Fortunately for young William, the Boston Athenaeum opened its doors to the public on Tremont Street, in a house very near his home. The Athenaeum was founded in 1807 by William S. Shaw, a gentleman who possessed a true passion for books, and who enjoyed sharing his collection with anyone who had an interest in learning. As a subscriber to the Boston Athenaeum, the elder Prescott was in receipt of two tickets of admission, one of which young William evidently used to peruse the library. He would spend much of his free time leafing through the unique collection of books stored at this newly-opened library. The Athenaeum had been granted possession of the private library of John Quincy Adams, who at the time was the American minister to Russia. The Adams library consisted of nearly 10,000 books, and the curious Prescott would spend many hours reading whatever piqued his interest, which was quite broad.

Judge Prescott frequently brought his family to his childhood home in Pepperell, a roughly 250-acre estate located some 40 miles to the north of their Boston residence and situated very near the border of New Hampshire. The widow Abigail Prescott, the grandmother of young William, still resided at the white New England farm house. Many years later, the historian wrote of Pepperell: "The land is well studded with trees—oak, walnut, chestnut, and maple—distributed in clumps and avenues, so as to produce an excellent effect. The maple, in particular, in its autumn season, when the family are there, make a brave show with its gay livery when touched by frost."[9] A small pond behind the house was surrounded by a cluster of trees. William Prescott made additions to the two story home, which included extending the rear of the house to provide room for guests and a study for the younger William. Years later, after he inherited the estate, William H. Prescott made further modifications to the home that had belonged to his grandparents and father.

The historian always appreciated the natural charm of the hills, woods, streams, and ponds of the region surrounding Pepperell, an idyllic location he fondly referred to as the Highlands. Prescott also enjoyed gazing upon Monadnock, a more than 3000-foot-high mountain that rests in nearby New Hampshire. The family maintained a small boat that they used to float along the Nissitissit, a small river which flows to the south of their Pepperell residence. Father and son often went on long walks while vacationing at Pepperell—their favorite destination being the Nissitissit stream.

The Prescott family generally spent eight or nine weeks at their Pepperell country home, which they usually departed during the third week of July. In 1836, William wrote of his appreciation of Pepperell's tranquil surroundings: "The country in its delicious green, the leaves out on every tree, and the air loaded with perfumes from a wilderness of blossoms. How poetical it makes one, to get out of the prison of brick and mortar."[10]

In the summer of 1811, William H. Prescott prepared for admission to Harvard College by receiving private tutoring from Levi Frisbie, a member of the school faculty. On August 22, 1811, William attended an exam that he needed to pass for advance placement. He was joined by another applicant, the 16-year-old Arthur Middleton of South Carolina, a grandson of one of the signers of the Declaration of Independence. The two very nervous students appeared at the home of President John Thornton Kirkland at precisely eight in the morning. The Reverend Kirkland, who was president of Harvard from 1810 to 1828, sought to put the anxious students at ease with an offering of fresh pears. The entrance exam was divided into two parts. The morning test was administered by Levi Frisbie, William's tutor, who proceeded to access their knowledge and understanding of Latin. After breaking for lunch, the two aspiring students returned to face questions from Dr. Henry Ware, Hollis Professor of Divinity. William managed to turn the tables on the professor by asking a theological question, one which elicited a hearty laugh that compelled the professor to place both hands over his face. The examination concluded by mid-afternoon; Prescott and Middleton were delighted to learn that they had passed the exams and were now Harvard sophomores.

Pleased with his performance, William wrote to his father, who at the time was in Maine tending to business before the Supreme Court of Portland: "As you would like to know how I appeared, I will give you the conversation, *verbatim*, with Mr. Frisbie, when I went to see him after the examination. I asked him, "Did I appear well in my examination?" Answer, "Yes." Question, "Did I appear very well, Sir?" Answer, "Why are you so particular young man? Yes, you did yourself a great deal of credit."[11]

Prescott's sophomore curriculum was composed of classes in Greek and Latin, geometry, rhetoric, logic, and mathematics. He was taught Greek by Professor Ashur Ware, and Latin was instructed by his tutor and entrance examiner, Levi Frisbie. Mathematics and geometry, two fields of study that were of little interest to William, were taught by Professor John Farrar. Levi Hedge was his instructor in logic and the Rev. Joseph McKeon taught his rhetoric course. History lessons for sophomores were conducted every Saturday for one hour, which was followed by declamations. The devout William made it a point to visit the chapel every morning and evening, and regularly attended church services on Sunday.

In 1812, William was accorded membership in the Porcellian Club, a social group whose aristocratic members often appeared more interested in physical pleasures than intellectual pursuits. While still a sophomore, Prescott befriended Franklin Dexter and Jonathan M. Wainwright, both seniors. Franklin was destined to follow his distinguished father into the field of law and would become a member of the Prescott family when he married Catherine Elizabeth Prescott, William's younger sister. Jonathan M. Wainwright would join the clergy and remained a good friend to Prescott, especially during the historian's latter years.

Counted among the juniors who had close ties to William was Charles Folsom, a future scholar who would later play a crucial role as proofreader and editor of Prescott's historical manuscripts. Other friends from the Harvard class of 1813 included Henry Warren, John Ware, and William Jones Spooner. His sophomore friends included Arthur Middleton, Francis William Pitt Greenwood, and Thomas Bulfinch.

During his junior year, William took additional courses in Greek and Latin, as well as metaphysics, theology, natural philosophy, and mathematics. The bookish student made full use of the Harvard library: School records show that during the year 1813 he checked out a number of history books, a list that included Charles Rollin's *Ancient History*, volumes 1 and 2; William Mitford's *Greece*, volume 1; and all three volumes of Robert Watson's *Philip II*. Fourteen years later Prescott reread Watson's work while carrying out research for his historical account of the reign of Ferdinand and Isabella, but it was clear that he did not think very highly of this historian. He wrote in his literary memorandum that Watson was "a meagre, unphilosophical chronicler of the richest period of Spanish history."[12]

While Prescott excelled in his studies of Greek and Latin language it was quite obvious that he had a difficult time coping with mathematics. His failure in this subject was not from a lack of effort on his part—he rigorously set aside an allotted period of time for his studies—but was the result of a processing disorder that kept him from comprehending many basic mathematical calculations. This disability would contribute to a lack of interest in this topic, which, in turn, prevented him from keeping pace with his classmates. Making resolutions to improve himself, a practice which took root in college to overcome his deficiency in math, was a ritualistic exercise he would continue to follow throughout his life. These college resolutions revolved around how much time he would grant to the study of each course. However, he made a strict point to never study any longer than the time limit he had established for a particular course, even if it was just a mere minute longer. William also set limits on how many times per week he would permit himself to attend social gatherings, such as dances and the theater.

William's intellectual curiosity, or some unforeseen manner of temptation, often caused him to stray from his plan of study. Knowing that his attention could be easily diverted, Prescott sought to correct this flaw by inflicting monetary punishments for his failure to adhere to a strict regimen of study. In the end, William would donate his accrued monetary fines to charity. He eventually raised the stakes by making wagers with college friends that he would accomplish a specific goal by a certain date or forfeit a pecuniary penalty for his failure. These small bets were based on an honor system; He would never tell anyone when he won, only when he lost. Prescott would later use this form of incentive to stay on track while working on his *History of the Reign of Ferdinand and Isabella, the Catholic*.

William Gardiner made mention of his friend's peculiar proposals: "This habit of forming distinct resolutions about all sorts of things, sometimes important, but often in themselves the merest trifles in the world, grew up rapidly to an extent that became rather ludicrous; especially as it was accompanied by another habit, that of talking aloud, and concealing nothing about himself, which led him to announce to the first friend he met his latest new resolution. The practice, I apprehend, must have reached its acme about the time when he informed me one day that he had just made a new resolution, which was,—since he found he could not keep those which he had made before,—he would never make another resolution, as long as he lived. It is needless to say that this was kept but a very short time."[13]

It was during his junior year that William Prescott fell victim to a freak accident which would forever alter his life. As he was leaving dinner in the Commons Hall, William's attention was drawn to the clamor of horseplay between a number of undergraduates. When he reached the door of the Hall, Prescott turned to see what was all the commotion. It was at that very moment a large and extremely hard crust of bread flung with great force by an unruly student struck his open left eye. The direct hit to the cornea caused an instantaneous shock to his system and William swiftly collapsed into an unconscious state from the violent force of this small projectile. He began vomiting and exhibiting other symptoms commonly associated with a concussion.

A number of caring friends and acquaintances assisted the injured William to his Boston home, where he soon regained consciousness. Dr. James Jackson, the family physician, was immediately summoned and arrived within a few hours of the crippling injury. Those who tended to William were deeply concerned about his weak pulse, pale complexion, and immobile state. His mind, however, was still alert; he could recall all that had transpired before and after the accident. Even after he regained a degree of mobility, William was deeply troubled by the fact that he was unable to sit up.

Though there was no outwardly disfigurement to the damaged left eye, William's vision remained severely impaired. Dr. Jackson described the injury as a paralysis of the retina, which was beyond his power to heal. There was little that the doctor could do for his young patient except to recommend complete rest. The shock to his system slowly subsided after a few days and William was able to return to school within a few weeks. Unfortunately, his injured eye would never fully regain its vision; the eye appeared normal but could only faintly distinguish between shades of light and dark. Oculists who were later consulted could only detect a difference in the eye through the aid of a powerful lens, and even then the injury appeared slight. All would agree that there was little that could be done to correct his loss of vision.

Prescott knew the young man who had caused irreparable damage to his eyesight, but he bore no grudge against him. In fact, William rarely mentioned him when recalling the incident, which he referred to as simply an accident. The juvenile offender, however, was not nearly as gentlemanly; he never bothered to apologize or express remorse for his wrongdoing. William would never use his damaged eye as an excuse, for in his mind God had seen fit to leave him with one good eye.

The injury to William's left eye forced him to ignore the leisurely distractions of the past and to dedicate himself anew to his college studies. Courses which previously were of little interest, such as philosophy and logic, he studiously applied himself to learning. His incredible memory served him well in his literary studies, but mathematics continued to be a source of extreme frustration. Failing to comprehend even the most basic equations, and knowing that he needed to pass this subject in order to graduate, Prescott resorted to memorizing with precise exactness the mathematical lessons of the day. Several friends were in on this scheme, which succeeded for a brief period. However, his lack of comprehension made him realize that he was merely deceiving himself. Ashamed of his clever ruse, William arranged a meeting with his Professor and told him of his dilemma; confessing that he never understood geometry and probably never would, and that he had resorted to memorization in a desperate effort to keep pace with the class. The Professor admired his honesty and excused him from further numerical recitations. The instructor's sole requirement for granting Prescott a passing grade was that he must attend all classes. William was very grateful for the Professor's understanding of his unique situation.

William studied mathematics, theology, political philosophy, and natural philosophy during his senior year. His hard work paid off with admission to Phi Beta Kappa, a society whose membership was restricted to a select number of the best scholars of the junior and senior classes. The historian always felt that this was the greatest honor he ever received at college.

Prescott had a nervous laugh that frequently caused him much embarrassment. William Gardiner wrote of his best friend's sporadic lack of impulse control: "He had a sense of ludicrous so strong, that it seemed at times quite to overpower him. He would laugh on such occasions,— not vociferously indeed, but most inordinately, and for a long time together as if possessed by the spirit of Momus himself." Gardiner goes on to state: "This original ludicrous idea he seldom succeeded in communicating; but the infection of laughter would spread, by a sort of animal magnetism, from one to another, till I have seen a whole company perfectly convulsed with it, no one of whom could have told what in the world he was laughing at, unless it were at the sight of Prescott, so utterly overcome, and struggling in vain to express himself."[14]

One such instance of hysterical laughter occurred during a private lesson on elocution with a college professor. William was suddenly overcome with laughter after just a few sentences into his speech. The instructor gave him a cold glare, which merely made Prescott laugh even harder. Believing that the student was mocking him, the angered instructor chastised William in the harshest tone. After several attempts, Prescott managed to regain his composure and continued with his speech. At this point the professor began to laugh, which, in turn, caused William to resume laughing. The exchange of laughter lasted until the professor managed to regain his composure long enough to say, "Well, Prescott, you may go. This will do for to-day."[15]

William Hickling Prescott read his original poem titled *Ad Spem* at the 1814 Harvard commencement ceremonies. Sadly, no copy of his Latin poem pertaining to hope has been located. A proud Judge Prescott and Catherine Hickling Prescott would dispatch hundreds of invitations to attend their private party to celebrate the graduation of their son. On July 26, 1814, more than 500 guests attended the Prescott's lavish and festive reception. A large canvas shielded the welcome visitors as they sat at tables set upon the lawn to enjoy a magnificent feast provided by their hosts and to toast young William's success. Prescott's good friends William Howard Gardiner and George Ticknor were among the many Bostonians in attendance.

2

Worldly Views

Truth cannot be drawn from one source, but from complicated and often contradictory sources.[1]

Unexpected Complications

William moved back into the family home once he had completed his studies at Harvard College. He made an effort to follow in the footsteps of his father by studying law in his office, a necessary step to prepare for his admittance to the bar. But from the very beginning it was clear that William's heart did not burn with desire for entering the legal profession. Instead of studying the Blackstone law books or other requisite legal manuscripts, William would have preferred spending his time reading classical literature or historical accounts. However, the dutiful son did not want to disappoint his father and therefore pursued his law studies without complaint.

In January of 1815, William's expected career path was derailed after he was suddenly stricken with a painful inflammation around his right eye. The swelling steadily increased and before long he could barely see out of his only good eye. William's delicate condition was further complicated by a persistent high fever and a racing pulse.

On the 15th of January, Dr. James Jackson, who, in due course, would be regarded as "New England's foremost physician,"[2] was called upon to examine the ailing Prescott, who complained to the doctor that it was extremely painful to move his eye. The family physician prescribed the application of leeches to the temple and a medicinal salve, treatments that temporarily relieved his patient's condition. However, the pain and inflammation steadily increased during the night and by the next morning William's eye had become so swollen that he was unable to see at all. Dr. Jackson made note of the fact that Prescott's cornea was noticeably opaque, his pulse was quite rapid, and his skin was very hot to the touch. The gravely concerned physician was at a loss to identify the cause of his young patient's ailment. The eminent Dr. John Collins Warren, a good friend of Dr. Jackson, was called in to consult.

William was bled numerous times in an effort to rid him of this unknown affliction, and for a brief time this course of treatment seemed to help. But Prescott's discomfort returned with a vengeance during the night and his suffering increased significantly the following nightfall. For five days the inflammation intensified despite all efforts to treat it. Doctor Jackson noted that during this period the patient lost around seven pounds of blood from the continual bleedings and that "the vessels of the conjunctiva were divided twice, with a view to arrest the disease in the cornea."[3] Because of the sensitivity of his patient's eyes to light, the doctor's efforts were hampered by the necessity to perform these medical procedures with as little light as possible. William's inflammation began to recede on the sixth day and by the morning of the seventh day it had faded almost entirely, which coincided with a significant improvement in his overall health. Unfortunately, Prescott's vision in the right eye was still impaired, and the doctor feared the damage to the retina might be permanent.

On the afternoon of the seventh day of William's malady, Judge Prescott became extremely concerned after he noticed that the infection had suddenly spread to his son's right knee, which was now quite swollen, reddened, and a source of tremendous pain. He informed Dr. Jackson, who, oddly enough, felt this was actually good news, for now he could identify the perplexing disorder as acute rheumatism, an illness also referred to as acute rheumatic fever. Even though this was a debilitating disease, and it was rare for such an affliction to attack the eyes, the physician was relieved to finally know what sort of ailment he was dealing with. Doctor Jackson felt confident that William's eye would not suffer any permanent damage and that his vision would soon return to normal. Shortly thereafter, the young patient appeared to have made a full recovery.

Unfortunately, William would soon suffer a relapse, and over the next three months he had to endure two more severe flare-ups. The swelling was noticeably less with each reoccurrence, but he would still have to briefly cope with total blindness until the malady subsided. The torturous remedies of blistering and bleeding also accompanied these agonizing attacks. The rheumatism ravaged the joints of his lower extremities with such excruciating pain that the ailing William was unable to walk for a period of 16 weeks. The affliction also spread to his neck and groin. Dr. Jackson would improvise various medicinal concoctions containing experimental portions of opium, cinchona, or antimonial. Throughout this ordeal William was confined to his bedroom, which was bereft of light.

It wasn't until late April before William's eyes were able to tolerate any amount of light in his room. Though the pain and swelling had departed, his vision was still not fully restored. There was no visible sign of damage to the cornea, but the doctor feared that the severe nature of these recurring inflammations had inflicted permanent harm to his retina. The family doctor noted, "In the latter part of April and in May electrical shocks were applied to the head three times a day. Also mercurials were used moderately—one grain of Calomel every night. The eye recovered partially, but not entirely."[4]

Dr. Jackson was able to trace William's rheumatic condition to his mother's side of the family. He learned that Catherine Prescott suffered from rheumatism, and that two of her cousins had experienced several attacks which had seriously affected their eyes—one of whom was nearly rendered blind by this ailment. The doctor concluded that William had inherited a susceptibility to this affliction and that it was sure to reoccur periodically during his life.

Throughout this long and painful ordeal William refused to allow these sufferings to dampen his spirits; he never complained or felt sorry for himself, and friends who visited made note of the fact that he was always in a cheerful mood. Unfortunately, Prescott would have to endure recurring attacks of rheumatism for the rest of his life, and forever after he was haunted by the troubling thought that one day he might permanently lose his sight.

After much deliberation, William and Catherine Prescott agreed that a trip abroad might prove beneficial to their son's health. This was a popular recommendation of the era for those who were fortunate enough to afford such a long and restful journey. They decided to send him to the Azores, where it was hoped he would find the island climate more healthful. There he would vacation for six months with his maternal grandfather, Thomas Hickling, who was the Consul of the United States at St. Michaels, a post he would hold until his death at the age of 91. Afterwards, William was to sail to England for the purpose of consulting with prominent oculists and doctors about the poor condition of his eyes.

Island Life

On September 26, 1815, the 19-year-old William Prescott bid his family farewell and boarded the *Legal Tender*, a small American sailing vessel.

Captain Lindsay steered his ship out of Boston harbor and followed a course that he routinely plied between the waters of Massachusetts and the Azores. The very first day on the water the novice seafarer suffered terribly from sea sickness, but by the third day William's body had become reasonably adjusted to the rigors of ocean travel. His cabin opened onto the deck, a placement which made it susceptible to the ravages of both wind and water.

An infestation of cockroaches and rats that roamed freely about the ship and the steady rocking caused by the ocean were but a few of the miserable conditions that William had never before experienced. He found the offering of food barely edible—rye pudding topped with a sprinkling of salt served as his main source of sustenance. In addition to the typical hardships of a long sea voyage, Prescott suffered yet another debilitating bout of acute rheumatism and severe swelling around his right eye, recurring maladies which kept him confined to his dark and dank cabin. Blood sucking bedbugs and salt water leaking into his small cabin were a source of much discomfort for the confined ship passenger. The voyage lasted 22 long and dismal days.

The *Legal Tender* docked at the island of St. Michaels on the 18th of October. St. Michaels, or São Miguel, was first settled in 1444 and is one of the nine islands that make up the Azores. This archipelago, which rests roughly 800 miles west of the Iberian Peninsula, had long served as an important stopover for Spanish and Portuguese sailing vessels. Spanish treasure ships would rendezvous at the Portuguese islands during their return from the New World.

William was greeted at the Ponta Delgada dock by two uncles who promptly escorted him to his grandfather's *Yankee Hall* residence at Rosto de Cão. The 72-year-old Thomas Hickling, Consul of the United States at St. Michaels, had an elegant country house nestled in a serene valley at Rosto de Cão, which was situated a few miles from Ponta Delgada, the capital of the island. The estate was enhanced by luscious gardens and aromatic orange groves, all of which combined to fill the air with a sweet and pleasant fragrance. William felt as if he had stepped into a tropical paradise, especially after having been confined for such a long period in his dingy cabin aboard the *Legal Tender*.

William Prescott was warmly received by his relatives, especially his young aunts and uncles, who went out of their way to make sure that he felt at home. His grandfather had long ago taken a second wife, a lovely woman from Philadelphia named Sarah Falder, who now called St. Michaels her home. The happy couple had 14 children, some of whom were approximately the same age as William. Two of Thomas Hickling's daughters had wed men from the island who were of Portuguese descent. His aunt Fanny's husband was a graduate of the University of Coimbra and William greatly enjoyed conversing with him in French, especially after having learned that he was a doctor. Aunt Charlotte's husband, however, was cut from a different cloth; William found him quite dull, which he attributed to his lack of education, as well as being an overly jealous husband. William's two young aunts, Amelia and Harriet, constantly showered him with attention.

During his stay at St. Michaels, William developed a rather unflattering view of the native inhabitants of the Azores. "I believe there is an original inferiority in the nature of the Portuguese, and if it were possible to dissect the Soul, I suspect in three fourths of the nation, the anatomy would be composed solely of knavery and stupidity, with an equal chance, which of these two ingredients should predominate."[5] This opinion was formed after noticing that peoples daily lives were dictated by their dependence on a capricious government and overly superstitious religious beliefs. Naturally, such harsh judgments did not apply to the loving family of his grandfather and step grandmother.

William went on numerous walks around the *Yankee Hall* estate, taking much delight in the mild climate of the island and the pleasant aroma emitted from the nearby orange groves. Though he enjoyed basking in the scenic landscape of St. Michaels, he was, however, greatly concerned by the earthquakes that periodically shook the island. In a letter to his sister, William wrote, "Scarcely a year passes without an earthquake. I have been so fortunate as to witness the most tremendous of these convulsions within the memory of the present inhabitants. This was on the 1st of February, at midnight. So severe was the shock, that more than forty houses and many of the public edifices were overthrown or injured, and our house cracked in various places from top to bottom. The whole city was thrown into consternation."[6] He noted that this violent tremor had lasted a full three and a half minutes.

Prescott suffered some minor inflammation shortly after he had arrived at the island, which he simply attributed to the arduous sea voyage he had just undertaken. The bright sunlight and native cuisine, however, seemed to exacerbate his delicate condition. His affliction was compounded by a lack of medicine, for he had inadvertently left his supply of medication aboard the ship. Within a fortnight of his arrival William's eye once again became inflamed, a severe flare up that kept him confined to a large bedroom lacking blinds which could control the amount of sunlight that entered the room. Instead, the shutters to the windows were closed, which made his room entirely dark.

Concerned about his ailing grandson, Thomas Hickling had William moved to his Ponta Delgada residence, where he rested in a room that faced toward the north and which was adorned with windows that were shaded with varying thicknesses of baize, a cotton or woolen material napped to resemble felt. His medical attention was overseen by the uncle who was a doctor. The uncle supplied him with healthy portions of beef to help restore his strength. A bland ration of vegetables, bread, milk, gruel, and pudding rounded out his daily diet. William's grandfather provided him with healthy doses of aged Madeira wine, a libation which helped to lift his spirits. William's confinement began on the first of November and extended all the way to the first of February, six weeks of which were passed in total darkness.

To provide himself with some sorely needed exercise and to help relieve boredom, William would spend several hours walking about his unlit bedroom. He would jut out his elbow to warn himself of the approach of a corner of the wall, a means of detection that caused a fair amount of damage to the plastering. He sometimes exercised by walking on the piazza, making sure to shield his sensitive eyes from glare with a handkerchief tightly tied over his protective goggles. Prescott had followed a similar routine while confined to his room in Boston. Forevermore, William would have to take precautions to avoid exposing himself to glare, dust, sunlight, dampness, wind, and night air, or any other irritant that might trigger an inflammation. During this period of convalescence young Prescott was saddened to learn in a letter from his father of the death of two dear friends, Theodorick Randolph and Haskett Pickman.

William sought to improve his mood by singing and reciting poetry aloud while he sat alone in the dark. Thankfully, he was cheered by regular visits from his adoring cousins and aunts. Prescott also passed the time dictating letters to his parents, his sister, and his good friend William Gardiner, whom he affectionately referred to as Will. His young aunt Amelia would pen numerous letters for her ailing nephew. Amelia also entertained him by reading books on Greek and Roman History. Aunt Harriet, whom he fondly thought of as a sister, read him the works of William Shakespeare and Sir Walter Scott as well as Homer's *Iliad and the Odyssey*, and a number of travel books about England and Scotland.

Day by day, William's health grew stronger, but his vision still remained very poor. Eventually, he felt well enough to mount a saddle horse provided by his grandfather. William was keen on taking long walks and on occasion he would run into residents who fondly remembered meeting his young mother when she visited her father at the island. He particularly enjoyed a visit to the hot springs in Ribeira Grande, which is located toward the north of the island. Later, a fit William Prescott went on an excursion in the company of approximately 20 fellow travelers to visit the volcanic phenomenon known as *the Furnace.* This group of island adventurers rode donkeys over mountainous terrain and across lands of sublime scenery before finally reaching their destination, a wondrous site that did not disappoint young Prescott.

In a letter addressed to his father shortly before leaving St. Michaels, William wrote of his concerns regarding suitable professions that might be available to him: "The most unpleasant of my reflections suggested by this late inflammation are those arising from the probable necessity of abandoning a profession congenial with my taste, and recommended by such favorable opportunities, and adopting one for which I am ill qualified, and have but little inclination. It is some consolation, however, that this latter alternative, should my eyes permit, will afford me more leisure for the pursuit of my favorite studies. But on this subject I shall consult my physician and will write you his opinion."[7]

A Visit to London

On April 8, 1816, an emotional farewell took place at the Ponta Delgada dock as William Prescott prepared to board a boat bound for the distant shores of England. His step-grandmother wept profusely and tears steadily rolled down the cheeks of his grandfather as he declared, "God knows, it never cost me more to part from any of my own children."[8]

Once again the rigors of the sea proved rather upsetting to the delicate condition of the novice voyager. Shortly after setting sail, William was once again plagued by a painful bout of rheumatism and the added discomfort of swelling around his good eye. The voyage lasted 24 days, and for 22 of those days the ailing young man was once more exiled to a dark and dank cabin. He sufficiently recovered in time to catch a view of the spectacular White Cliffs of Dover.

Shortly after docking at the port of Dover, a naive William fell victim to a swindler who had touted his services as a guide. After this unpleasant experience, Prescott boarded a stagecoach that would transport him to London. The curious traveler elected to sit in the coachman's seat so that he could pose questions to the driver about the surrounding countryside.

William thoroughly enjoyed the scenic views along this route, especially those he spotted at Kent and Canterbury. While visiting the cathedral that was once home to a shrine to Thomas Beckett, Prescott noted, "I immediately threw myself on my knees on the very spot, ... much to the astonishment of my poor guide, though, if the truth were known, not so much from religious veneration, as from my respect to antiquity."[9] The carriage proceeded to pass through Gravesend and Greenwich before arriving at the bustling city of London. A letter of introduction in his possession helped William obtain lodging at the West End in Pall Mall.

Adhering to the sound guidance offered by Dr. Jackson prior to his departure from Boston, William sought out Mr. Astley Cooper (later Sir Astley) and Dr. John Richard Farre for advice concerning his visual defects. Cooper was an eminent surgeon who received a baronetcy in 1820 and four years later was named surgeon to King George IV. Both physicians agreed there was little that they could do for him; the maimed left eye was totally and permanently paralyzed, and the right eye would always be at the mercy of his recurring bouts of acute rheumatism. Dr. Farre would prescribe a host of medicines, but Prescott soon believed this course of action was strengthening the purse of the Apothecary Shop more than his health. After three weeks had passed, William asked Dr. Cooper to recommend a qualified oculist. The name of Sir William Adams was provided for him.

Following an intensive examination, Sir William Adams correctly concluded that his young patient's paralyzed left eye would never regain its full power of sight. But the oculist was convinced that with the proper treatment it would be possible to make some noticeable improvements to the damaged eye. As for Prescott's delicate right eye, the doctor felt that a change in diet would help strengthen his health, which, in turn, would reduce his susceptibility to inflammation. He prescribed ample amounts of meat and fish, which was to be washed down with a sizable glass of wine. Sir William also applied various lotions and unguents to both the lid and eye of his patient.

Following the unfavorable diagnosis of these London specialists, a disheartened William Prescott wrote: "As to the future, it is too evident I shall never be able to pursue a profession. Gods knows how poorly I am qualified and how little inclined to be a merchant. Indeed, I am sadly puzzled to think how I shall succeed even in this without eyes."[10]

William chose to place his trust in the advice of the distinguished British oculist. Per Sir William Adam's recommendation, Prescott relocated to a room overlooking Regent's Park. After noticing there was a marked improvement in his condition, a very pleased William wrote to his parents, "My eye is entirely free from inflammation and it has already acquired considerable strength under Sir William Adam's treatment."[11] The letter was penned for him by a man named McCandlish, whom Prescott had hired as his personal secretary for the sum of $12 per month.

Prescott's letters of introduction granted him an audience with John Quincy Adams, U.S. Minister at the Court of St. James, and his wife Louisa at Boston House, their residence in suburban Ealing. This eldest son of President John Adams would become the sixth president of the United States a mere eight years after meeting with the young fellow Bostonian. William was a frequent guest at the Adams' home and even joined them on a journey to Windsor Castle, where the minister's influence gained them access to parts of the castle that were not open to the general public. They also visited Eton, Hampton Court, and Slough. The latter site provided William an opportunity to see the telescopes designed by Sir William Herschel, the eminent German born astronomer.

While at London, William was introduced to Colonel Thomas Aspinwall and his charming wife Louise. Thomas Aspinwall had studied law at Harvard and graduated with honors in 1804. After graduation he accepted a position at the law office of William Sullivan, where his hard work and exceptional abilities soon led to him being named a partner. He later started a private practice but closed shop at the onset of yet another war with England in order to enlist in the military. Aspinwall was appointed commander of the Ninth Infantry of Massachusetts during the War of 1812, and lost his left arm to a musket shot during the siege of Fort Erie. Thomas was just beginning a new career in the service of the American consulate when he first met William Prescott. Colonel Aspinwall was appointed United States consul at London in 1824, a title which he held until his retirement. In addition to his many diplomatic duties, Aspinwall also served as the London literary representative for a number of American writers, a list that would eventually include such distinguished authors as Washington Irving, James Fenimore Cooper, Fitz-Greene Halleck, John Lloyd Stephens, and an historian by the name of William Hickling Prescott.

During his stay in London, William had the opportunity to visit Richmond Hill, London Tower, the House of Parliament, St. Paul's, Westminster Abbey, Greenwich observatory, and several other sites of historical interest. Prescott also found time to enjoy some of London's more entertaining events: he viewed the Stevens-Robinson boxing match, watched the horse races at Epsom, toured Bullock's Museum, and attended a performance of skilled jugglers from India. William also saw the splendid cork models of ancient temples on display at Dubourg's Museum, visited the exhibit of exotic animals at Stephens Polito's Royal Menagerie, and viewed the many creative devices on show at Weeks's mechanical exhibition.

William visited the British Museum and Westminster Abbey on multiple occasions. He also developed an interest in art, especially after having attended an exhibition of Benjamin West's work, which included the artist's *Christ Rejected by the Jews* and *Christ Healing the Sick in the Temple*. This led to an extended private meeting with the renowned and elderly painter, an American born artist who was a founder and president of the Royal Academy as well as a painter to King George III. The artist was noted for his grand paintings of well-known historical events, biblical episodes, and mythological themes. *The Death of General Wolfe* is considered by many to be one of West's best and certainly most recognizable work of art.

Always on the lookout for a good book to read, or have read to him, William perused the local libraries and rummaged through the numerous bookshops of London, especially those located along Paternoster Row. He wrote, "I take great delight in looking into their scarce and valuable editions, collections such as I have never before witnessed."[12] Though he found that most of these books carried a hefty price tag, he still managed to purchase a few titles of interest that were difficult to find at home.

Per his father's request, William found time to observe the English judicial system at work. He wrote, "I have heard some excellent arguments in the cockpit, the Court of Appeals from the Colonies, and Admiralty decisions."[13] Overall, William viewed the legal proceedings as rather tedious and dull. He was even more disappointed with the activities of the House of Commons.

The few letters that William penned to his family were delayed by infrequent shipping schedules, especially those he had written during his stay in the Azores. Once at London, he decided to postpone sending any letters home until he had some positive news to report about the treatment of his eyes. This lack of news was disconcerting to his parents. Catherine Prescott wrote a scathing letter to her negligent son, "Had it not been for the attention of our friends we should not even have heard of your arrival in London; does the amusements of that gay city, and the pleasures that surround you, banish from your remembrance the Parents, who promoted your going there, the father who daily labours to support you there, and the friends who feel so much anxiety for you, no that can not be, yet I am weary of conjecture, and tired of apologizing."[14] From then on William made sure to honor his parents with letters on a more frequent basis.

In a letter dated July 28, 1816, William wrote to his parents that he had learned from Mrs. Delafield, a woman who had taken an interest in his delicate condition, of a new device that might prove very useful to him: "Last evening.... I heard of a new invented machine by which blind people were enabled to write. I have been before indebted to Mrs. D. for an ingenious candle screen. If this machine can be procured, you may depend upon it you will feel the effects of it."[15]

A week later William was able to purchase this new mechanism from Ralph Wedgwood, Jr., a London inventor who held the patent for this machine known as a noctograph. He would purchase a second noctograph, which was kept in reserve just in case the other broke down. Though he never owned more than two such writing devices during his lifetime, he would, overtime, purchase many others to give to individuals he knew who suffered from a similar lack of vision. The noctograph proved invaluable to Prescott's future profession, which he religiously used to write the drafts for his historical accounts.

William provided a detailed description of the noctograph, a device he states was composed of "a frame of the size of a common sheet of letter-paper, with brass wires inserted in it to correspond with the number of lines wanted. On one side of this frame is pasted a leaf of thin carbonated paper, such as is used to obtain duplicates. Instead of a pen, the writer makes use of a stylus, of ivory or agate, the latter better or harder. The great difficulties in the way of a blind man's writing in the usual manner arise from his not knowing when the ink is exhausted in his pen, and when his lines run into one another. Both these difficulties are obviated by this simple writing case, which enables one to do his work as well in the dark as in the light."[16] The noctograph allowed for up to 17 lines per sheet of paper that measured approximately seven and three-quarters by ten inches.

While there were numerous advantages in using the noctograph, there were, however, a few significant disadvantages to writing with this mechanical device. The user was unable to make erasures or corrections, which meant there was little choice but to continue forward with their writing. There were occasions when Prescott forgot to load a sheet of paper and proceeded to write a full page before discovering his mistake. Such problems forced him to make sure that the contents of his compositions were fully organized and composed in his mind before committing them to paper, a process that Washington Irving described as "pre-thinking." His proficiency with the noctograph became easier and faster over time. William would often refer to his writing as being just as difficult to decipher as ancient hieroglyphics, a remark made in jest.

Continental Travels

Eager to explore some of Europe's historic cities, William soon began making plans for a tour of the European continent. Sir William Adams made sure to provide his young patient with precise dietary instructions and necessary medicinal supplies for his upcoming travels. The oculist also advised him to treat any sudden recurrence of inflammation with thorough applications of cold water. William also made sure to store in his luggage the newly-acquired noctograph. After an enjoyable stay of three months in London, the suddenly venturesome William Prescott sailed across the channel in the company of a gentleman known only as N. Amory to take up residence in Paris, the romantic *City of Light*.

Shortly after arriving in Paris, William was tormented by a recurrence of the much dreaded inflammation to his good eye. But by assiduously following Sir William's explicit instructions, the malady subsided after a mere three days and did not bother him again during his two-month-long stay in Paris.

William used his noctograph for the very first time to compose a letter to his parents. He found the machine quite difficult and tiresome but was confident that practice would make it much easier to use. In a letter dated August 24, 1816, William stated, "You must excuse this writing dear Parents it is my *coup d' essai* with my machine for writing without looking, is doubtless illegible and filled with blunders, as I have not seen a word of it; the invention however is certainly a very fortunate one for me, but the process is so tedious."[17]

While at Paris the ever-inquisitive William Prescott visited the museums, libraries, palaces, churches, and numerous other sites of interest that the city had to offer. He was awed by the magnificent book collections stored at both the Bibliothèque du Roi and the library of the French Institute. It was during this visit that William had the pleasure of making the acquaintance of Albert Gallatin, the elder American statesman who had recently been appointed minister to France. Years later these two men, both of whom having developed a keen interest in early Mexican history, would correspond on a regular basis. Prescott had a chance meeting with another American tourist; John Chipman Gray, a good friend and fellow graduate of Harvard, who was an heir to a very prosperous shipping family in Salem.

William decided that he would spend the winter months touring the warm and sunny region of Italy, where he hoped the salubrious climate would prove beneficial to his rheumatic condition. John Gray agreed to accompany him on this journey. Wishing to travel in style, the two American tourists purchased from a Parisian seller a chariot suitable for gentlemen such as themselves, a cost of comfort that amounted to a hefty 2000 francs. William found it necessary to purchase matching green curtains to hang over the carriage windows as a means of reducing the harmful glare of the sun. He would also purchase a pair of sheets to hang over windows at inns that might not have sufficient blinds or curtains in place. On October 7, 1816, William and John set out on their Italian tour in the company of a Swiss-born manservant named Fribourg, a valet hired to handle their baggage, negotiate room rates with innkeepers, and attend to their various personal needs.

Their first stop after leaving Paris was La Grange, where Prescott and Gray were fortunate to enjoy the gracious hospitality of Marquis de Lafayette, the famous French officer who had rallied to the side of the American colonists during their desperate struggle for independence. They would spend the night at the six-century-old castle belonging to the Marquis. The next morning, following a quick tour of Lafayette's vast estate, the young adventurers resumed their journey to Italy. In 1825, when Marquis de Lafayette returned to America and stopped at Boston, William H. Prescott was there to welcome the visiting hero with open arms.

During their ten-day journey to the Italian border, William Prescott, John Gray, and their faithful manservant passed through the regions of Avallon, Autun, Mâcon, Bourgoin, Chambéry, and St. Jean de Maurienne. Though the scenery was not quite as charming as he had expected from his inquiries about these provinces, William still found the journey very enjoyable. The American companions followed a route through France and Italy that would pass by the cities of Lyon, Turin, Genoa, Milan, Venice, Bologna, and Florence before arriving at Rome.

William enjoyed Italy immensely, an observation made evident in a letter he wrote to his parents on November 15, 1816: "I never expect to feel again similar emotions to those I felt when I set foot on this sacred land." In that same letter Prescott wrote of his impression of the Po river, "It is a noble river, and well deserves the immortality to which Ovid has consigned it."[18]

Continuing along the road that passed through Genoa, Prescott and

Gray paid a visit to Marengo, the site of a famous Napoleon victory. They shared lodgings at the towns of Asti and Novi with a host of fleas that made sleep virtually impossible. Their journey took them across the battlefield where Francis I, the king of France, was forced to surrender to Charles V, king of Spain and Holy Roman Emperor. William and John continued on to Milan, which served as a base for visits to lakes Maggiore and Como. They also visited the Milanese site where it was said an echo would reverberate 50 times. The two Massachusetts travelers put this tale to the test by firing off their pistols, which thundered with a sound comparable to an artillery barrage.

Prescott and Gray visited an amphitheater at Verona, which at the time served as the stage for a visiting circus. William and his traveling companion toured the home of Livy, one of ancient Rome's greatest historians. They also viewed the birthplaces of Catullus, the celebrated Roman poet, and Pliny, the renowned Roman scholar. The towns of Modena and Bologna were visited prior to their reaching Florence. William found Florence to be a very charming city, declaring, "Italian society is in its perfection at Florence." He added, "It is the modern Athens; and the arts seem to have selected it, as their last retreat."[19] Here at the city generally recognized as the birthplace of the Renaissance, William encountered Rafaello Morghen, an esteemed engraver whose work he admired so much that he bought ten of his engravings for 180 francs, regretting that he could not afford to buy more.

William enjoyed good health for most of his Italian adventure. While the mild climate certainly seemed to agree with him, Prescott also acknowledged that the medication and excellent advice provided by Sir William Adams, the London oculist, played a major role in his continued well-being.

Rome offered an abundance of time-honored sites to satisfy Prescott's interest in classical antiquities. There were the ancient Roman amphitheaters, temples, tombs, baths, sculptures, circuses, and bridges to observe and reflect upon. He also paid his respects at several Christian churches, the most memorable being St. Peter's Basilica.

William suddenly realized that his expenditures were rapidly exceeding his allowance and consequently was compelled to tighten his purse strings. Such cutbacks interfered with his opportunity to meet His Holiness Pius VII. The cost of a specially tailored outfit that conformed with proper etiquette for meeting the Pope, a suit which he would never again have a use for, seemed frivolous and therefore he decided to pass on this invitation.

The two intrepid adventurers remained in Rome for roughly six weeks before heading to Naples for a month-long visit. William found that the prices at Naples were excessively high—rampant price gouging was directly related to the steady increase in the number of wealthy English tourists. Because of rapidly rising rents, William and John had to relocate several times during their four-week stay in Naples. Prescott was sidelined for four days at the city by a sudden recurrence of swelling around his eye. Once he had recovered, Naples would serve as a base for their excursions to Portici, Vesuvius, Pozzuoli, Pompeii, Cumoe, Salerno, Eboli, and Baia. Prescott even felt strong enough to climb the crater of the still active Vesuvius volcano.

After a stay of four weeks at Naples, William and John realized that the time had come for them to begin their long journey back to France. The two American wayfarers returned to Rome to spend a few days visiting the historical sites they had not yet seen. Afterwards, the traveling companions made their way to the city of Florence. They trekked through the Arno Valley to arrive at Pisa; their five-month tour of Italy would come to an end at Livorno (aka Leghorn). On the twelfth of March, Prescott and Gray boarded a ship that sailed past Genoa, Nice, and Toulon. They decided to stop for a brief visit at Marseilles before proceeding by chariot to Nismes, Avignon, and Vaucluse. While at Avignon the two young men visited the tomb of Laura de Noves, the woman who is said to have captured the heart of Francesco Petrarch, the famous Italian scholar and poet. The two adventurers then headed to Fontainebleau, which they reached on the thirtieth of March.

William returned to Paris on the seventh of April only to find himself confined to a darkened hotel room for an entire week because of yet another recurrence of inflammation around his right eye. Fortunately, Prescott's good friend George Ticknor was to check into the same hotel just as he had begun to feel better. George was returning from nearly two years of studies at Göttingen, Germany, which he attended with Edward Everett, who was a close friend of both Ticknor and Prescott. George Ticknor was preparing to return to Boston to accept the Smith Professorship of French and Spanish Language and Literature at Harvard. Ticknor's presence helped to lift Prescott's spirits and he soon felt strong enough to take a stroll through the streets of Paris with him and a gentleman who served as the banker for both young gentlemen. After dinner they returned to the Hotel de Montmorency, whereupon William complained that he was feeling slightly feverish. Ticknor immediately summoned for Prescott's personal physician, who ordered immediate bed rest for his ailing patient. George Ticknor stayed by William's side throughout the night.

Prescott's condition would continue to worsen. George Ticknor now had a much better understanding of the painful ordeal that his younger friend had to periodically endure, and was struck by the fact that William never complained about his ailment. Many years later, Ticknor recalled his Parisian encounter with the ailing Prescott, "It was in that dark room that I first learned to know him, as I have never known any other person beyond the limit of my immediate family."[20] He was a frequent visitor at Prescott's bedside during this unpleasant ordeal, which further strengthened the bond between them, a friendship that flourished for nearly five decades. William's affliction lessened after three or four days, and in less than two weeks he felt well enough to leave his room. A week later his ailment had completely vanished.

Once his strength had returned, William took the time to enjoy more of the city's many attractions. He also did some shopping and visited several Parisian hostesses, including Madame de Staël, a celebrated woman of letters who would pass away shortly after their meeting. Prescott would mention Madame de Staël in his article titled "Italian Narrative Poetry," which was published in the October 1824 edition of the *North American Review*. Afterwards, Prescott and Gray decided to prepare for their return to England. They were able to sell their chariot to another American traveler for 1250 francs. Prior to sailing to England, William spent a week at the estate of Dr. Daniel Parker at Draveil. Prescott and Gray traveled to Dieppe in mid–May, and there they boarded a boat that ferried them across the English Channel.

A Return to England

After docking at Brighton, Prescott made his way to London, where he stayed for approximately six weeks. He made sure to visit Sir William Adams to report on the state of his health. Prescott had faithfully adhered to the doctor's recommendations during his travels in France and Italy, a treatment plan which included following the oculist's recommended diet, properly shielding his eyes from the glare of the sun, regular applications of astringent lotions, and the consumption of two glasses of wine per day. The young patient enjoyed the wine so much that he always had it served in the largest available glasses. William also added brisk walks to his daily regimen. Dr. Adams was encouraged by the results and instructed him to continue this course of treatment.

Prescott had intended to take a tour of Scotland but abandoned this plan so that he could have more time to further explore the many interesting and historic sites that London had to offer. This also provided William an opportunity to do some additional shopping for himself and his family. He also found time to once again view the ongoing debates in the House of Lords and the House of Commons. Mr. McCandlish, William's secretary, was kept busy penning his letters, reading to him, and performing various other services during his residence in the West End.

William traveled by stagecoach to visit Oxford, Blenheim, and the Wye, a journey that provided him an opportunity to view the striking Gothic architecture of New-College Chapel and the ruins of Tintern Abbey, both nestled in a scenic valley that served to enhance their pastoral charm. He also visited Gloucester and Bristol on this whirlwind tour that lasted an entire week. William returned by way of Salisbury before heading to Cambridge armed with letters of introduction to respected fellows and professors. While at Cambridge, Prescott paid a visit to King's College Chapel, where he had a chance to view the manuscripts of John Milton and Sir Isaac Newton. He then returned to London to pack his belongings and say his goodbyes. On July 30, 1817, William Prescott set out for Liverpool, where he had booked passage on the *Triton* for his return voyage to Boston.

3

Scholarly Pursuits

A man must find something to do.[1]

First Literary Effort

As one might expect, young William's return to Boston in late summer of 1817 was a joyous occasion for the entire Prescott family. Even though his health had not been fully restored, William and Catherine were satisfied that their son had made every effort to attend to his well-being. William would continue to minister to his health by regulating his diet, curbing the use of his eyes, exercising regularly, and dramatically limiting his social activities. The return from his lengthy overseas adventure marked a brief period where William felt rather self-conscious about his condition, and therefore he became somewhat of a recluse.

While William was off on his overseas adventure, Judge Prescott had moved the family out of their Otis Place home and taken up residence at a house he purchased on the north side of Pond Street, which in 1821 was renamed Bedford Street. Their new home was a large brick house painted yellow that stood very close to the street, but which had an enormous backyard that was shaded by a number of towering elm and horse-chestnut trees. At the end of the lot stood a big brick stable that housed the family horses. In addition to a master bedroom and separate rooms for the three siblings, there were additional bedrooms to comfortably accommodate guests. The new Prescott house also boasted a lavish library and a sizable parlor.

In anticipation of the return of her oldest child, Catherine Prescott had his drab room made more cheerful with a fresh coat of white paint and some brightly colored wallpaper. Sadly, William found that the room was far too bright for his sensitive eyes; the white paint was redone in gray, and the wallpaper and carpet were replaced with material containing greenish hues. The changes helped somewhat but a return of poor health compelled William to relocate to the family's newly-leased house in the country, which was shaded by numerous trees. Unfortunately, the damp and cool climate, triggered another flare up of his acute rheumatic ailment. William would return to town, where he would remain confined to his darkened room for most of the winter season.

The bond between William and his sister Elizabeth, which had always been close and affectionate, grew even more intimate following his return. Nearly 18 when her older brother came home, Lizzie had blossomed into a young lady who had a passion for the arts. She was also an avid reader and would spend many an evening reading to her brother from a varied assortment of books that piqued and broadened his literary interests. Unfortunately, an age gap of nearly eight years between William and Edward interfered with their developing a closeness like that which William shared with Lizzie. Furthermore, Ned did not share the same intellectual curiosity as that of his older brother.

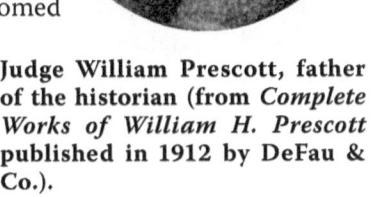

Judge William Prescott, father of the historian (from *Complete Works of William H. Prescott* published in 1912 by DeFau & Co.).

William Gardiner, who was pursuing a career in law by starting off as a clerk in Judge Prescott's office, dropped by almost daily to chat and read the classics of literature to his oldest and dearest friend. Lizzie would read novels and other literary works to her brother once Gardiner had finished his visit. Since William's bedroom had to be kept in a darkened state, Elizabeth often had to position herself along the floor at the face of the door in order to catch the small amount of light that seeped in through the threshold. These readings, which helped keep William's mind active during this trying period of convalescence, would continue for many hours and often went late into the night. Such lengthy reading sessions were reminiscent of those that had occurred while he was confined to his room in St. Michael's listening ever so intently to various family members who voluntarily entertained him with tales of romantic adventures and lively historical accounts.

William gradually recovered and by the spring of 1818 he felt strong enough to venture outside. This would soon prove to have been a hasty move on his part, for come May he was once again sidelined by a sudden and painful recurrence of inflammation. However, by early July, Prescott was well enough to resume his daily regimen of walks and balanced consumption of wine. Once his vision had sufficiently improved, William was able to remove the blinds that barred the sunlight from his room.

Young Prescott made it a point to awaken early, which was no easy task for him. Prior to his marriage, the family servant, Nathan Webster, had the daily duty of making sure Master Prescott was wakened before sunrise. The Prescotts also employed another longtime servant named Lucy. Once awake, William would count to 20 before leaping out of his bed. Mr. Webster would then inform him of the current temperature and weather conditions so that he might dress accordingly for his morning exercise. Once readied, he would mount his horse for a brisk ride to Jamaica Plain, a location less than four miles away, where he would patiently wait to greet the rising sun. He performed this task daily, regardless of how bitter cold it might be. The only exceptions were periods of extremely severe weather or times when he suffered from poor health. Judge Prescott often rode with his son. Their respective horses were brought to the front of the house, and once mounted, father and son rode side by side for awhile, but always parted ways at a designated spot.

Alone with his thoughts, William could not help but wonder what the future might hold for him, particularly regarding his choice of a career. Fortunate to come from a family of means, he could have relaxed and simply enjoyed life as a gentleman of leisure, but this was unthinkable to a young man such as himself who thirsted for knowledge. Since the fields of law or business were no longer viable options, he contemplated what sort of profession might be available that could hold his interest.

Motivated by his love of books and the encouragement of his sister, William decided to try his own hand at writing. He kept his writing project a secret until the article was finished, which he turned over to Lizzie to make a more legible copy. The story was sent to the *North American Review*, a barely two-year-old regional journal that had already earned a fair measure of respect amongst a steadily growing following of New England readers. Since some of his friends and acquaintances were connected with this journal, William decided to submit his article anonymously. He merely wanted to see if it would be approved on its own merit. More than a week passed before he received a rejection letter from the editor. He asked his sister, who seemed to take the bad news even harder than he did, to keep this failed effort a secret. The aspiring author complained, "There! I was a fool to send it!"[2] Though disappointed by the result, William learned from this experience that he would have to hone his writing skills if he ever hoped to succeed as an author.

Meanwhile, William's father, the Honorable William Prescott, LLD, was steadily adding to his growing fortune by making sound investments in local business firms, particularly in the expanding fields of transportation, insurance, and industry. Judge Prescott played an important role in the incorporation of the Massachusetts Hospital Life Insurance Company, serving first as a director (1823–1827) and then as its president (1828–1842). His close association with many of Boston's financial and business leaders provided beneficial inside information which, in turn, led to profitable speculation in trade. Judge Prescott also partnered with his good friend David Sears to invest in land, principally properties located in Maine.

William's mother was actively involved in a number of charitable institutions. Catherine Prescott frequently visited and comforted the sick and dying at the Lying-in Hospital. Much of her free time was consumed by work at the Female Asylum, where she was a manager for 39 years, the last 17 of which she served as the Asylum's first female director. Her association with the Female Asylum continued until the time of her death. The charitable activities of his parents clearly had a deep and lasting impact on William's benevolent behavior.

Social Gatherings

William eventually decided that the time had come for him to shed his reclusive life and resume socializing with friends and acquaintances. These renewed associations led to the formation of a literary club that included members of similar age and interests who regularly gathered to rub elbows and discuss literature. The first meeting took place on June 13, 1818, which was attended by Prescott and eight other like-minded Boston gentlemen. Membership would grow to 12 by the second gathering. This scholarly group, however, never numbered more than 24 members. The list of Harvard colleagues included Franklin Dexter, his soon to be brother-in-law; Theophilus Parsons, who studied law with Judge Prescott; Jared Sparks, future publisher and editor of the *North American Review*; and his best friend William Gardiner. The other group members were also graduates of Harvard, many of whom were members of the Porcellain

Club, who were currently embarking on careers in law, the clergy, medicine, or business. Since William Prescott had yet to find his calling, the other members nicknamed him *the gentleman*. This literary group was referred to as simply the *Club*.

Prescott greatly enjoyed attending these meetings and therefore rarely missed a session. The members would discuss literature and read their own compositions to the group, who then proceeded to amuse themselves with friendly critiques of one another's writings. Before long, the group felt their work was good enough to be shared with the public. William and the other members decided to publish a periodical that they called *The Club-Room*. In addition to contributing several of his own stories, Prescott served as editor for the local periodical. This experience helped improve his writing technique and provided the motivation he needed to give serious thought to pursuing a literary career. Out of concern for his health, Prescott would excuse himself no later than 12 o'clock from these meetings.

Despite vowing to never again attempt to publish his writings after his first literary effort had been so roundly rejected, Prescott willingly contributed three articles to the project: a romantic story titled *Vale of Alleriat*; a gothic tale called *Calais*; and *The Club-Room*, which was a light-hearted account of the naming of the periodical and its intended purpose. In the latter feature, William wrote that it took as many as seven meetings for the group to agree on a name for their publication: "The Cynics recommended *Tales of the Tub*, and the Peripatetics proposed *Velocipede*. In this crisis, being, as usual, unanimously divided in our opinions, we determined to follow the example of the ancient Greeks, who when each man had voted himself the best general at the siege of Troy, wisely balloted for the second-best; and in precisely the same manner did we at length resolve upon the very ingenious name of the Club-Room."[3]

Regrettably, *The Club-Room* had a very short literary life. The first issue was published on February 5, 1820. Five hundred copies of the 40-page periodical were printed at a price of 37 and one-half cents. The 44-page second edition was released on March 10, 1820, for the same price. The third issue, which at 54 pages was their largest edition, was published on April 26, 1820, at the increased fee of 45 cents. The fourth and final edition of *The Club-Room* was a 39-page issue distributed on July 19, 1820. Even though each edition had managed to yield a small profit, their inability to reach a wider audience and the stress of so few members contributing stories worthy enough to print had spelled the inevitable demise of the project. The *Club*, however, continued to have a great many more meetings, and William Prescott remained an active member for some 40 years.

Marriage

The hospitable Judge Prescott and his wife would occasionally host large and lavish dinner parties. In remembrance of their Puritan lineage, Thanksgiving Day was a time when family and friends gathered at the Prescott home. William took great pleasure in joining the parlor games that were played at these gatherings, and was particularly fond of taking part in blindman's buff and puss in the corner, which he played with youthful zest even as an adult. Another favorite was Albano, a card game similar to puss in the corner, which was introduced to him by some friends who had played it in Rome. He was also passionate about playing a challenging game of chess. There were times when a jubilant William Prescott would unexpectedly burst into song, a particularly favorite began "O, give me but my Arab steed."[4] He also developed a fondness for attending the theater.

William relished the social interaction and stimulating conversation he freely engaged in at the balls held either in his house or the home of friends. He especially enjoyed dancing and his favorite dance partner was the young Miss Susannah Amory, best known to her friends as Susan. She was the daughter of Thomas Coffin Amory, Esq., a prosperous merchant who, before he passed away in 1812, had amassed a sufficient amount of wealth to ensure a comfortable life for his family. Susan's mother, Hannah Linzee, was the daughter of Captain John Linzee, a British naval officer who had commanded the frigate *Falcon*, a war vessel which had participated in the bombardment of Bunker Hill during its occupation in 1775 by troops under the command of William's grandfather. Susan would inherit the military sword that belonged to her grandfather. Her brother, William Amory, was one of Prescott's oldest and dearest friends.

Determined to win Susan's affection, William serenaded her with selected poems of Thomas Moore, Lord Byron and James Macpherson. In August of 1819, Susan's smitten suitor sent her the following stanza, which is a near verbatim quatrain by the Irish poet Thomas Moore:

> And sweetly did the pages fill
> With fond device and loving lore
> And every leaf she turn'd was still
> More bright than that she turn'd before.[5]

While William was courting Susan Amory, his sister, Catherine Elizabeth Prescott, agreed to marry Franklin Dexter, the son of Samuel Dexter, a highly respected lawyer and statesman, and on September 28, 1819, the couple entered into wedlock. Theirs was a happy marriage that produced four sons.

One of the losing bets that William felt compelled to honor was paid to Theophilus Parsons, a wager pertaining to his soon to end status as a bachelor. In a letter dated May 3, 1820, Prescott wrote to Parsons: "It is so long since the bet became due that I ought to pay interest, but such a thing, I believe, is contrary to the code of honor, and is still more contrary to the laws of love, which have a right to preside over our bet. However if I lost my money I have got my wife, and I am very willing to pay it as a discount upon the high prize."[6]

William and Susan were married on the following day, May 4, 1820, which so happened to be Prescott's 24th birthday. They said their vows at Mrs. Amory's home, located at 21 Franklin Place, and the service was followed by an elegant feast. After much celebration, the newlyweds retired to the Prescott family home, a mere two blocks away from where they were married. Coincidentally, their Bedford Street home was the same house where Susan's parents were married 25 years earlier. William and Susan lived quite happily at this house until 1845, the year they decided to relocate to Beacon Street. Shortly thereafter, the old mansion was torn down.

George Ticknor provided a description of William Prescott that paints a rather vivid picture of how the historian looked at the time of his marriage to Susan Amory: "my friend was one of the finest-looking men I have ever seen; or, if this should be deemed in some respects a strong expression, I shall be fully justified, by those who remember him at that period, in saying that he was one on the most attractive. He was tall, well formed, manly in his bearing but gentle, with light-brown hair that was hardly changed or diminished by years, with a clear complexion, and a ruddy flush on his cheek that kept for him to the last an appearance of comparative youth, but, above all, with a smile that was the most absolutely contagious I ever looked upon."[7] The following year, George Ticknor ended his days as a bachelor by marrying Anna Eliot, the daughter of Samuel Eliot, a prosperous merchant and banker. A few years later, George and Anna moved into their house at the corner of Park and Beacon Streets.

Susan was a timid and innocent young woman, but grew comfortably into her role as wife and mother. She remained, however, an introvert who never felt comfortable mingling in society or venturing beyond the city limits, except for visits to their country and seaside homes. Susan tenderheartedly looked after the health of William and enjoyed reading to him. William always found time to spend with his wife—part of his daily routine was to enjoy the pleasure of her company at dinner and until shortly after sunset before tending to his other interests. Prior to their marriage, Susan and her family had faithfully attended Trinity Church on Summer Street, where Dr. John S. J. Gardiner was the rector. Neither William, who was a Unitarian, or Susan, who was an Episcopalian, wished to turn their back on their respective churches, so they compromised by alternating attendance at their Unitarian and Episcopal services.

Intellectual Pursuits

Shortly after his marriage to Susan, William resolved to formulate and follow his own plan of studies that would enable him to become a respected man of letters. In the spring of 1822 he wrote in his journal, "I am now twenty-six years of age, nearly. By the time I am thirty, God willing, I propose with what stock I have already on hand to be a very well read English scholar; to be acquainted with the classical and useful authors, prose and poetry, in Latin, French, and Italian, and especially in history…. The two following years, 31–32, I may hope to learn German and to have read the classical German writers; and the translations, if my eye continues weak, of the Greek. And this is enough for general discipline."[8]

Now that he had set his sights on becoming a scholar, William committed himself to perfecting the writer's craft. Just as he had done in college, he would allot himself a fixed amount of time each day for study, dividing his inquiries among topics he felt would make him a better writer. Prescott established a work schedule that aspired to seven and a half hours a day, a little less on Sundays. He split his studies into shifts; his morning schedule began between 8:30 and nine o'clock in the morning, and would conclude, depending upon his starting time, at around two o'clock or half past two in the afternoon. He would resume work around four or five o'clock. The final work session would last for two hours. Naturally, allowances were made for interruptions, both for social and health reasons.

Schedules were maintained for nearly every aspect of Prescott's daily routine: there were specified hours to wake, eat, exercise, work, enjoy the company of family and friends, and retire. His diet was regulated by rules as was his manner of dress. Shoes, of which he had a great many, were always lined up and ready to wear for the proper occasion. There would always be an orderly method to controllable events that affected his everyday life. As mentioned earlier, William hated to wake early but knew that he must if he wished to fulfill his ambition of becoming a man of letters. To avoid bothering his wife, Prescott left strict instructions with Nathan Webster, the family manservant, to awaken him before dawn and authorized him to strip off his covers if he failed to arise when called.

William kept a journal to periodically record his literary ambitions, achievements, opinions, concerns, and estimates for completing various tasks. Many of his early journal entries were opinions of works he had just read during his determined quest to become a man of letters. The aspiring writer referred to these journals as his literary memoranda. Overtime, Prescott filled nearly 12 notebooks, each containing roughly 100 pages, which covered the period from mid–1823 until late 1858. His notes were written in ink but there are also miscellaneous notes jotted down in pencil. Approximately one-third of the writings in these journals were penned in his own hand, while the majority were written by either a succession of secretaries, his wife, his sister, or whomever else might be available to record his pressing thoughts. These notebooks offer a fascinating glimpse into the mind of a man who was committed to becoming a scholar and author of note.

In keeping with his practice of setting goals for himself, William often designated the fourth of May, his birthdate, as a day when he expected to achieve a specific objective of major importance. He also would make note of any personal fault on a piece of paper, which he stored in a large envelope. Prescott would periodically review these recognized failings and if he determined that he had permanently corrected that particular shortcoming he would discard the slip of paper. New faults were continually added throughout his life. This ritual was known to only a few friends and family members. After his death, this envelope containing his list of

Prescott at work (showing use of the noctograph) (from *Complete Works of William H. Prescott* published in 1912 by DeFau & Co.).

perceived shortcomings was discovered, which Prescott had clearly marked "To be burnt." His written wish was honored.

Prescott began assembling a collection of books germane to his studies, the first step taken toward amassing what would become a large and impressive library. He selected a variety of reading materials that would be of intellectual interest and which would provide him with a solid grounding in the essential characteristics of exemplary writing styles. William dedicated himself to learning his chosen craft by studying the principles of grammar, proper writing techniques, and acquainting himself with the style of the finest prose writers. The aspiring author familiarized himself with selected works of such noted English authors as Roger Ascham, Sir Philip Sidney, Sir Francis Bacon, Sir Thomas Browne, Sir Walter Raleigh, John Milton, and concluded with the works of prominent contemporary English writers. William would spend nearly a year studying the styles of these noted English prose-writers. He also read a number of Latin classics, which included those penned by Tacitus, Livy, and Cicero.

Judge Prescott wholeheartedly supported his son's scholarly pursuits. The elder Prescott, who was an enthusiastic reader, was delighted to see that his son now had a goal and therefore was no longer content to be thought of as merely *the gentleman*, the title bestowed upon him by fellow members of the *Club*. The Judge provided his son with a generous allotment of rental properties that would furnish the hopeful scholar with his own source of funds. Now that he was married, William assumed the responsibility of managing his own portfolio, which included investments in local banking, insurance, manufacturing, real estate, and later the railroad industry. Sound financial advice was freely provided by his knowledgeable father.

William's trio of stories for *The Club-Room* were his early entries as a writer, but these were self-published works that did not have to pass the keen scrutiny of a skillful editor. In order to succeed in his scholarly ambitions Prescott knew that he would need to have his writing published by a respected source. Such an opportunity occurred in 1821 when the *North American Review* and its editor Edward Everett decided to publish his essay titled "Byron's Letter on Pope." This was the beginning of a more than 30-year-long relationship between William Hickling Prescott and this distinguished literary magazine.

In 1821, while still pursuing his scholarly studies, William wrote: "I will write a review no oftener than once in three numbers of the 'No. American Review.' No *oftener*, and *print* only what I think will add to my reputation…. In the interim I will follow a course of reading and make the subjects of my reviews, as far as I can, fall in with this course.... Pursue this course till I am thirty.... Mem. I will never engage to write for a number."[9]

From 1821 to 1833, Prescott continued to contribute what he referred to as his "annual peppercorn" to the *North American Review*, the periodical affectionately referred to by many, including William, as the *Old North*. Initially, these reviews were little more than a means of honing his writing skills and an opportunity to be recognized for his literary abilities. His essays contained little in the way of literary criticism or new insight into the author or topic he was reviewing. However, William's essay titled "Italian Narrative Poetry," which was published in the *North American Review* in 1824, was met with criticism from Signor Lorenzo da Ponte, an Italian poet living in New York, who was best known for writing the libretto to Mozart's *Don Giovanni*. Prescott responded to Signor da Ponte's complaints with a firm but respectful 50-page article titled *"Da Ponte's Observations,"* which appeared in the July 1825 edition of the *North American Review*. Since there was no reply from the Venetian poet, it appeared that the matter had been satisfactorily resolved by Prescott's polite and lengthy response.

William also made a commitment to protect and strengthen his one good eye, which he could use for only a limited period of reading and writing. In 1821 he wrote: "I will make it my principal purpose to restore my eye to its primitive vigor, and will do nothing habitually that can seriously injure it."[10] Silken screens were placed on his glasses to shield him from direct sunlight during his daylight strolls through town or the countryside. Occasionally, he felt that his eyes were strong enough to do without the silk shades.

While the noctograph allowed Prescott to write without having to look at what he was writing, he still had to rely on his vision to correct what he had written. He took the precaution of limiting the use of his good eye for correcting his writings. The entries in his journal and corrections to his manuscripts had to be written without the aid of the noctograph. In an effort to write legibly, Prescott adhered to his axiom, "Write a large and straight and unequivocal, and broad hand—black ink."[11]

During a period in 1821, Judge Prescott was among a group of 13 men who drew up a report proposing that the township of Boston change its legal status by incorporating as a city, which was subsequently approved by a ballot vote. The elder Prescott would serve as one of four councilmen for the Ninth Ward of the newly-incorporated city. He also was president of the Common Council, which consisted of 47 male citizens of Boston.

In February of that year Pond Street, where the Prescott home was located, was officially changed to Bedford Street. The younger William sat on the Committee of Managers of the Boston Asylum for Indigent Boys while his mother was involved with its sister charity, the Female Asylum. It was during this year that the Prescott family mourned the passing of Abigail Prescott, the beloved mother of the Judge and grandmother of the aspiring scholar.

William's predilection for history is revealed in a memo from 1822: "History has always been a favorite study with me and I have long looked forward to it as a subject on which I was one day to exercise my pen. It is not rash, in the dearth of well-written American history, to entertain the hope of throwing light upon this matter. This is my hope."[12]

In 1822 the Boston Athenaeum moved to a larger building on Pearl Street. The Judge and William continued to be passionate supporters of this illustrious institution, and both regularly donated funds to the independent library. George Ticknor became a trustee in 1823, a post that William H. Prescott assumed in 1832 and held for the next 15 years. Franklin Dexter, William's good friend and brother-in-law, also served on the board of trustees of the Boston Athenaeum. In 1849 the Boston Athenaeum moved into a newly-constructed building on Beacon Street, where it still stands.

Beginning in 1822, and continuing into the following year, William turned his attention to the study of French literature. He was not, however, overly impressed with the style of French authors; he thought that their writing, on the whole, lacked the richness and originality he had found in classic English literature. But he did enjoy a number of writings by Michel de Montaigne, Blaise Pascal, Jacques-Bénigne Bossuet, Pierre Corneille, and Jean-Baptiste Poquelin, the latter who is better known as Molière. While acquainting himself with French literature, Prescott gathered ample material for a study of Molière, which he planned to write at a future date.

In June of 1823, William Prescott continued his scholarly pursuits with a study of poetry up through the Middle Ages. A few months later he embarked on an in-depth study of Italian literature, which exposed him to the writings of Giovanni Boccaccio, Dante Alighieri, and Francesco Petrarch. He greatly admired the richness and elegance of Italian prose and poetry, a literary style he felt eclipsed the quality of English writers. He made numerous notes pertaining to the style of the authors that appealed to him, which in turn had a positive influence on his own literary approach. The imaginative writings of Dante's *Divine Comedy* and Boccaccio's *Decameron*, were particular favorites; William often returned to passages from these popular works that had stirred his imagination. George Ticknor, his friend and mentor, and an Italian scholar residing in Boston, provided him with much guidance on this topic of study. Prescott became so enamored with these inquiries that for a time he considered composing a history of Italian literature. He would later write two articles on Italian poetry that were published in the *North American Review*: "Italian Narrative Poetry" was published in the October 1824 issue, and "Poetry and Romance of the Italians" appeared in the July 1831 edition.

Prescott found the Germanic language far more difficult to learn and much less appealing than he had envisioned. William soon realized that it would take far too long to sift through the voluminous classical works he had planned to study and, after much consideration, he decided to abandon his Germanic studies. Prescott viewed this as a major setback, but he was of the mind set that the only way to approach a subject was to learn it thoroughly, and the Germanic tongue seemed to be beyond his ability to master. The Romance languages clearly had a far more satisfying appeal to Prescott.

On September 24, 1824, Susan gave birth to a daughter, the first child for her and William. Their healthy nine pound baby girl was christened Catherine Hickling Prescott, a name that paid homage to William's mother. The Prescotts' bundle of pride and joy was affectionately referred to as either Kitty or Kate.

Spanish Studies

During the ensuing period of frustration brought on by unexpected difficulties pertaining to the field of Germanic studies, Prescott was fortunate to find his interest gravitating toward the study of Spanish literature. This awakening was sparked by his good friend George Ticknor, who, in the autumn of 1824, read him some of his lectures on this topic for a course he was about to teach at Harvard. Ticknor knew that his younger friend was despondent over having to abandon his plan to learn the German language and felt that the Spanish tongue would make a suitable replacement for his scholarly studies. Finding himself entertained by Ticknor's lectures on Spain's literary history, William decided to incorporate Spanish literature into his study plan.

George Ticknor compiled for William Prescott a list of essential Castilian writers that he would need to include in his Spanish curriculum. Meanwhile, Ticknor and his family were slated to be away from their

Boston residence for much of the winter, and knowing that William did not have the necessary Spanish books at his disposal, the distinguished Hispanicist generously offered his friend full access to his large and well stocked library as a place to pursue his Castilian studies. Prescott gladly accepted his offer.

Ticknor's library, which overlooked the historic Boston Common, housed a numerous collection of books penned by many of Spain's most celebrated authors. A portrait of Sir Walter Scott, the Scottish historical novelist, hung above the fireplace in the Ticknor library. It was here that George Ticknor spent many an evening working on his comprehensive *History of Spanish Literature*, a scholarly work that took him 20 years to complete.

William first read *Conquista de México* by Don Antonio de Solís, one of the many authors that Ticknor had recommended to him. Prescott also read the works of Miguel de Cervantes, the celebrated author of *Don Quixote*; Jean C. L. Sismondi, a Swiss economist and historian; Friedrich Bouterwek, the German philosopher; as well as the chivalrous tales of *Amadis de Gaula*—the adventure books that he had enjoyed as a child and which were fervently read by many of the Spanish conquistadors. The four-volume series of *Amadis de Gaula* served as Cervantes' inspiration for *Don Quixote*, the immensely popular work that is widely regarded as the first modern novel.

Realizing the need to become proficient in what he read and what was being read to him, William began taking Spanish lessons on December 1, 1824, from a private teacher. Since few books in this language had been translated into English, the ability to read and comprehend Spanish was essential to his scholarly studies. A few days after receiving instructions in grammar Prescott wrote: "I snatch a fraction of the morning from the interesting treatise of M. Jossé on the Spanish language and from the *Conquista de México*, which, notwithstanding the time I have been upon it, I am far from having conquered."[13]

Initially, William Prescott had his doubts about studying Spanish, which he revealed in an 1824 Christmas day letter to his friend George Bancroft, "I am battling with the Spaniards this winter but I have not the heart for it, I had for the Italian. I doubt whether there are many valuable things, that the key of knowledge will unlock in that language."[14]

Shortly thereafter, William had an epiphany, a moment of realization that opened the door to his fully comprehending proper Castilian. In a letter penned on January 24, 1825, to George Ticknor, he wrote: "Did you never, in learning a language, after groping about in the dark for a long while, suddenly seem to turn an angle where the light breaks upon you all at once? The knack seems to have come to me within the last fortnight in the same manner as the art of swimming comes to those who have been splashing about for months in the water in vain."[15] After Ticknor returned to Boston, Prescott felt confident enough in his grasp of Castilian to write him notes in Spanish. William would learn to read, write and speak fluent Spanish, but never fully mastered Spanish diction—the Boston historian always spoke the language like a foreigner.

4

Their Catholic Majesties

I must discipline my idle fancy or my meditations will be little better than dreams.[1]

Maintaining Discipline

William Prescott was eager to find a fitting direction in which he could channel his scholarly studies. A sense of urgency appeared to have set in after his younger brother graduated from Harvard on August 31, 1825, and began studying law at their father's office. On the 16th of October, William jotted down in his memorandum: "I have been so hesitating and reflecting upon what I shall do, that I have, in fact, done nothing." Two weeks later he noted: "I have passed the last fortnight in examination of a suitable subject for historical composition. It is well to determine with caution and accurate inspection."[2]

For a brief period, William would contemplate the notion of focusing his energy on the annals of America's history. But by Christmas of 1825 he seemed to have a good idea which course he truly wished to pursue: "I have been hesitating between two topics for historical investigation,— Spanish history from the invasion of the Arabs to the consolidation of the monarchy under Charles V., or a history of the revolution of ancient Rome, which converted the republic into a monarchy. A third subject which invites me is a biographical sketch of eminent geniuses, with criticisms on their productions and on the character of their times. I shall probably select the first, as less difficult of execution than the second, and as more novel and entertaining than the last."[3]

It mattered little to Prescott how long it might take to achieve his goal, provided that it involved a topic of interest that was worthy of his time and effort. Success was merely an afterthought; he wished to prove to himself that in spite of his poor eyesight and frail health he had something to offer for posterity. On January 8, 1826, William posted in his journal that he had cast aside the subject of Roman history. He also mentioned that a biography of Ferdinand and Isabella, the Catholic king and queen of Spain, was a refreshing change of direction to consider for his first historical account.

Just when he seemed to have finally settled on a topic to pursue, William was once again diverted by his interest in Italian studies, particularly the history of the Roman Empire. After careful reflection, however, Prescott concluded that such a broad subject would require an extensive knowledge of Italian literature, history, and a thorough command of the language, after which there might be little that he could add to a subject already covered by numerous historians. Looking for something new to write about, William returned to his plan to focus on the rich history of Spain.

On January 19, 1826, William noted in his memorandum: "I believe the Spanish subject will be more new than the Italian; more interesting in the majority of readers; more useful to me by opening another and more practical department of study; and not more laborious in relation to authorities to be consulted, and not more difficult to be discussed with the lights already afforded me by judicious treatises on the most intricate parts of the subject, and with the allowance of the introductory year my novitiate in a new walk of letters. The advantages of the Spanish topic, on the whole, overbalances the inconvenience of the requisite preliminary year. For these reasons, I subscribe to the History of the Reign of Ferdinand and Isabella."[4] In May of 1847, William penciled in an addendum to his renewed commitment, "A fortunate choice."

There were three Spanish works in particular that steered William's interest toward Spain's sudden and rapid emergence as a worldwide empire: Alonso de Ercilla's *La Araucana*; Antonio de Solís's *Conquista de México*; and Juan de Mariana's *Historia de rebus Hispaniae*. Alonso de Ercilla was a Spanish conquistador who began writing his epic poem *La Araucana* while serving in Chile in the fight against the Araucanians. The esteemed Spanish author and historian Antonio de Solís published in 1684 his classic account of the conquest of Mexico by Hernán Cortés and his small but zealously devoted band of conquistadors. Juan de Mariana, a Spanish Jesuit, historian, and philosopher, wrote a continuing series of books that covered the history of Spain from its founding on up to the beginning of the reign of Philip IV in 1621.

Unfortunately, when William began to immerse himself in the rich language, literature, and history of Spain, he had to rely on the assistance of a reader by the name of George R. M. Withington, who, after much practice, could adequately mimic the Castilian dialect but failed to comprehend what he was reading. Alexander Everett, a fellow graduate of Harvard and the brother of Edward Everett, learned of Prescott's dilemma and obtained for him the services of George Lunt, a young man who could read and speak proper Castillian. A graduate of Harvard's class of 1824, the 21-year-old Lunt was hired to work set shifts of six days a week at the Prescott residence. It was understood by both parties that this was a temporary arrangement. When Lunt left after only a few months to seek more gainful employment, he was replaced by Hamilton Parker, another recent college graduate, who would serve as Prescott's personal secretary, amanuensis, and reader for a year-long period beginning in 1826.

On January 27, 1826, Susan and William Prescott celebrated the birth of their first son. He was christened William Gardiner Prescott, a name that paid tribute to his loving father, William Prescott, and his best friend, William Howard Gardiner.

Research Materials

On January 22, 1826, Prescott compiled a long list of books he needed to acquire for his research into the reign of Ferdinand and Isabella, which he included in a letter addressed to Alexander Everett in Madrid. Everett, who served as U.S. minister to Spain from 1825 to 1829, agreed to help locate any available material but advised William that he would certainly find it worth his while to pay a visit to Spain, at which point he could help him gain access to the books and manuscripts he wished to obtain. In response, Prescott agreed that such a trip would certainly be beneficial to his work, but his recurring rheumatic inflammation, the poor condition of his one good eye, and the discomforts of ocean travel deterred him from undertaking such a long journey.

In the course of composing his letter to Alexander Everett, William suffered from what he described as "a stiffness of the right eye" which progressed into a painfully "new disorder." Once again, he found himself confined to a bedroom devoid of natural light. Numerous remedies were attempted to treat his condition, including the old remedy of cupping, which involved applying glass cups to his temples in an effort to draw blood away from the affected area. This procedure merely succeeded in leaving permanent marks on his skin. Unable to maintain the methodical schedule he had established for his historical inquiries, William soon slipped into a melancholy state. But as he had done before, Prescott bore his suffering with quiet dignity.

Prescott made mention of his difficult situation in the Preface of his *History of the Reign of Ferdinand and Isabella, the Catholic*: "Soon after my arrangements were made early in 1826, for obtaining the necessary materials from Madrid, I was deprived of the use of my eyes for all purposes of reading and writing, and had no prospect of again recovering it. This was a serious obstacle to the prosecution of a work, requiring the perusal of a large mass of authorities, in various languages, the contents of which were to be carefully collated, and transferred to my own pages, verified by minute reference. Thus shut out from one sense, I was driven to rely exclusively on another, and to make the ear do the work of the eye."[5]

William was forced to endure this debilitating condition for four interminably long months. By the summer of 1826 he finally felt well enough to resume his studies. All that he was unable to read on his own was read to him by his secretary. Fearful of a relapse, William put temporary limits on how much time he would devote each day to his project. These reading sessions, regardless of how well he felt, now ranged from four to six hours each day. It was his hope that even at this slower pace he would still be able to finish his work on the historic reign of Ferdinand and Isabella within the next five or six years. However, the sheer breadth of this topic combined with an array of unexpected interruptions were foremost among the many circumstances which caused him to take twice as long as he had anticipated to complete his first book.

The aspiring historian established a meticulous work plan to help him achieve his literary objective. "My general course of study," he states, "must be as follows: 1. General Laws, &c. of Nations. 2. History and Constitution of England. 3. History and Government of other European nations,—France, Italy to 1550, Germany, Portugal. Under the last two divisions, I am particularly to attend to the period intervening between 1400 and 1550. 4. General History of Spain,—its Geography, its Civil, Ecclesiastical, Statistical Concerns; particularly from 1400 to 1550. 5. Ferdinand's Reign *en gros*. 6. Whatever concerns such portions of my subject as I am immediately to treat of. The general division of it I will arrange when I have gone through the first five departments."[6]

In spite of all the precautions he had taken to protect his vision, William still managed to aggravate his good eye while perusing Montesquieu's *Esprit des Lois* (Spirit of Laws), the first research step taken toward achieving his ambitious literary goal. For the next three months the frustrated scholar did not attempt any manner of reading. Prescott privately wondered if the project was beyond his physical capabilities, and worried about what the future would hold if he should permanently lose his vision. Disheartened by this complication, Prescott once again chose to reverse course, this time postponing the Spanish topic in favor of a proposed *Historical Survey of English Literature*.

After five weeks pursuing this new subject, William realized that he had made yet another mistake and vowed to resume work on his previous topic. On November 5, 1826, Prescott recorded in his literary memorandum: "I have again & trust finally determined to prosecute my former subject, the Reign of Ferdinand and Isabella. In taking a more accurate survey of my projected literary history, I am convinced it will take at least five years to do anything at all satisfactory to myself, and I cannot be content to be so long detained from a favorite subject & one for which I shall have such rare & valuable materials in my own possession." He concluded by stating, "And I am now fully resolved nothing but a disappointment in my expected supplies from Spain shall prevent me from prosecuting my original scheme."[7]

Prescott believed that after he had committed a full year of studying material pertinent to the reign of Ferdinand and Isabella he would be fully prepared to begin writing his own historical account of the esteemed Spanish monarchs. However, the arrival of the great number of books he had ordered from Madrid made him realize that far more time would be required to complete a scholarly study of this truly eventful period in Spanish history.

Numerous books were read to Prescott during his initial research into the celebrated rule of Ferdinand and Isabella, a list that included Adam Smith's *Wealth of Nations*, Henry Hallam's *View of the State during the Middle Ages*, John Muller's *Universal History*, Charles Mills' *History of Chivalry*, William Robertson's *Charles the Fifth*, and Robert Watson's *Philip the Second*. In addition, William listened intently to translations of passages from the classic works of Plato, Marcus Aurelius, and Cicero.

William also lent his critical ears to lengthy recitations of Christoph Wilhelm Koch's *Revolutions de Europe*; Voltaire's *Essai sur les Moeurs*, and José Antonio Conde's *Spanish Arabs*. Digging deeper into this topic, he listened intently to Juan de Ferreras's *General History of Spain*, Abbé Mignot's *Histoire de Ferdinand et Isabelle*, and other notable works that complimented his topic of interest.

Prescott read an average of 24 pages an hour, which, after much experimentation, he found to be an acceptable speed to absorb and retain the knowledge required for his research. William continued to have Spanish grammar read to him to ensure that he had a firm grasp of the language. After only a year of study William had become proficient enough in the Castilian dialect to correct improper pronunciations uttered by those who read to him.

In the autumn of 1827, James Lloyd English replaced Hamilton Parker as William Prescott's secretary. Newly graduated from Harvard College, James had been highly recommended for this position by George Ticknor, who was now the head of Harvard's department of literature. James English would prove to be a valuable assistant for the next four years. He worked six hours each day, which was divided into a morning shift that began at ten o'clock and continued until two o'clock, and an evening stint that started at six o'clock and ended at eight o'clock. These evening work sessions were subject to cancellation whenever William had a scheduled meeting of his literary group or was slated to attend a social event in the company of his wife.

William Prescott and James English worked out of the large study that Judge Prescott had added to the rear of the house. The two side walls of the family library were occupied by well-stocked bookcases that rose from floor to ceiling. A third wall had a large green screen which Prescott faced while seated at his desk. Behind him was a large window, with a set of light blue muslin shades which could be adjusted to regulate the outside light in proportion to the sensitivity of William's delicate vision. Mr. English sat at a desk near a second window, where he read and took dictation. William often sat in a comfortable rocking chair, especially when listening to the books that were read by his secretary.

William proudly hung two crossed swords over a bookcase in his Bedford Street study; one was the sword of Colonel William Prescott, his grandfather, which he wielded while commanding the Colonial militia at the Battle of Bunker Hill; the other was the sword of John Linzee, the grandfather of Susan Prescott, who commanded a British war ship during the siege of Bunker Hill. These crossed swords would later hang above a fireplace in the Prescott library in the family's new Beacon Street residence.

The first batch of books and manuscripts arrived from Madrid shortly before Mr. English was hired as Prescott's new secretary. But because of another recurrence of inflammation to his right eye these books would long remain unopened. Many years later in a letter to George E. Ellis, a Boston theologian and a good friend, Prescott reflected, "I well remember the blank despair which I felt when my library treasures arrived from Spain, and I saw the mine of wealth lying around me which I was forbidden to explore. I determined to see what could be done with the eyes of another. I remembered that Johnson had said in reference to Milton that the great poet had abandoned his projected History of England, finding it scarcely possible for a man without eyes to pursue an historical work requiring reference to various authorities. The remark piqued me to make the attempt."[8]

Whenever Mr. English read a passage of interest Prescott would instruct him to mark it, which the secretary did by penciling lines at the margins. Afterwards, William would use his noctograph to make extensive notes of these relevant points. This sizable collection of notes were later copied in large print by the secretary for the author's future reference. With regard to his penmanship on the writing device he had brought back from England, Prescott stated, "The characters thus formed made a near approach to hieroglyphics; but my secretary became expert in the art of deciphering, and a fair copy—with a liberal allowance for unavoidable blunders—was transcribed for the use of the printer."[9]

Much to the amazement of James English and succeeding secretaries, Prescott was able to commit to memory a prodigious amount of material from these lengthy reading sessions. Even though progress was much slower than he had anticipated, William felt emboldened by the completion of each task; every accomplishment, regardless of how small, was viewed as a significant step toward the realization of his grand and confidential project.

On June 7, 1828, Prescott once more had a change of heart: "Renewed studies in Italian literature make me hesitate whether I should not prefer it as a matter of history to the Spanish subject which I had already chosen." An entry to his memorandum on the 22nd of June notes yet another resolution: "I confirm my previous decision.... Shame on my doubtings, delays, and idleness!" This commitment, however, was not etched in stone until July 3, 1828: "Finally, for the hundredth time, after a full and accurate reflection on the whole matter, I confirm my preference and choice of the Spanish subject."[10]

William continued to adhere to a strict daily regimen: He awoke early to ride his horse, a time used to exercise both his body and mind. During these morning jaunts he would review and organize the numerous pages of notes he had committed to memory. Prescott would return from his ride shortly before breakfast feeling exhilarated and eager to pursue his studies. After indulging in a moderate breakfast he would retire to the library, where, for an hour or more, he conversed with his wife or listened as she read to him from the newspapers or a favorite book. His secretary usually arrived around ten o'clock, at which point the two would pick up where they had left off the previous day. Work would continue for the next three to four hours. Afterward, William would take a vigorous walk of between one and two miles in order to be alone with his thoughts about the events surrounding the reign of Ferdinand and Isabella. The morning horse rides generally lasted an hour and a half while his walks were usually around a half-hour in length.

Prescott would return from his midday hike with a healthy appetite for dinner, which was generally served around three o'clock. This was a time when the family gathered around the table and engaged in lively conversations. William would indulge in a glass of wine, the alcoholic beverage he had experimented with to determine how much he could safely drink for medicinal purposes. Over a period of two years and nine months he maintained a detailed record of how much wine he consumed each day and carefully noted its effects on his good eye and his overall health. He concluded from these calculations that two and a half glasses of either sherry or Madeira was an acceptable amount of wine for him to consume on a daily basis.

After dinner William usually enjoyed smoking a cigar while he conversed with Susan or listened to stories that she read to him. He relished listening to a good novel, and found the works of Sir Walter Scott and Maria Edgeworth to be very entertaining. Afterwards, he would take another walk before returning home for a refreshing cup of tea. Prescott would then retire to the library for a two hour, or slightly longer, work session with his secretary. Once finished with his work, he spent time enjoying the company of his family or entertaining friends who paid a visit to their home. He would end the day spending precious time with his dear wife.

By this time, Prescott's work ethic had become so deep-rooted that he would feel tremendous guilt whenever he was unable to perform his literary tasks, especially when he was unexpectedly sidelined by his recurring ailments. In one such instance, a return of acute rheumatism made it far too painful for him to sit up, so rather than take a break from composing, he positioned his noctograph on the floor and continued to write while lying next to his writing device—an awkward routine that he performed for numerous hours over the course of nine consecutive days.

Even writing letters to friends and acquaintances, correspondence which William normally enjoyed, suddenly felt as if such an obligation to stay in touch was interfering with his efforts to establish himself as an historian. In spite of this concern, Prescott's ingrained social graces would not permit him to let any letter go unanswered. William wrote his letters with the aid of the noctograph. His secretary would be entrusted with the difficult task of deciphering the contents, a chore which often required Prescott's help. The more legible copies made by the secretary were signed by Prescott and then dispatched. The original drafts were summarily filed away.

William's literary plans were known to only a few family members and friends. According to George Ticknor, no more than a half dozen people outside the family circle knew of his intentions to write an historical account. Knowing of William's fondness for books, many simply thought that the long hours he spent in his library was merely time set aside for pleasurable reading. Early on in his journal Prescott wrote, "Nor shall any one else If I can help it, know that I am writing."[11] He remained quiet about his plans even when unaware friends and acquaintances urged him to find a worthwhile pursuit that would provide his life with a sense of purpose.

Mr. Prescott Goes to Washington

In the spring of 1828 William Prescott decided to take a break from his painstaking research and journey south for a visit to the Federal city of Washington. William was accompanied by George Ticknor, his good friend and Spanish mentor, on this circuitous route to the nation's capital. The two young men traveled by coach from Boston to Providence, where they boarded a steamboat bound for New York. Once they had docked, Prescott and Ticknor stepped aboard a carriage that carted them all the way to Philadelphia. The Boston gentlemen then booked passage on a steamboat which transported them approximately 50 miles down the Delaware River to the town of New Castle, and from there the two friends traveled by coach through the rugged roads of Maryland to French Town, located near Elkton. Prescott and Ticknor then boarded a steamboat to Baltimore, after which they obtained passage on a carriage that took them across a scenic farmland region that led directly to the District of Columbia.

William Prescott and George Ticknor spent a pleasant week in Washington, D.C., meeting with a number of prominent politicians, which included audiences with such distinguished statesmen as Daniel Webster, John C. Calhoun, and Martin van Buren. William also had an opportunity to meet with Henry Clay, Secretary of State, whom he described as "worn and thin as a dyspeptic—he is killed by care and anxiety. His manners, though far from graceful, are very amiable."[12] The two visitors from Boston attended a dinner at the White House hosted by President John Quincy Adams, a fellow Bostonian whom Prescott had the pleasure of meeting in London when Adams was serving as America's minister at the Court of St. James. William also had an opportunity to tour the halls of Congress.

Prescott and Ticknor were guests at a magnificent feast hosted by the British minister Charles Richard Vaughn, which was attended by numerous dignitaries. There were 20 varied and succulent dishes served at this lavish event, a menu that included fresh lobsters and halibut from New York, tasty truffles from France, and tender olives from Seville, Spain. William found Mr. Vaughn to be an extremely charming and interesting host.

William Prescott and George Ticknor decided to pay a visit to Mount Vernon, the Virginia estate of George Washington. Unfortunately, their carriage broke down along the way, which meant that both men had to trudge four miles over a muddy path in order to reach their intended destination. Their long-awaited view of Mount Vernon proved disheartening to these weary visitors. Prescott wrote that Washington's plantation was "in the finest situation in the world—but ... in the most shocking state of dilapidation and ruin."[13] The beloved home of the nation's first president would continue to fall into ruin until it was purchased in 1858 by the Mount Vernon Ladies Association, which raised money for the restoration of this historic estate.

Prescott made sure to bring his noctograph on this trip, which he used to write 11 letters home to loved ones during his three-week-long adventure. The homesick scholar soon longed for the day when he would be reunited with his loving wife, children, and parents. On April 28, 1828, a day when his journey was coming to a close, William wrote in his letter to Susan, "Nothing short of life and death, shall ever send me upon such another tremendous journey and exile. The more I see of tavern life and stages, and steamboats and strangers, the more I long to be at home—home—however Pepperell is a journey quite distant eno' for my time of life."[14]

During their return journey, Prescott and Ticknor stopped once again at the city of Baltimore. They used this opportunity to pay a visit to Charles Carroll, a wealthy businessman and retired politician who was the sole surviving signer of the Declaration of Independence. In a letter to Susan, William wrote of an unusual encounter during his brief stay at Baltimore:

In the evening I was introduced to a phrenological society in Baltimore—composed chiefly of doctors, who, after reading a very satisfactory (to themselves) lecture on the science of craniology, proceeded to a careful examination of my pericranium. They measured it with a variety of instruments, until they had ascertained a complete map of my skull, with all its flats and elevations. When what do you think was the result?

The organ of *firmness* was found predominant above every other. Far above that of Mr. Webster's, of which they had a scale. I was very low in the development of *parental affection*. So you will not accuse me of loving Kate too much again. And the organ of *secrecy*, was found in high perfection. The other qualities came pretty right.

I told them they were never more mistaken in their lives—that I was totally destitute of *firmness*, being remarkably weak of purpose on most occasions; and that I never kept a secret in my life. They were a good deal annoyed, and insisted upon it that I did not know my own character.

There were lying upon the table the skulls of five or six pirates—who had been executed at Norfolk, who had certain developments not unlike mine. So much for this profound science.[15]

The next morning Prescott and Ticknor resumed their journey to Boston.

On July 27, 1828, Susan Prescott gave birth to a second daughter, who, in honor of William's sister, was named Elizabeth. That same year, Judge Prescott, who was now 66 years old and recently retired from private practice, decided to purchase a parcel of land at East Point, Nahant. The lot was located at the edge of a small promontory just south of the town of Lynn, where the Judge ordered the building of a rather plain looking two story wood cottage that overlooked the water. The Nahant peninsula, which stretches several miles out to the ocean, provided its residents with a scenic view interspersed with the rhythmic surge of waves breaking against the shore, an occasional chorus of whistling winds, and the soft spray of saltwater. The rugged landscape is punctuated with cliffs along the coastline that rise from between 20 to 60 feet—the bluffs of Nahant soar 50 feet above the coast. The cool breeze of the ocean made for ideal temperatures to escape the oppressive heat that hung over Boston during the summer season.

Now that he finally had some free time for leisurely activities, Judge Prescott agreed to sit for a portrait by Gilbert Stuart, which was very likely the acclaimed artist's last such work. This was one of eight paintings by Stuart that were on display at the Boston Atheneum's 1828 art exhibition. The elder Prescott was an early investor in the Atheneum and in 1827 he transferred the title of his certificate bearing the number 76 to his son William.

During the year 1828, William Prescott was disappointed to learn that a new article he had written on the topic of Italian literature had been rejected. Eager to see his work published in England, Prescott had sent this manuscript, which numbered an estimated 50 printed pages, to his friend Jared Sparks in London, whom he hoped could use his literary influence to strike a deal with either the *Edinburgh Review* or the *Quarterly Review*, two periodicals that Prescott held in the highest regard. He was disappointed to learn that neither of these distinguished British journals were interested in his essay. In a letter to Sparks dated September 28, 1828, Prescott stated: "I should have been not a little chagrined to have gone so far out of my way to write for a foreign journal and to have had my article returned on my hands, a catastrophe which from an ominous passage in your first letter did not appear to me very improbable—so that I began to regret that I had sent the piece. But it is all *comme il faut* and I am much obliged to you for the part you have taken in forwarding my designs."[16]

In 1829 Judge Prescott and his family made Nahant their summer residence for the very first time. Their Nahant cottage rested on a cliff which protrudes over Swallows' Cave. The family nicknamed their newly-built home *Fitful Head*, a name taken from a location in the Shetland Islands that appeared in Sir Walter Scott's novel *The Pirate*. The windows at Nahant offered a sweeping view of the Atlantic Ocean, and on a clear day William could see the ships that passed to and from Liverpool—the very route that ships would one day follow to transport his manuscripts and books across the open water.

William did not care much for Nahant at first; he complained that the bright reflection of the sun bouncing off the water was terribly hard on his sensitive eyes and the dampness of this location posed a serious threat to his rheumatic condition. There was also a lack of trees that could provide much needed shade from the sun. After having suffered a temporary impairment to his vision, the hopeful historian was convinced that he would never be able to accomplish any work at this picturesque home by the sea. However, Prescott chose to tolerate their new summer residence because he knew it was beneficial to the persistent cough that affected his father. But over time, William was able to adjust to the tranquil seashore surroundings and would eventually look forward to spending time at Nahant.

The Prescotts' periodic change of residences was dictated by the change of seasons. During the summer, the family would depart Pepperell in mid–July and return to Boston for a week, a brief stay that was used to prepare for departure to their seaside home at Nahant, which they arrived at during the third-week of July. The *Fitful Head* cottage was a good deal smaller than their country home. Because of its close proximity to Boston, their seashore residence generally received more guests, which translated into increased interruptions—most of which William viewed as a welcome break from his daily routine of research and composition. The invigorating scenery and climate at Nahant inspired Prescott to take long morning and evening walks, daily strolls that rigorously followed the same path. He would amble through the main street that led to a beach just over two miles in length, and only turned back after arriving at a particular rock situated along the sandy shore that he had designated as the end of the journey. For his midday walks, the historian followed a path through a meadow shrouded with just enough trees to provide welcome shade from the heat and sunlight.

During his visits to Pepperell, William enjoyed taking long walks along the unspoiled countryside. The calm and splendor of nature was a stark contrast to the hustle and bustle of the city. He was particularly fond of a path behind the house that provided a magnificent view of Monadnock mountain. Beyond the path could be seen a thick grouping of trees that he called "the Fairy Grove," which he later took delight in telling his children that this was an enchanted realm inhabited by fairies and elves.

In a letter to a friend, William described Pepperell as "a plain New England farm, but I am attached to it, for it is connected with the earliest recollections of my childhood, and the mountains that hem it around look at me with old familiar faces."[17] Prescott always made sure to bring along an umbrella on these leisurely strolls, which he used, whenever necessary, to shield his eyes from the sun. William viewed the quiet solitude of this splendid country setting as his "Muse of History." A great many chapters of his books were composed during these wanderings along a well worn path paved by his daily footsteps.

A Test of Faith

On February 1, 1829, an unexpected and devastating tragedy befell the Prescott family: the four-year-old Catherine, the first and favored child of William and Susan, passed away. Her sudden death was a painful and difficult loss for the entire family to bear, especially for William, who loved his young daughter very dearly and always found time to spend with her once he had finished with his studies. Young Catherine was so adored by her father that he even permitted her to enter his study, which Mr. English, the secretary, viewed as a most welcome interruption to their taxing work sessions. She had an endearing personality that charmed anyone who came into contact with her. The Prescott household lapsed into a prolonged state of mourning; the mother, grandfather, and grandmother required much consoling for the grief experienced over having lost their dearly beloved Kate.

A fortnight after the passing of little Catherine, William wrote in his diary: "The death of my dearest daughter on the first day of this month, having made it impossible for me at present to resume the task of composition, I have been naturally led to more serious reflection than usual, & have occupied myself with reviewing the grounds of the decision which I made in 1819 in favor of the Evidences of the Christian revelation. I have endeavored & shall endeavor to prosecute this examination with perfect impartiality & to guard against the present state of my feelings and my mind any farther than by leading it to give to the subject a more serious attention. And so far such influence must be salutary & reasonable, & far more desirable than any counter influence which might be exerted by an engrossing occupation with the busy cares & dissipation of the world. So far, I believe I have conducted the matter with sober impartiality."[18]

Overcome with grief, William sought solace by conducting an intensive search for empirical evidence that he would be reunited with his precious daughter when death called upon him. He had his secretary read to him numerous books and treatises authored by a number of true believers as well as ardent skeptics, all of whom were learned men who had closely examined the various supernatural events surrounding the tenets of Christianity, particularly topics that focused on the immortality of the soul. These readings included *Essays on Miracles and a Future State*, by the philosopher and historian David Hume; the selected writings of the historian Edward Gibbon; the English writer Conyers Middleton's *Free Inquiry into the Miraculous Powers*; Richard Watson's *Apology for Christianity*; and the theologian William Paley's *A View of the Evidences of Christianity*. He also studied *The Analogy of Religion*, by Joseph Butler, the Bishop of the Church of England; *Internal Evidences*, by the poet and essayist Soame Jenyens; and *Statement of Reasons for Not Believing the Doctrines of Trinitarians*, by the American preacher Andrews Norton. Naturally, the Bible was frequently consulted, especially the Four Gospel accounts that appear in the New Testament, with a close examination into the miracles of Jesus that were recorded by these Four Evangelists.

Judge Prescott joined his son in these inquiries into the mysteries of the afterlife. Williams wrote "that an examination of miraculous testimony with an old and cautious lawyer, like my Father, is a sufficient pledge of the severity of my scrutiny."[19] Although he never found the answers he sought concerning the immortality of the soul, William clung to his faith and accepted as probable that the afterlife offered the comforting thought that souls would be reunited in heaven. He decided not to trouble his mind any longer with exploring the relation between God's infinite being and man's finite being and chose to simply follow his own credo, which was "To do well and act justly, to fear and to love God, and to love our neighbors as ourselves—in these is the essence of religion. For what we can believe, we are not responsible.... For what we do we shall indeed be accountable. The doctrines of the Saviour unfold the whole code of morals by which our conduct should be regulated."[20]

Return to Studies

Those several weeks that Prescott spent occupying his thoughts with thorough religious examinations had helped to soothe his deep sense of sorrow, a necessary healing process which enabled him to return to work on his chronicle of the reign of Ferdinand and Isabella. The birth of William Amory Prescott on January 25, 1830, helped to bring some much needed joy back into the household. The new addition to the family was named after William Amory, his wife's brother and a long-time friend of William Prescott.

During this period when William resumed his work, there arrived from Spain and France another batch of books as well as numerous copies of manuscripts discovered in the archives which were thought to be useful to his research. The hopeful historian and his secretary spent a great deal of time sifting through this treasure trove of material in a concerted effort to determine what was relevant, much of which still had to be translated.

The London book-dealer Obadiah Rich played an essential role in helping William Prescott obtain books that were germane to his biography of the Spanish monarchs. A native of Cape Cod, Massachusetts, Obadiah was appointed by President James Madison in 1816 as American consul in Valencia, Spain, and seven years later he was named to the same post in Madrid. Afterwards, Obadiah, who was an avid bibliophile, moved to London to establish his own book selling business, which was located at 12 Red Lion Square. He was joined in this venture by his son James. Obadiah would frequently travel to the Continent to hunt for rare or unique books for customers of his shop. His American clients included several prominent institutions and a number of well-known individuals, most notably George Ticknor—a fact which was known to Prescott. Per William's request, Obadiah Rich managed to locate Luis del Mármol Carvajal's book on the history of the Spanish Moriscos. A delighted Prescott wrote: "The arrival of ... Mármol's Moriscos came as quick upon the trigger as if I owned Aladdin's lamp. You are certainly a prince of Genii in the Bibliopolical way."[21]

Over a span of five years, Obadiah Rich shipped a vast number of books that would greatly benefit Prescott's research and adorn the author's ever-expanding library. William would periodically compile a list of books that he wished to acquire and Rich would do his very best to fulfill his requests. Their business relationship came to a close when the London bookseller accepted an offer to serve as U.S. Consul to Minorca, a small Spanish island that is part of the Balearic archipelago in the Mediterranean.

Prescott's principal instructions to his many foreign aides was that they should locate for him applicable books and manuscripts that were reasonably priced and in fairly good condition, preferably editions with large type set on quality paper. Payment for these invaluable literary services rendered by assistants abroad were processed through an account the historian had established with the London based banking firm of Baring Brothers.

William took the time to acquaint himself with the writings of Augustin Thierry, a French historian whose scholarly research and writings caused his vision to deteriorate, and who, just like Prescott, had to rely on the eyes of his secretaries, especially after 1830, a time when his eyesight failed him completely. William, who could empathize with Thierry's visual handicap, a factor which probably had more effect on him than the scholar's actual writings, greatly admired the French historian's dedication to his work. It is understandable that William Prescott would demonstrate a deep compassion for those with vision problems similar to or worse than his.

Reflecting on his own need to rely on the sight of another, Prescott wrote: "The difficulty of recalling what has once escaped, of reverting to, or dwelling on the passages read aloud by another, compels the hearer to give undivided attention to the subject, and to impress it more forcibly on his own mind by subsequent and methodical reflection. Instances of the cultivation of this faculty to an extraordinary extent have been witnessed among the blind, and it has been most advantageously applied to the pursuit of abstract science, especially mathematics."[22]

Unfortunately for Prescott, the return to his studies also marked a recurrence of his vexing eye problems, which considerably slowed his pace. William persevered in spite of these difficulties and by the end of summer he had managed to prepare a detailed synopsis of his proposed historical account.

William's quest to write a grand history encompassing the life and times of Spain's Ferdinand and Isabella was an intensive learning period for an aspiring historian whose only previous writing experiences were but a few published reviews of no great length. He embarked on a meticulous search for a style of his own while making sure to adhere to the formal approach of a true historian. Prescott tried to emulate the best writing style of authors that he admired and merge them into his own manner of composition—one which he hoped would appeal to the scholar and casual reader alike. William provided insight into his pursuit of finding his own voice by stating, "Whoever would write a good English style, we should say, should acquaint himself with the mysteries of the language as revealed in the writings of the best masters, but should form his own style on nobody but himself. Every man, at least every man with a spark of originality in his composition, has his own peculiar way of thinking, and, to give it effect, it must find its way out in its own peculiar language. Indeed, it is impossible to separate language from thought in that delicate blending of both which is called style; at least, it is impossible to produce the same effect with original by any copy, however literal."[23]

Prescott maintained a strict daily regimen during his determined effort to see this massive project to its fruition. Small steps were taken each day in order to achieve such a lofty objective. Resorting to the disciplinary tactics he had employed at Harvard, William periodically made small wagers with his secretary Mr. English that he would accomplish designated writing goals by a specific date. Prescott would formalize these agreements on paper, which he signed and induced his secretary to sign. James English later remarked that often he did not know what he was signing, but trusted that it was in his interest and that of Mr. Prescott's to do so. The secretary remembered being paid winnings on two separate occasions, and recalled only one instance when he was told that he had lost between $20 or $30. William, however, refused to collect on the wager.

As mentioned previously, William took copious notes of what was read to him and these entries were later copied in large and legible print by his secretary so that he could refer to them as needed. There were times when the historian would personally read his vast collection of notes but usually they were read to him. Prescott would commit these writings to memory, and then would spend several days arranging these extensive notes into a flowing and engaging narrative. Even though he was blessed with a prodigious memory, William still had to train himself to remember relevant facts, dates, names and then shape them line by line, and paragraph by paragraph into an account which he felt comfortable with. He managed to teach himself to compose and memorize whole chapters before committing the story to paper. Once perfected, this method helped him to complete his writing much faster. Prescott noted in his memorandum, "Never take up my pen until I have traveled over the subject so often as to be able to write almost from memory, not from invention as I go along. This is the only way for me."[24]

Riding his horse or taking long walks were solitary moments that William used to mull over the extensive notes he had committed to memory. He would write the story in his head while completely tuning out everything around him. Prescott would keep going over the text, making corrections and alterations, until he felt it was worded exactly the way he desired. This mental exercise would last roughly three days, sometimes longer. There were occasions when he was interrupted by acquaintances who wished to engage him in friendly conversation or simply tag alongside him. Even though he was clearly annoyed by such untimely interruptions, William was always courteous to those who approached him. When one such intrusive acquaintance made a habit of meeting him on horseback, the historian countered by altering his morning route. There was, of course, an element of risk in these equestrian excursions. In September of 1834, William was thrown from his horse, a spill that injured both of his arms just as he was preparing to compose the eighth chapter of his *History of the Reign of Ferdinand and Isabella, the Catholic*.

Once satisfied with the arrangement of the material he had consigned to memory, Prescott proceeded to write it down with the aid of his noctograph. His secretary was charged with the difficult task of deciphering what was written and to legibly rewrite it so that it could be read back to his employer. William carefully weighed each sentence for errors in grammar and to make sure the statements were factually accurate. After the necessary corrections had been implemented, the secretary would make a revised copy in large lettering, so that his employer could go over it once more, at which point the historian would make additional emendations, comments, quotes, and incorporate new reference material. The secretary then had the daunting task of copying the newly-revised edition in large print for Prescott to read. The process continued until the historian was fully satisfied with the chapter. This painstaking procedure was repeated for all subsequent chapters.

Prescott was determined to develop a writing style that was distinctly his own. He recorded in his literary memorandum: "The only rule is, to write with freedom and nature, even with homeliness of expression occasionally, and with alteration of long and short sentences; for such variety is essential to harmony. But, after all, it is not the construction of the sentence, but the tone of the coloring, which produces the effect. If the sentiment is warm, lively, forcible, the reader will be carried along without much heed to the arrangement of the periods, which differs exceedingly in different standard writers. Put life into the narrative, if you would have it take. Elaborate and artificial fastidiousness in the form of expression is highly detrimental to this. A book may be made up of perfect sentences and yet the general impression be very imperfect. In fine, be engrossed with the thought, and not with the fashion of expressing it."[25]

In a later entry pertaining to the search for his own literary voice, Prescott wrote: "There are certain faults which no writer must commit: false metaphors; solecisms of grammar; unmeaning and tautological expressions; for these contravene the fundamental laws of all writing, the object of which must be to express one's ideas clearly and correctly. But within these limits, the widest latitude should be allowed to taste and to the power of unfolding the thoughts of the writer in all their vividness and originality. Originality—the originality of nature—compensates for a thousand minor blemishes."[26]

Taking his craft very seriously, Prescott assiduously studied the literary styles of the great historians of ancient Greece and Rome. He learned from Herodotus and Livy the importance of developing a flowing narrative, while Tacitus and Thucydides made him aware of the need to incorporate a degree of drama in his work.

William was greatly influenced by the works of Abbé Gabriel Bonnot de Mabley, a celebrated French philosopher he referred to as "a perspicuous, severe, shrewd, and sensible writer, full of thought, and of such thoughts as set the reader upon thinking for himself."[27] He read Mabley's *Etude de l'Histoire*, numerous times for inspiration; an obscure work that William found helpful in setting the tone and direction of his first book as well as his later accounts of the Spanish conquests of Mexico and Peru. Mabley's work made him mindful of the need to maintain the readers interest by providing vivid details of important incidents, stressing the significance of related recorded events, and offering the colorful orations of central figures. Regarding the latter, Prescott was not particularly keen on speeches, especially those he suspected were merely the imagined words of the author, but understood the importance of using them in certain instances.

Prescott also found *Elogio de la Réina Doña Isabel*, by Don Diego Clemencin, a contemporary Spanish historian, to be a valuable resource that he often consulted during his exhaustive research into the life and times of the Catholic monarchs. Prescott would later refer to this book, which had provided him with significant insight into the political ambitions of the Spanish rulers, as "a most rich repository of unpublished facts, to be diligently studied by me at every pausing point in my history."[28] Henry Hallam's *View of the State of Europe during the Middle Ages* was greatly admired by Prescott and served as a model for his book about the important events surrounding the reign of Ferdinand and Isabella.

William Prescott was extremely critical of his own writing, as evidenced by the notation he made in his literary journal regarding the articles he had written for *The Club Room*: "Too many adjectives; too many couplets of substantives, as well as adjectives, and perhaps of verbs; too set; sentences too much in the same mould ... sentences balanced by *ands*, *buts*, and semicolons; too many precise emphatic pronouns as *these*, *those*, *which*, &c., instead of the particles *the*, *a*, &c."[29]

To acquaint himself with the proper approach to writing a biography, Prescott stated that he focused on five biographies to help him determine what worked and what did not: Lucy Aikin's *Memoirs of the Court of Queen Elizabeth*, Voltaire's *The History of Charles XII of Sweden*, William Roscoe's *The Life of Lorenzo de' Medici*, Amable Barante's *Histoire des Ducs de Bourgoyne de la maison de Valois*, and Augustin Thierry's *Histoire de conquête de l'Angleterre parles Normands*. Prescott found Akin's and Voltaire's works interesting and well written, but of little benefit to his specific purpose. The other works, however, he found quite useful in helping to develop his own style. Foremost, William learned the importance of composing a flowing narrative that would enable the reader to better envision the historical events which he sought to convey. The aspiring historian also became aware of the importance of providing detailed notes to back up his statements and conclusions.

On October 6, 1829—some three and a half years after he had begun research on his selected topic—Prescott started composing on the noctograph the first chapter of his account of the reign of Ferdinand and Isabella. This endeavor was preceded by three months of thoroughly reviewing his notes, and then composing and committing to memory the opening chapter. Another significant reason for the need to memorize his text and all revisions was that the cumbersome noctograph made corrections and alterations practically impossible. It would take him a full month to write the first chapter. Two months later he had managed to complete the third chapter of his book.

Although he found himself lagging well behind his own schedule, Prescott was encouraged by what he had managed to accomplish, which provided him with the incentive he needed to continue his ambitious project. On May 13, 1830, William felt confident enough with his progress to propose in his journal that this work would be completed by January 1, 1833, a prediction which would prove to be yet another of his many missed deadlines. Four days later he wrote: "I cannot make my history profound. I have neither the knowledge or talent for this. I can make it *entertaining*. My materials will furnish me with novelties. Be my care to select such as will be the most interesting. Ever keep this in view as the principle of my operations."[30]

Prescott's *History of the Reign of Ferdinand and Isabella, the Catholic* was originally conceived as two volumes but expanded to three books once the author realized how much ground needed to be covered. It would take the historian a full 16 months to write the first 300 pages of his book. The persistent Prescott managed to complete the majority of his writing by early 1834, but he would spend the next two years incorporating changes that helped to make his work much tighter and more cohesive.

Work on Ferdinand and Isabella, the Spanish monarchs whom William fondly referred to as "their Catholic Majesties," was periodically interrupted by the onset of his recurring ailments or the continuation of his annual contributions to the *North American Review*. In the late spring of 1829 William completed a review of José Antonio Conde's *Historia de la dominación de los Arabes en España*, but decided not to submit it after determining that he could incorporate it into his *History of the Reign of Ferdinand and Isabella, the Catholic*, which would prove to be a perfect fit for chapter eight of his work—a section that provides an overview of the Spanish Arabs prior to the War of Granada. Instead, Prescott decided to submit to the *North American Review* an article he wrote about Washington Irving's *Conquest of Granada*.

There were a number of public-spirited endeavors that occupied a great deal of Prescott's spare time. Empathizing with the plight of the blind and anyone who suffered from severe visual impairments, Prescott became actively involved with the work of the New England Asylum. Founded on March 2, 1829, by Dr. John Dix Fisher, Samuel Gridley Howe and 29 other benevolent benefactors, the institution was later known as the Perkins School for the Blind.

Prescott wrote an article in the July 1830 edition of the *North American Review*, titled "Asylum for the Blind," to help foster public awareness of the urgent need for a humanitarian institution such as the one recently established in Boston. He wrote:

> No suitable institutions, until the close of the last century, have been provided for the nurture of the deaf and dumb, or the blind. Immured within hospitals and almshouses, like so many lunatics and incurables, they have been delivered over, if they escaped the physical, to all the moral contagion too frequently incident to such abodes, and have thus been involved in mental darkness far more deplorable than their bodily one.
>
> This injudicious treatment has resulted from the erroneous principle of viewing these unfortunate beings as an absolute burden on the public, utterly incapable of contributing to their own subsistence, or of ministering in any degree to their own intellectual wants. Instead, however, of being degraded by such unworthy views, they should have been regarded, as, what in truth they are, possessed of corporeal and mental capacities perfectly competent, under proper management, to the production of the most useful results. If wisdom from one entrance was quite shut out, other avenues for its admission still remained to be opened.[31]

Beginning in 1830, William Hickling Prescott served on the Board of Trustees of the New England Asylum, and in May of 1833 he helped to raise $50,000 for the institution. Prescott attempted, without success, to recruit the Rev. Thomas Hopkins Gallaudet, who in 1817 founded the American Asylum for Deaf-Mutes at Hartford, Connecticut, to serve as the institute's overseer. The name of the New England Asylum was changed to the Perkins School for the Blind to honor the memory of Colonel Thomas H. Perkins, a wealthy Boston merchant who made an extremely large charitable donation to the school.

The Perkins School earned international acclaim after it was able to successfully demonstrate that a young deaf and blind girl could have a truly meaningful educational experience. Laura Dewey Bridgeman, who was born at Hanover, New Hampshire, in 1829, was stricken with scarlet fever at the age of two, an affliction which left her deaf and blind. She also lost much of her sense of smell and taste. Laura's difficult situation was brought to the attention of Samuel Gridley Howe, headmaster of the Perkins School for the Blind, and at the age of eight Laura was enrolled in the Boston asylum. Formulating his own plan of instruction, Samuel Howe patiently worked with the severely handicapped Laura to teach her the alphabet by means of touch and association, which eventually led to her learning how to read. Charles Dickens, who had a deep and abiding interest in the welfare of underprivileged children, made a point to meet Laura Bridgeman during a visit to the school in January 1842, and wrote of both her and Samuel Howe in his book *American Notes*. At age 20, Laura felt comfortable enough to spend the summers with her family. She would return to the Perkins School, where she lived with the other students until her death on May 24, 1889.

In early June 1831, William traveled in the company of approximately ten other Boston residents on a tour of upstate New York and the neighboring nation of Canada. He was recovering from yet another bout of illness and hoped that a change of scenery would benefit his health. The group toured the Hudson and Mohawk Valleys, visited Niagara Falls, sailed over lakes Ontario, Champlain, and George, and took a leisurely cruise down the St. Lawrence River. The travelers also had an opportunity to tour the Canadian cities of Montreal and Quebec. William had a less than favorable impression of Montreal, but Quebec he considered to be one of the finest cities he had ever visited. He returned from his five-and-a-half-week-long journey feeling rejuvenated and eager to return to writing: "I now propose to resume my labors systematically and industriously and to pursue them unbroken, without the intervention of so much as a review for a year to come."[32]

Between 1832 and 1833, William Prescott wrote three articles for *The New-England Galaxy*, a paper owned and run by his younger brother Edward. Still searching for his niche in life, Ned was also studying to become a lawyer and would leave the weekly publication shortly before the third article by his brother was printed.

At the request of Jared Sparks, who was putting together a series of American biographies, Prescott agreed to write an essay on Charles Brockden Brown, a writer of gothic tales who had a major impact on Nathaniel Hawthorne and Edgar Allan Poe. The 64-page biography of the man considered by many as the "father of the American novel" was completed in a mere two weeks at his Nahant retreat, for which he was paid the sum of $44.80. William wrote that he began work on this topic on July 14, 1833, and on July 29 of that year he noted in his journal, "Finished Brown's Life and Writings. Written at the rate of 3 and 4 noctographs per day. I am afraid it will verify the proverb of 'easy writing,' etc. The subject proved not at all to my taste.... I could not have finished one of his novels unless as a job."[33] This article was less a biography and more of a review of William Dunlap's biography and other critiques of the American novelist. After having written at least 23 articles by this point, Prescott's name had yet to appear as the author until the publication of his essay on Charles Brockden Brown.

William's essays and literary criticisms lacked the depth and insight that would make his historical accounts so interesting. He clearly had a hard time criticizing the work of others, which is quite evident in his treatise on Charles Brockden Brown. Jared Sparks was slightly disappointed with this essay, and even Prescott criticized himself for overly praising the writings of Brown. Eventually, William grew weary of writing critical reviews of the works of others. In 1843 he noted: "It is impossible for one who has done that sort of work himself to have any respect for it. How can one critic look another in the face without laughing?"[34] Prescott soon stopped writing such articles except for when he felt compelled to promote the work of another author.

Always willing to come to the aid of a friend in need, Prescott loaned $500 to Jared Sparks on January, 13, 1834 to help the fellow Harvard graduate and fellow member of the *Club* weather a temporary financial crisis. In May of 1838, William and his father would lend Sparks $2000, which provided him with enough cash to survive yet another economic downturn.

In September 1835, after four years of dedicated service as Prescott's secretary, Henry Simonds parted company with his employer. William had the highest regard for the young scholar who had assisted and provided him with noteworthy suggestions for *History of the Reign of Ferdinand and Isabella, the Catholic*. Sadly, Henry Simonds passed away in 1840. He was replaced by Elijah Dwight Williams, who would serve as the historian's secretary for the next five years. While acclimating the new secretary to his daily routine, Prescott suffered another affliction to his right eye, a brief ailment blamed on overuse of his good eye reading printed material in a foolhardy effort on his part to maintain his rigid work schedule during this difficult transition of assistants.

As he neared the end of his account of the reign of Ferdinand and Isabella, Prescott wrote to George Bancroft: "I have little more to do than bury and write the epitaphs of the Great Captain, Ximenez, and Ferdinand. Columbus and Isabella are already sent to their account. So my present occupation seems to be that of a sexton, and I begin to weary of it."[35]

5

Exceeding All Expectations

"It is enough for the novelist if he be true to the spirit, the historian must be true, also, to the letter."[1]

Lingering Doubts

William Prescott completed the last chapter of *History of the Reign of Ferdinand and Isabella, the Catholic* on June 25, 1836, but he would spend another year correcting his manuscript and dealing with lingering doubts as to whether or not this was a work worthy of being published. Regarding the latter concern, Prescott noted in his journal: "It is a satisfactory evidence to my mind of my moderate anticipations ... that I feel not only no desire but a reluctance to publish, and should probably keep it by me for emendations and additions at my leisure, were it not for the belief that the ground would be more or less occupied in the meantime by abler writers. I hear already of Southey's preparation for a history of the Spanish Arabs, and it warns me not to defer my own publication."[2] He sought advice from the man whom he respected the most, his father, who, in turn, told his son, "The man who writes a book which he is afraid to publish is a coward."[3]

On June 26, 1836, Prescott wrote of his expectations for his historical account of the Catholic monarchs who ushered in Spain's era as a dominant world power: "What do I expect from it now it is done? ... I do not flatter myself with the idea that I have achieved anything very profound, or, on the other hand, that will be very popular. I know myself too well to suppose the former for a moment. I know the public too well, and the subject I have chosen, to expect the latter. But I have made a book illustrating an unexplored and important period, from authentic materials obtained with much difficulty, and probably in the possession of no one library, public or private, in Europe. As a plain, veracious record of facts, the work therefore, till some one else shall be found to make a better one, will fill up a gap in literature which, I should hope, would give it a permanent value."[4] He concludes by writing, "Come to the worst, and suppose the thing a dead failure, and the book born only to be damned. Still it will not be all in vain, since it has encouraged me in forming systematic habits of intellectual occupation, and proved to me that my greatest happiness is to be the result of such. It is no little matter to be possessed of this conviction from experience."[5]

In 1833, during a period when he was halfway through his manuscript, William contracted with a printer by the name of Dickinson to type set his writings. Once work on *Ferdinand and Isabella* was completed, Prescott again turned to Dickinson to convert the remainder of his written manuscript into a printed book, instructing that it was to be "in the same style as the previous portion, at the rate of twenty-five cents per page, text, and notes."[6] He paid Dickinson $456.10 for a corrected proof and three complete copies of the finished work.

Prescott had several good reasons for doling out so much money to have printed copies of his text made before beginning his search for a publisher. One purpose was to see how the completed work looked in print and to make last minute corrections and alterations before submitting it to a publisher. He also wished to have a bound copy for his close friends to read and critique. Another motive for prepublication copies was to have an opportunity to simultaneously submit his work to publishers in America and England. Lastly, William wanted the satisfaction of seeing his work assume a cherished place among the vast collection of books in his private library in the event it failed to get published.

When William finally made it known to all that he had written a book about the reign of Ferdinand and Isabella the news took many friends by surprise, as very few knew of his plans to become an historian. George Ticknor wrote that "most of his friends thought that he led rather an idle, unprofitable life, but attributed it to his infirmity, and pardoned or overlooked it as a misfortune, rather than as anything discreditable."[7]

In February of 1836, Prescott was fortunate to make an important contact during a dinner party that took place at his Bedford Street home. He was once again introduced to Colonel Thomas Aspinwall, the U.S. Consul in London, whom Prescott had first met 20 years earlier during his visit to England. Currently home on leave, Thomas Aspinwall, a native of Massachusetts, was born to a distinguished family from the nearby town of Brookline. He was a graduate of Harvard College, class of 1804, where he had prepared for a career in law. As mentioned previously, Aspinwall's lawyerly ambitions were abruptly sidetracked by a call to service during the War Of 1812, in the course of which he lost his left arm to a musket ball during an assault on Fort Erie. In 1816, Aspinwall was assigned to the American consulate in London and eight years later he was named head consul. In addition to his diplomatic duties, Thomas Aspinwall served as the London literary agent for a number of American authors, a distinguished group that currently included James Fenimore Cooper, Washington Irving, and Fitz-Greene Halleck.

Both Obadiah Rich and George Ticknor told Prescott that Thomas Aspinwall would be an excellent choice as a literary agent to solicit his book to publishers in England. William had thought of Obadiah as his best hope for presenting his work to publishers in London, but the bookseller made it clear that he was not interested in acting as a literary agent. When the suggestion was put forward, Colonel Aspinwall gladly agreed to serve as William Prescott's literary agent.

Once a copy of *History of the Reign of Ferdinand and Isabella, the Catholic* arrived at the American Consulate in London, Colonel Aspinwall wasted no time in presenting William Prescott's book to a number of English publishers. Since correspondence was slowed by the pace of transatlantic shipping schedules, several months would pass before Prescott would hear any news regarding his situation. What made the wait even more unbearable for William was the pledge he had made to himself to hold off seeking an American publisher until he had secured a deal in England, an endorsement he felt would surely enhance his prospects at home. Unfortunately, this long and worrisome wait began to sow seeds of doubt in Prescott's mind.

On February 25, 1837, Prescott wrote to Jared Sparks, a fellow graduate of Harvard and a founding member of the *Club*, for advice related to publishing *Ferdinand and Isabella*: "I wish to consult you fully as to the best way of getting out the book—the size of the volumes etc.—I count on you for all the information relative to the mysteries of the trade."[8] As editor of the *North American Review*, Jared Sparks had published nearly a dozen of Prescott's articles. Though no longer at the helm of the "Old North," Sparks still knew much about the field of publishing from his experience as both editor and author. His *Writings and Life of Washington* was released in 12 volumes between the years 1834 and 1838. Sparks also wrote biographies of Benjamin Franklin and Gouverneur Morris.

At a dinner held at Prescott's house on February 28, 1837—nearly one year after having met with Colonel Aspinwall—friends in attendance, who included Jared Sparks, William Amory, and Henry Wadsworth Longfellow, were engaged in a lively conversation that soon turned to offering opinions and literary advice on the book written by their gracious host. Jared Sparks, who had read several chapters of William's book, had already told his friend, "The book will be successful, bought, read, and praised."[9] While the group discussed the various intricacies of getting published, Sparks advised Prescott to have his finished manuscript stereotyped, a duplicating procedure that emerged in the 18th century which was already beginning to make good on its promise to lessen costs and speed up the printing process. By 1830, stereotyping was enthusiastically embraced by a great many American printers. This technique involved making a mold of each printed page. Molten metal was then poured into the mold and allowed to cool until it hardened into a plate that replicated the original page. The author was entirely responsible for the cost of creating these durable printing plates.

The next day, after mulling over the suggestions of his friends, William stated in a letter to Jared Sparks, "The more I think of the stereotyping the better I am pleased with the arrangement—if I can secure the services of a good midwife to bring my bantling into the world."[10] Prescott then sought to learn about the expenses associated with stereotyping his work. He wrote to George Bancroft, a friend who had recently published his first volume of *History of the United States*, to inquire about the terms and costs involved in this relatively new printing process. It would take Bancroft four decades to finish his monumental ten-volume study of America's history, a worthy effort which led many to refer to him as the father of American history.

John Pickering, a celebrated Salem scholar, wrote an encouraging note to Prescott on May 1, 1837: "Being uninterrupted last evening, I had an opportunity to finish the few pages that remained of your work, and I now return the volumes with many thanks. I cannot, however, take leave of them without expressing the high satisfaction I feel that our country should have produced such a work,—a work which, unless I am mistaken, will live as long as any one produced by your contemporaries either here or in England."[11] His good friend William Gardiner, who had reviewed his manuscript before it was seen by Sparks, was supportive of his literary effort and freely offered advice in the form of criticisms and corrections, some of which were heeded by Prescott.

Pursuing Publishers

Unfortunately for Colonel Aspinwall, his efforts to find a London publisher for William Prescott's book proved to be a far more daunting task than he ever anticipated. The publisher John Murray declined without even bothering to examine this new work. Meanwhile, the firm of Longman & Company did take a look at Prescott's manuscript but chose not to make an offer. Prescott was stung by these rejections and began to wonder if he had simply wasted his time and effort on this work—a common fear of any fledgling author who has encountered their first string of rejections. The Boston historian was convinced that the English writer Robert Southey, who he had heard was preparing a work on the history of the Spanish Arabs, had persuaded the Longman firm not to publish his book. The simple truth was that the publisher did not wish to commit to a three-volume historical account, especially one by an unknown author.

The dutiful Colonel Aspinwall refused to give up his search for a publisher. His persistence paid off on March 20, 1837, with the signing of a contract with Richard Bentley of 8 New Burlington Street. Bentley was known for his willingness to publish American authors, a list of overseas authors which greatly exceeded that of any other English publisher. Richard Bentley's Publishing house was later titled as Richard Bentley & Son. George Bentley had joined his father's publishing firm in 1836 and several years later he was made a partner. For his services as literary agent, Prescott paid Aspinwall a commission of "ten percent on the proceeds of books published on half profits"[12] and reimbursed him for postage and any other expenses related to his work.

Richard Bentley had succeeded in 1833 in getting himself appointed Publisher in Ordinary to His Majesty. In a letter to Prescott dated October 19, 1840, Jared Sparks addressed the topic concerning the flowery title that Bentley would imprint on his publications: "Next to Colburn he [Bentley] has the character of being the most familiar of any publisher in London with the small tricks of his trade. He has lately had the vanity to get himself made 'Publisher to her Majesty,' which is mere vapor. Now there are divers 'Leather Breeches Makers to the Queen' in London, though it is not positively known that her Majesty ever wore leather breeches; but she has certain equerries, huntsmen, and grooms, who sometimes bedeck themselves in that habiliment, and Albert may now and then want a pair when he goes upon his sporting excursions; so that the tailors make some good account of royal breeches makers. But who ever heard of the Queen or any of her household publishing a book? Yet Bentley attaches this foolish appendage to all his title-pages, and it will doubtless adorn the next edition of Ferdinand and Isabella."[13] Ironically, Queen Victoria did publish a book in 1867 titled *Leaves from the Journals of our Life in the Highland*, which bore the name of another publisher. Bentley was said to have been extremely embarrassed by this royal snub.

Prescott made sure to file for a copyright at the Boston branch of the clerk of the District Court for the District of Massachusetts, a protective measure which he applied to all of his historical accounts. The American copyright law, which had only offered an author 14 years protection from someone infringing upon their work, was expanded on February 3, 1831, to 28 years, with the right to renew for another 14 years. Publishing difficulties abroad were largely attributable to the lack of an international copyright accord. America failed to participate in any of the international copyright arrangements that were being forged in Europe. Prussia would lead the way in 1836 by instituting a law whereby any nation could procure a copyright for its authors provided it accorded the same courtesy to Prussian writers. Germany followed suit in 1837, and the succeeding year England instituted a similar international pact.

On February 2, 1837, a petition signed by 56 British authors was sent to Congress asking for protection from unscrupulous American publishers who were flaunting the absence of reciprocal international copyright accords. Several of these signers, such as Henry Hallam, Charles Lyell, Henry H. Milman, and Maria Edgeworth, were soon to become good friends of William Prescott. Two days later, a similar appeal signed by 30 American authors requesting passage of an accord that would protect their rights in England was sent to lawmakers. Soon thereafter, a reciprocal copyright law was introduced in Congress, which would require amending the current law. However, the bill offered by Henry Clay's committee failed to come to a vote. The bill was reintroduced by Clay, but by this time opposition to the passage of an international copyright law had grown in strength. The proposed piece of legislation failed and the current American law remained intact.

The failure to enact an international copyright agreement meant that American and British authors had to rely on what was known as "trade courtesy" when their writings were published in each others country. Such works could be exploited without any obligation for payment of fees and royalties, for which the violated author had no legal recourse. Even though such actions were deemed by many as piracy, the absence of reciprocal international copy right laws paved a licit course for publishers to impinge on the writings of foreign authors. There were, however, a few publishers who were guided by a moral obligation to pay a fair royalty to foreign authors. Because of the popularity of their works, British authors were more prone to such exploitation than their American counterparts. Charles Dickens, who was widely abused by American printers, paid a visit to America in 1842 to publicly criticize this illicit trade. Because of

5. Exceeding All Expectations

this lack of an international accord between the United States and Great Britain, Prescott sought to avoid any legal entanglements by selling his copyright to the publisher Richard Bentley.

Back home, Hilliard, Gray & Company and the American Stationers' Company were two Boston firms that had expressed an interest in publishing Prescott's *Ferdinand and Isabella*. The author, who was deeply concerned with the details regarding the design of his book, decided that the American Stationers' Company, a new publishing firm founded by men who were committed to producing quality books, was the best fit for his needs. It also helped that the publishing house was just a few blocks from his home. The contract, which was signed on April 10, 1837, stipulated that Prescott was to supply the stereotype plates and engravings for his book, and, in return, the company agreed to print 1250 copies to sell over a span of five years.

To reproduce his manuscript onto stereotype plates William Prescott turned to Folsom, Wells, and Thurston of Cambridge, a firm that had a reputation for superior work in the printing of American books. Charles Folsom, a fellow Harvard graduate and *Club* member who was charged with overseeing the printing of Prescott's book, critiqued the work and marked the proofs with thoughtful suggestions and necessary corrections. Having served as the librarian of both Harvard College and the Boston Athenaeum, William had good reason to trust Folsom's literary advice and therefore agreed to implement a number of his recommendations. The correcting of these proofs was a responsibility that the historian usually assigned to his secretary. George Ticknor helped his good friend by supervising the type setting of *History of the Reign of Ferdinand and Isabella, the Catholic*.

Prescott preferred to pay someone else to perform the tedious and time consuming task of creating an index for his book. The librarian John Langdon Sibley, a resident of Union, Maine, was recommended by Jared Sparks for indexing the three-volume set of *Ferdinand and Isabella*. Prescott paid the indexer $100 for the comprehensive list that numbered 42 pages, a fee which the historian thought was excessive. However, Sibley did such an outstanding job that Prescott would again employ his services in 1848 to index his next book, which was his classic work titled *History of the Conquest of Mexico*.

As for Richard Bentley, Prescott would only send him the proof sheets produced from the stereotype plates. No metal plates were ever shipped across the Atlantic during his long-standing relationship with the London publisher. As an added precaution, William would ship his work piecemeal to avoid the possibility of the entire manuscript being lost at sea. Fortunately, none of his copies ever suffered such a terrible fate. The Boston historian often shipped his papers in a secure diplomatic pouch, a benefit of having friends in high places.

William corresponded frequently with his publisher regarding suggestions and demands he felt were necessary for the betterment of his forthcoming book. The author suggested the use of high quality black ink, insisted on the finest paper, demanded the best binding, requested a faster completion of the index, and sought extra copies to distribute to respected reviewers. He also inquired about the best approach toward producing the title page, how many lines and letters there should be per page, and the placement of postscripts. After enduring the many trials he had encountered to publish his first book, Prescott would often refer to the publishing field as the "slippery trade."

A memo dated April 30, 1838, provides a detailed account of the expenses that Prescott incurred to publish his manuscript:

> Paid to Folsom Wells and Thurston for plates, extra corrections included: $2,143.90
> Paid to Andrews for one engraving ... $400
> Paid to Stone: for two engravings ... $160
> Paid to Sibley: for making index ... $ 100
> Total: $2,803.90

If to these I add:

> Paid Flagg for portrait of Isabella for Andrews $40
> Paid Dickinson for first printed copy $456.
> Finally, for cost Spanish books and MS. $1,200
> Total: $4,499.90

"Of this, $1,000 for Spanish works was defrayed by my father, so that I was out of pocket by the expenses of publication $3,500."[14]

Prescott turned to George Bancroft and Jared Sparks for help in getting his work reviewed, an essential step toward promoting awareness both in and outside the Boston market. The list of newspaper and magazine editors that the two accomplished authors compiled for their friend was shared with the American Stationers' Company in advance of the book's release.

The three-volume set of *History of Ferdinand and Isabella, the Catholic,* which was bound in tan floriated cloth, was priced at $7.50, an amount that was slightly beyond the affordable budget of an average family and still a steep outlay for those of means during the current economic downturn that was forcing many to cut back on the purchase of luxury items such as books. A portrait of Queen Isabella, by J. Andrews, appeared on the front piece of the first volume. King Ferdinand and Cardinal Ximenez de Cisneros, both by G. F. Storm, graced the second and third volumes, respectively. The set went on sale Christmas day 1837, which helped to make it a popular holiday gift amongst the residents of Boston. The London edition was published in early 1838. The dedication read:

Ferdinand the Catholic (1452–1516), King of Sicily, married Isabella (courtesy Historical Findings and Library of Congress).

> To
> the Honorable
> William, Prescott, LL.D.,
> the guide of my youth,
> my best friend in riper years
> These Volumes
> with the warmest feelings of filial affection,
> are respectfully inscribed

The American Stationers' Company spared no expense in promoting William Prescott's book, which they advertised well in advance of its release. Advertisements for the publication of *History of the Reign of Ferdinand and Isabella, the Catholic* appeared in the *Courier, American Traveller, Daily Advertiser, Boston Recorder, Mercantile Journal, Daily Evening Transcript*, and the *Evening Mercantile Journal*. Convinced there would be little demand for this title outside of the northern region, the Boston publisher decided to ignore the markets of the south. The first edition was limited to 500 copies simply because the publisher feared risking a larger number for the narrow New England market. The American Stationers' Company had to rethink their marketing strategy when half of the books were sold within the first ten days of release and sold out entirely after only five weeks.

History of the Reign of Ferdinand and Isabella, the Catholic sold far better than either the author or publisher had anticipated, but such figures were tempered by the fact that these purchases were confined to the New England region, where the Prescott name was well known. Seeking to perfect his work, William compiled an errata list that noted the errors spotted by himself and several friends, which he submitted to the printer so that the necessary corrections could be implemented for the next edition. A second edition of 1250 copies was quickly brought to market and by the first anniversary of its initial release the *History of the Reign of Ferdinand*

and Isabella, the Catholic had sold approximately 2800 copies in America.

Universal Acclaim

Prescott's friends did their very best to make sure that the public took notice of his newly-released *History of the Reign of Ferdinand and Isabella, the Catholic*. William Howard Gardiner, the author's lifelong friend and confidant, praised his work in Boston's *North American Review*. Francis William Pitt Greenwood, a fellow Harvard classmate, commended the book in the March 1838 edition of the *Christian Examiner and General Review*; the classicist John Pickering paid tribute to the historian in the April 1838 issue of the *New York Review*; and George Bancroft, another close friend, lauded *Ferdinand & Isabella* in the May 1838 publication of the *United States Magazine and Democratic Review*. Jared Sparks helped Prescott's cause by making sure that copies of the book found their way into the hands of influential reviewers. Sparks later recalled telling his friend after he had reviewed *Ferdinand and Isabella*, "there could be but one opinion about it; that I had read the book with great delight, and thought he had written one of the most successful works of its kind that had come before the public."[15] As a critic himself, William knew just how much a favorable review could stimulate public interest.

William Gardiner's review addressed the broad appeal of Prescott's *Ferdinand & Isabella*: "The scholar will find a rich treat of literary mingled with political history. The general reader cannot fail to be interested and surprised at the number of striking incidents and blood stirring adventures crowded into the compass of a few years. And the gentler sex may find in the life of Isabella, not only something to excite their domestic sympathy, but much excellent example also, even for those who are not born to grace a throne. They will be particularly struck with the harmonious action by which the royal couple accomplished their united purposes; that happy mingling of interest, affection, and authority, which cherished mutual respect, and claimed mutual support, without compromising the dignity or independence of either; and that graceful division of the cares of sovereignty which assigned the foreign relations and military movements of Ferdinand, while his queen regulated the internal affairs of the great national household, not neglecting, meanwhile the humbler domestic duties, which fall within the ordinary sphere of a wife and a mother."[16]

William greatly appreciated the efforts of his friends but secretly feared they were blinded by their close relationship with him. Those concerns quickly faded when critical praise was received from a number of prominent reviewers both at home and across the Atlantic.

During this period there existed a general prejudice in European literary circles that good writers could only be found in the Old World. The contemporary English critic Sydney Smith had bluntly stated his objection to the literary efforts of American authors: "Why should Americans write books when a six weeks' passage brings them in their own language our sense, our science and genius in bales and hogsheads.... In the four quarters of the Globe, whoever has read an American book?"[17] At the time, American authors who could support themselves through writing were few in number. Washington Irving was one of the first to earn his keep solely from writing. Most, however, had to work full time jobs while pursuing their literary craft. William Prescott was in the enviable position of not having to worry about earning money from his writing endeavors.

George Ticknor was traveling abroad when Prescott's book was released. During his tour of the European continent, the accomplished Boston scholar helped to support the work of his good friend by making sure that copies of Richard Bentley's edition of *Ferdinand and Isabella* were placed in the hands of such distinguished reviewers and scholars as Martín Fernández de Navarette, Nicolaus Heinrich Julius, Friedrich von Raumer, Francois Guizot, Charles Fauriel, and Count Adolphe de Circourt. The latter gentleman wrote a highly favorable review that appeared as a series of five installments between 1838 and 1840 in the *Bibliotheque Universelle de Geneve,* which an appreciative Prescott felt obliged to respond with a sincere letter of appreciation.

Isabella the Catholic (1451–1504), Queen of Castile, and Leon, Crown of Castile (courtesy of Historical Findings and Library of Congress).

While in England, George Ticknor made sure a review of *Ferdinand and Isabella* found its way into the *Edinburgh Review.* Ticknor met with Macvey Napier, editor of the quarterly magazine to see if they would print a review of Prescott's work. Napier agreed but stipulated that the review must be written by Dr. John Allen, Lord Holland's secretary and librarian who was known for his extensive knowledge of Spanish History. While Dr. Allen was impressed with Prescott's book he turned down Ticknor's request to write a review. Luckily, a young Spanish friend of Dr. Allen, by the name of Pascual de Gayangos volunteered to examine this book about the Catholic Monarchs of Spain.

George Ticknor first met Pascual de Gayangos at a dinner held at Holland House on June 3, 1838. The Spanish scholar was currently performing essential work on a number of historical and literary manuscripts for the British Museum. Ticknor believed the young Gayangos would be an excellent choice to replace Dr. John Allen as a reviewer of Prescott's *History of the Reign of Ferdinand and Isabella, the Catholic*. Though the American and Spanish scholars would never again meet in person they would continue to correspond on a regular basis, friendly missives which terminated upon the death of George Ticknor in 1871.

Ticknor's efforts on behalf of his friend quickly paid off; William was the recipient of something rarely accorded American authors—widespread literary acclaim. These accolades were a source of pride for Prescott, for unlike reviewers in America who were somewhat familiar with his name, these were by critics who had never heard of him. He wrote: "These tributes from another quarter of the world, without the bias of national partiality, come like the voice of posterity, not to be bribed or bought."[18]

William was also pleased to receive glowing reviews for his work from such noted historians as Jean Charles Leonard de Sismondi, Augustin Thierry, and Patrick Fraser Tytler. He had, as Daniel Webster would declare, "burst upon the world like a comet."[19] Prescott's *Ferdinand and Isabella* was that rare example of a scholarly work that appealed to a wide audience. He was praised by many for his objective and impartial views, attention to detail, and compelling writing style. He was also widely acknowledged for setting a higher standard of documentation for primary and secondary sources. William Hickling Prescott was the first American historian to be recognized as an equal of the European historians of his day.

As mentioned, the Spanish scholar Pascual de Gayangos y Arce would write a highly favorable review of *Ferdinand and Isabella,* which appeared in the January 1839 edition of the *Edinburgh Review*. As a Spaniard, Pascual de Gayangos was certainly intrigued by the topic that William Prescott had chosen, and as a scholar he was very moved by the American author's breadth of knowledge and grasp of Spain's rapid rise as a united and powerful European nation. Gayangos noted in his review of *Ferdinand and*

Isabella, "Mr. Prescott's work is one of the most successful historical productions of our time."[20]

Pleased with this flattering review, William felt compelled to express his heartfelt appreciation in a note to the Spanish scholar. In a letter dated March 20, 1839, Prescott thanked Pascual de Gayangos for his praise and the gracious manner in which he pointed out his inaccuracies: "if I have erred, anywhere, from want of authentic documents, I should be happy to correct it. Will you also allow me to ask if, among your papers, you have any which can throw light on the history of Cortes or Pizarro; a subject which I am now meditating, and for which I have collected some valuable materials, both from Madrid and Mexico."[21] William also pledged to send him a copy of his latest American edition of *History of Ferdinand and Isabella, the Catholic,* a promise which he kept.

A response from Pascual de Gayangos arrived in late March 1840: "Nothing could be so gratifying ... as to enter into a correspondence with the author of Ferdinand and Isabella." The scholar spoke of the numerous manuscripts in his possession, and was especially proud of an account of the correspondences between Gonzalo de Córdoba, the Great Captain, and King Ferdinand. The Spanish scholar stated, "I need not tell you that this and every one of the historical manuscripts in my collection is at your service."[22] This was the beginning of a nearly 20-year friendship that continued until the death of the Boston historian.

Born in Seville in 1809, Pascual's father, José Gayangos y Nebot, was an officer in the Spanish army who, between 1816 and 1820, served as the military governor of the Mexican province of Zacatecas. The family was transferred to France, where the father soon passed away. Influenced by the lectures of the orientalist scholar Silvestre de Sacy, Pascual chose to remain in Paris to pursue his interests in Arabic and Moorish history and Spanish literature.

It was during this period of studies that Pascual de Gayangos met and fell in love with a young English girl on holiday by the name of Frances Revell, or Fanny to her friends and family. The lovesick Pascual followed Fanny to England, where he courted and married her at Round Oak, Windsor, in May 1828, a mere month before his 19th birthday. Pascual's mother was adamantly opposed to her son's marriage on the grounds that he was much too young and the differences in their faith. Remaining in England, Gayangos resumed his scholarly studies while supporting himself and his wife by working a variety of jobs, which included stints as a bibliographer, book seller, translator, and copyist. He supplemented his income by contributing articles to the *Penny Encyclopaedia*, the *Westminster Review*, and the *Edinburgh Review*. By the time he was 28, Pascual had already earned acceptance as a serious and respected literary scholar. Gayangos was primarily interested in the Arabic period of Spanish history. The first volume of his *History of the Mohammedan Dynasties in Spain* was published in 1840 and a second volume was released three years later.

Not all critics were kind to Prescott in their reviews of his *History of the Reign of Ferdinand and Isabella, the Catholic*. The English critic Richard Ford complained about the American author in his 1839 article for the British *Quarterly Review*: "His style is too often sesquipedalian and ornate, the stilty wordy, false taste of Dr. Channing without his depth of thought; the sugar and sack of Washington Irving without the half-pennyworth of bread—without his grace and polish of pure, grammatical, careful Anglicism."[23] Richard Ford was the author of several works, most notably *Handbook for Travellers in Spain*.

William was deeply troubled by Richard Ford's harsh criticisms, which caused him to question his own style of writing. After fretting about the English critics stinging review he decided, "I will not hereafter vex myself with anxious thoughts about my style when composing. It is formed. And if there be any ground for the imputation that it is too formal, it will only be made worse in this respect by extra solicitude. It is not the defect to which I am predisposed. The best security against it is to write with less elaboration—a pleasant recipe which conforms to my previous views. This determination will save me trouble and time. Hereafter what I print will undergo no ordeal for the style's sake except only the grammar."[24]

It was around this time that Prescott received from Richard Bentley a copy of his British edition of *Ferdinand and Isabella*, which he noticed had been printed on a better quality of paper and with blacker ink, but the typeface appeared rather inferior to that of his American release. He was disappointed that his list of corrections had not arrived in time to appear in the overseas publication. Grateful for this opportunity to break into the British market, the Boston historian was generally pleased with the work that Bentley had performed on his behalf.

On April 30, 1838, William summed up his feelings about the favorable American reviews of his book: "From the time of its appearance to the present date, it has been the subject of notices, more or less elaborate, in the principal reviews and periodicals of the country, and in the mass of criticism I have not met with one unkind or sarcastic, or censorious sentence; and my critics have been of all sorts, from stiff conservatives to leveling loco-focus." He goes on to state, "Whatever is the cause, the book has found a degree of favor not dreamed of by me certainly, nor by its warmest friends. It will, I have reason to hope, secure me an honest fame, and—what never entered into my imagination in writing it—put, in the long run, some money in my pocket."[25]

While the American Stationers' Company had done an admirable job of fulfilling their contract with William Prescott, the publishing firm was hit hard by the financial panic that had erupted in 1837. Even the success of Prescott's book could not save the company from collapse during the spring of 1838. Unable to weather the financial storm, the publishing enterprise was forced to close its doors less than six months after the initial release of *Ferdinand and Isabella*. The stereotype plates, which the historian had paid a handsome price for, were stored at the Cambridge printers. Grateful they were not lost to the liquidation proceedings, Prescott would thereafter insist on retaining control of his stereotype plates. The printing firm would be responsible for any damage that occurred while using the metal plates for a print job and they were not allowed to be transferred without Prescott's express approval. William was fortunate to receive the promised $1000 flat sum for the 1250 copies of *History of the Reign of Ferdinand and Isabella, the Catholic*, a sum which fell far short of the expenses that the author had incurred to produce his book.

Because of the overwhelming success of his first book, Prescott had little trouble finding a new publisher. On May 14, 1838, William closed a deal with Charles C. Little and his partner James Brown, both of whom had learned the intricacies of the book trade during their employment with Hilliar, Gray & Company before branching out on their own. Little & Company agreed to publish 1700 copies of *History of the Reign of Ferdinand and Isabella, the Catholic* over a period of five years. William Prescott would receive $2975 for the rights to his work. The historian then provided his new publisher with the stereotype plates that had been produced by Folsom, Wells, and Thurston of Cambridge. The first Little & Company edition was released in August of 1838. Nine years later the publishing firm changed its name to Little, Brown & Company.

It was during this period that Prescott's book was introduced into Spanish circles by Ángel Calderón de la Barca, the former Spanish minister to the United States. Calderón had read this work while in New York and was so impressed with it that he arranged for copies to be sent to the queen of Spain and to the Real Academia de la Historia, the latter being Spain's leading historical society. On March 23, 1838, the Spanish diplomat wrote to Prescott. "I think it is the duty of every Spanish lover of literature to show his gratitude to one who like yourself has expended so much time and money to perpetuate for posterity, with the mastery that you have shown, the memory of the most glorious and interesting period in the history of Spain—perhaps of the world."[26] Ángel Calderón even volunteered to translate the book into Castilian.

William was elated to learn that such an influential member of the Spanish court had taken an interest in his work. He went to New York toward the end of March 1838 to meet with his enthusiastic supporter, an encounter that blossomed into a lifelong friendship. Unfortunately, Calderón's time-consuming diplomatic duties prevented him from ever getting around to translating Prescott's book into Spanish. The first Castilian translation of *Ferdinand and Isabella* was performed in Madrid by Pedro Sabau y Larryoya, and published in 1845.

On April 21, 1838, William Prescott sent a copy of his book to Tomás González, the keeper of the archives of Simancas, along with a note stating, "I now propose to assume a narration of the conquest of Mexico and Peru, if I can obtain such original and authentic documents as will furnish an apology for telling again what has been told more than once from inadequate sources. Your acknowledged courtesy in opening the archives of Spain to such scholars as are disposed to derive materials from them, encourages me in the belief that you will render the same good office to a stranger who devotes himself to the study and exposition of the materials himself. With this hope I have requested my friend, Mr. Arthur Middleton, Secretary of the Legation at Madrid, to employ some person to communicate with you on this subject, and to obtain your permission to copy such manuscripts in the archives as would further the objects I have in view."[27]

On April 30, 1838, William Prescott made the following notation in his literary memorandum: "Confined to my chamber by a fall from a horse, which has badly sprained my leg. I am now slowly recovering, but it will cause me a lameness for some time, and prove a wholesome lesson, I hope, not to meddle with half-broken colts again."[28]

In late June of 1838, the Prescott family was preparing to leave Pepperell to take up residence at Fitful Head, It was during this time that Catherine Hickling Prescott suddenly felt listless and her mind became very confused, ailments manifested by an abrupt swelling of her brain. William worried that his nearly-71-year-old mother was near death. But all were greatly relieved when she soon began exhibiting favorable signs that her health was on the mend. It was decided that the family should return at once to Boston, where his mother would spend the summer regaining her strength, which improved significantly over the ensuing weeks.

6

Continuing with the Spanish Theme

Poets may be born, but historians are made.[1]

Contemplating a New Project

While *Ferdinand and Isabella* was being prepared for publication, Prescott took some time to relax as well as ponder what new subject he might like to devote his time and effort to write about. He passed the time enjoying the company of family, friends and new acquaintances, many of whom showered him with praise—sincere expressions of adulation that William never let go to his head.

During this well-deserved period of respite from research and writing, Prescott gave serious consideration to working on an in-depth study of Jean-Baptiste Poquelin, the French actor and playwright more easily recognized by his stage name Molière, who was the subject of an article he had written for the July 1828 edition of the *North American Review*. In September of 1837, William wrote to George Ticknor, who was in Paris at the time, to inform him of his proposed biography of Molière and to issue a request for any materials or books that he might be able to locate on this subject. Ticknor complied by sending him some 50 volumes related to the French playwright, but by the time they had arrived William's interest in this topic had already waned.

There was also another biography that was being seriously considered by William Prescott; prior to the publication of *History of the Reign of Ferdinand and Isabella, the Catholic,* William toyed with the idea of writing a history of the long and eventful reign of Philip II. But lack of access to the archives of Simancas made it impossible to obtain the numerous historical documents he deemed necessary for a thorough account of the life and times of this Spanish monarch. This immense collection, which included millions of official papers relating to the history of Spain, had been placed in storage in 1536 by decree of Philip's father, Charles V. Prescott had sought to gain access to this vast storehouse of official documents, private letters, and correspondences by seeking help from friends in Madrid. Arthur Middleton responded by informing William that he knew of a scholar who had been granted permission to search the archives only to discover that the official documents prior to 1700 were stacked in large piles without any manner of order, a collection which would surely take more than the six months to sort through. On September 14, 1839, William disappointingly noted in his journal: "By advices from Madrid this week, I learn that the archives of Simancas are in so disorderly a state that it is next to impossible to gather material for the reign of Philip II."[2]

Determined that he would one day write a biography of Philip II of Spain, Prescott stated in a letter dated January 18, 1839, to Friedrich Wilhelm Lembke, "It is looking rather far ahead to be thinking of a second subject, before I have despatched the first. But I have often thought that if I should live to complete the Conquest of Mexico and Peru, I should turn my attention to the reign of Philip II of Spain. It is a reign which still remains to be written in English."[3]

After spending 18 months contemplating which subject he would like to tackle next, Prescott set his sights on writing a detailed account of the Spanish conquest of Mexico. He sent a letter to George Ticknor to inform him that he had once again altered his literary course, stating that he was switching from a study of the literary achievements of Molière to an examination of the daring exploits of Hernán Cortés. The success of his *History of the Reign of Ferdinand and Isabella, the Catholic* and his evolving interest in sweeping historical accounts, particularly those centered around the era of Spain's emerging empire, had certainly played key factors in this decision. In the end, the Spanish conquest of Mexico proved to be the reasonable and orderly choice for his next topic. William had made a reference to the legendary conquistador Hernán Cortés in the second volume of *Ferdinand and Isabella* as that "young adventurer who was destined, by the conquest of Mexico, to realize all the magnificent visions, which had been derided as only visions, in the lifetime of Columbus."[4]

Before delving into his next project, Prescott reached out to his friend James Rich in London to inquire if his father, Obadiah Rich, would be interested in seeking out books in Spain that pertained to the Spanish conquest of Mexico. The Boston historian made it clear that he was willing to spend as much as $1500 to acquire books and manuscripts that were relevant to this subject.

William acknowledged the previous works on this topic by the Spanish author Antonio de Solís and the Scottish historian William Robertson, but information that had recently become available necessitated a need to visit the subject once more. Prescott refused to be drawn away from work once he had fully committed to this project, which is reflected in his decision to decline an invitation to deliver the Phi Beta Kappa address at Harvard, as well as speak to an audience at the National Institute at Washington.

Collecting Data

William Prescott used his literary connections and ample source of funds to collect any available books germane to the Spanish conquest of Mexico. By means of a letter of credit drawn on Barings Bank, the historian paid $1500 to the noted London bookseller Obadiah Rich to acquire books on this subject, but was disappointed to learn just how few publications there were on this historic event. Prescott's new friend Don Pascual de Gayangos, the Spanish scholar residing in London who was also a friend of Obadiah Rich, came to his rescue by voluntarily combing numerous libraries and archives in London, Paris, and Madrid for manuscripts related to Hernán Cortés's conquest of Mexico.

In April of 1838, Prescott sent a formal request to the Royal Academy of History in Madrid for permission to copy portions of the extensive research material that had been assembled by Juan Bautista Muñoz, Spain's official historiographer of the Indies. Muñoz had been granted unrestricted access to the national archives in Spain and its colonies as well as all of their public and private libraries. In the course of his duties, Juan Muñoz assembled a massive collection of manuscripts but, unfortunately, the historiographer did not live long enough to complete his work. Following his death in 1799, Muñoz's immense compilation of historical documents was deposited in the archives of the Royal Academy of History. Don Vargas y Ponce, President of the Academy, continued to add to the late historian's collection by procuring similar texts, many of which were located in the archives of the Indies in Seville.

Prescott would enlist the services of Arthur Middleton, a Harvard classmate and former editor of the North American Review who was currently serving as secretary of the American legation in Spain, by stating in a letter, "You, my old friend, are on the very spot and situation which can lay this career open to me."⁵ Middleton replied that he would gladly do all that he could to help him.

Arthur Middleton complied with his friend's request by contracting the services of Friedrich Wilhelm Lembke, a German historian and member of the Royal Academy who was very familiar with the Spanish archives—knowledge he acquired while conducting research for his history of Spain up to the year 1800, titled *Geschichte von Spanien*. Dr. Friedrich Lembke supervised four copyists he had hired with Prescott's money to collate and transcribe this massive collection of unpublished documents and manuscripts which were to be shipped to America. In expressing his appreciation of Lembke's valuable assistance, Prescott wrote, "This learned Theban, who happens to be in Madrid, has taken charge of my own affairs and, like a true German, inspecting everything and selecting just what has reference to my subject."⁶ In November of 1838, Friedrich Lembke managed to finish preparing for Prescott's benefit this unique collection of papers related to the Spanish conquest of Mexico.

Prescott acknowledged and appreciated the liberal spirit that currently existed in Spain to openly share their historical information. Previously, the Scottish historian William Robertson had made a similar request, which was met with a swift refusal by Spanish authorities. William gave credit to this dramatic change in attitude to Don Martín Fernández de Navarrete, President of the Royal Academy of History. This eminent Spanish scholar even provided the American historian with access to his own collection of manuscripts on Spain's colonial history, particularly those pertaining to the settlement of Mexico by his homeland. Prescott was too modest to admit that his favorable treatment of Ferdinand and Isabella had helped to open doors to Spanish officials who were in a position to honor his research requests.

Valuable assistance was also rendered by a number of esteemed sources outside of Spain: Count Camaldoli at Naples; the Duke of Serradifalco in Sicily; and the Duke of Monteleone in Mexico. The latter nobleman, who was the representative of the Cortés estate, was kind enough to make the family records of the famed conquistador readily available to him. Prescott was also grateful that the French historian Henri Ternaux-Compans and Count Adolphe de Circourt made their abundant collection of manuscripts accessible for his research.

Meanwhile, Don Pascual de Gayangos perused the British Museum for any official documents relating to the Spanish conquest of Mexico, which he copied and translated for Prescott's benefit. Gayangos also brought to William's attention the pending sale in Dublin of the late Lord Kingsborough's voluminous *Antiquities of Mexico*. The Spanish scholar would also loan the Boston historian a number of books from his personal collection.

Prescott acknowledged a debt to the handful of historians and officials in Mexico who were kind enough to provide him with sound advice and valuable materials pertinent to the country's pre–Columbian civilizations, particularly those concerning the Aztecs, much of which had been overlooked by previous historians. Count Cortina; Carlos de Bustamante; Don Lucas Alamán, Minister of Foreign Affairs in Mexico; and Angel Calderón de la Barca, the Spanish minister to Mexico who was destined to become a good friend of William Prescott, were among those who willingly lent a helping hand on this obscure topic.

Friends and scholars would serve as the eyes of the lands that William Prescott had chosen to write about but was unable to visit. By meticulously seeking out detailed descriptions supplied by eyewitness accounts and reports of travelers who had covered the very ground he intended to write about, Prescott was able to add authentic coloring which helped to make his tale even more enjoyable for the reader. Frances Calderón de la Barca, the wife of the Spanish minister to Mexico, provided the Boston historian with a wealth of information about the diverse flora, fauna, and terrain of Mexico.

Frances Erskine Inglis was the maiden name of the former Scottish schoolmistress who was a descendant of the Earls of Buchan. Her widowed and near penniless mother left home to seek a better life for herself and her family in America. Landing in Boston, the mother founded a school, where Frances served as a teacher for several years. In 1838, the 34-year-old Fanny, as she was better known to her family and friends, married Don Angel Calderón de la Barca, who was the Spanish minister in Washington. The newlyweds traveled to Mexico, where Angel would serve as the first minister from Spain, now that the Spanish court had finally recognized Mexican independence, which had occurred in 1821.

In a letter to Fanny Calderón de la Barca, dated August 15, 1840, Prescott requested that she send him information about the geography of the regions that Hernán Cortés and his men had passed through on their way to the city of Tenochtitlán, the capital of the Aztec Empire. In addition to a detailed report on the flora and fauna of the region, Prescott wanted her to provide him with a description of the sacred snow-capped mountains named Iztaccihuatl (White Lady) and Popocatepetl (Smoking Mountain) that the conquistadors had viewed along the path to Tenochtitlán. Madame Calderón paid a visit to the ancient ruins of Teotihuacan (The Abode of the Gods), which she mistook for Tenochtitlán. Unfortunately, Madame Calderón was unaware of the fact that Mexico City was built atop the ruins of the Aztec capital. Prescott was quick to realize her error and therefore chose to rely on Alexander von Humboldt's description of the abandoned and forgotten city of Teotihuacan, which contained its own unique set of flaws.

On January 8, 1839, Prescott reached out to Joel Roberts Poinsett, the current secretary of war under President Martin van Buren, to help him procure from Mexico any materials related to the Spanish conquest. Poinsett's *Notes on Mexico, 1822*, which was published in 1824, was an insightful account of his experiences in Mexico. When his special diplomatic mission was finished, Poinsett returned home with a charming shrub bearing scarlet leaves that is native to Mexico and Central America, a plant which was renamed poinsettia in honor of the American statesman.

James and Obadiah Rich were able to satisfy Prescott's research requests by obtaining copies of books written by Giovanni Battista Ramusio and Andrés González Barcia. William also instructed the London booksellers to obtain a copy of Lord Kingsborough's *Antiquities of Mexico*, a limited set of folios which, at the time, was unavailable in America. Previously, Obadiah Rich had assisted Lord Kingsborough in obtaining a number of articles that were included in his *Antiquities of Mexico*. At first, William was hesitant about purchasing this massive work, especially after he learned that the Boston Athenaeum was seeking to acquire its own copy, which would have provided him full access at no cost. However, the library had placed a restriction to pay no more than $400 for this set of historical works. Not wanting to miss the opportunity to use this unique collection for his research, Prescott decided to purchase his own copy with the intention of donating it to the Boston Athenaeum—subject to his unlimited use. William paid the princely sum of $3500 to acquire the complete set of Lord Kingsborough's *Antiquities of Mexico*.

Lord Kingsborough was Edward King, a wealthy Irishman who was thoroughly convinced that the natives of Mexico were the direct descendants of the Lost Tribes of Israel. Published between 1829 and 1848, the nine-volume *Antiquities of Mexico* contained lithographed and handpainted copies of every known Mexican screen fold book and manuscript that Edward King was able to acquire. Finding himself unable to pay his accrued debts after having exhausted his entire fortune on this obsessive quest, Viscount Kingsborough was sentenced to Sheriff's prison in Dublin, where, after contracting typhus fever, he died at the age 42. The final volume of *Antiquities of Mexico* was posthumously published in 1848.

Prescott paid tribute to Edward King's magnificent collection by stating, "The drift of Lord Kingsborough's speculation is to establish the colonization of Mexico by the Israelites. To this the whole battery of his logic and learning is directed. For this hieroglyphics are unriddled, manuscripts compared and monuments delineated.... By this munificent undertaking, which no government, probably, would have, and few individuals could have executed, he has entitled himself to the lasting gratitude of every friend of science."[7]

In addition to Lord Kingsborough's *Antiquities of Mexico*, Prescott obtained copies of several other rare manuscripts pertaining to the history and culture of the native tribes that flourished in and around the Valley of Mexico, a list that included works by Motolinía (Toribio de Benavente), Bernardino de Sahagún, Fernando de Alva Ixtlilxochiltl, Juan de Torquemada, Lorenzo Boturini, Francisco Xavier Clavigero, and Antonio León y Gama.

The Boston historian's connections abroad did their job well; In the early spring of 1839 there arrived the first shipment of materials copied from the Spanish archives. After sifting through 2500 pages of transcriptions an elated Prescott declared, "Of course I have all the solid basis for prosecuting my labors."[8]

By the end of the year William Prescott was in possession of a massive collection of research material—much of which had never before been available to historians—concerning the Spanish conquest and settlement of the New World, particularly those pertaining to Mexico and Peru, the crown jewels of the Spanish empire. William stated that he received "about eight thousand folio pages. They consist of instructions of the Court, military and private journals, correspondence of the great actors in the scenes, legal instruments, contemporary chronicles, and the like, drawn from all the principal places in the extensive colonial empire of Spain, as well as from the public archives in the Peninsula."[9]

Roughly 5000 of those pages that were now in the possession of the Boston historian were obtained from the Spanish Academy, most of which were copies from the collection assembled by Juan Bautista Muñoz and Vargas y Ponce. The satisfied historian wrote, "The doubt as to the acquisition of the materials essential to the success of my undertaking is dispelled; and their materials, safe from all the perils of land and water, are now on my own shelves."[10]

Certain aspects of his chosen subject matter, however, weighed heavily on Prescott's mind: "The daring achievements of these bold adventurers is a striking subject to the imagination. But I confess I do not relish the annals or the conquest of barbarians, so much as those of civilized people."[11]

William Prescott was a great admirer of Alexander von Humboldt, the German scientist who is rightfully regarded as the greatest explorer and naturalist of his era. Humboldt traveled throughout Latin America collecting data on geography, people, fauna and flora, and ancient ruins he stumbled across. Alexander and his traveling companion, the botanist Aimé Bonpland, visited the great pyramid at Cholula and collected information pertaining to the ruins of, Teotihuacan, Mitla and Xoxichalco. His research aroused interest in the ancient civilizations of Mexico and Central and South America, especially after the release of his *Views of the Cordilleras and Monuments of the Indigenous People in America*, which was published in 1810. This scholarly work contained detailed depictions of Inca buildings, Aztec sculptures, engravings of the Maya Dresden Codex and other known Aztec, Zapotec, and Mixtec manuscripts. Humboldt's research induced King Charles IV of Spain to commission an expedition to explore and make a record of Mexico's pre–Columbian ruins.

In June of 1838, Prescott read with much interest Alexander von Humboldt's *Researches concerning the Institutions of the Ancient Inhabitants of America* and his *Statistical Analysis of the Kingdom of New Spain*. After reading these two major works Prescott wrote: "Humboldt is a true philosopher, divested of local or national prejudices, fortified with uncommon learning, which supplies him with abundant illustrations and analogies. Like most truly learned men, he is cautious and modest in his deductions and, though he assembles very many remarkable coincidences between the Old World and the New in their institutions, notions, habits, &c., yet he does not infer that the New World was peopled from the Old,—much less from what particular nation, as more rash speculators have done."[12]

William Prescott wrote of his determination to create works of lasting merit: "No motives but those of an honest fame and of usefulness will ever be of much weight with me in stimulating my labors. I never shall be satisfied to do my work slovenly or superficially. It would be impossible for me to do the job-work of a literary hack. Fortunately, I am not driven to write for *bread*, and I never will write for money."[13]

Conflict of Interest

No sooner had Prescott committed himself to this new topic, for which he had already assembled a vast amount of research material, did he suddenly become aware of an unforeseen obstacle that threatened to derail his plans. Mr. Joseph. G. Cogswell, the head of the Astor Library in New York, informed him that Washington Irving was currently working on his own book about the Spanish conquest of Mexico. Though celebrated as the author of such classic short stories as *The Legend of Sleepy Hollow, Rip van Winkle,* and *The Spectre Bridegroom,* Irving was also a respected historian who had already published a series of well-received historical accounts, which were titled *History of the Life and Voyages of Columbus, Chronicle of the Conquest of Granada, Voyages and Discoveries of the Companions of Columbus,* and *Tales of the Ahlambra.* The conquest of Mexico seemed a logical follow-up to the Spanish themes Irving had successfully pursued in the past. Prescott, however, did not want to abandon this project that was of great interest to him, and which he had already shelled out a hefty sum of money to obtain books and other materials pertaining to this subject.

On December 31,1838, William Prescott was considerate enough to pen a letter to Washington Irving in which he informed the celebrated New York author of his plan to follow up his account of the reign of Ferdinand and Isabella with a book on Hernán Cortés and his campaign to conquer and settle Mexico, and humbly sought his blessing to proceed with this topic. Prescott noted how much time and money he had already invested in this subject, and subtly suggested that he would consider it a great favor if he would yield the topic to him, but added that he would gracefully step aside if Irving wished to proceed with his own account of this epic event.

In preparing for his account of the Spanish conquest of Mexico, Washington Irving had read the writings of Antonio de Herrera y Tordesillas, Antonio de Solís, and Bernal Diaz del Castillo, which he said were to serve "as guide-books" for his work. Just like Prescott, Irving found the history of Spain a topic of boundless fascination. But early into his research he was plagued by doubt: "Ever since I have been meddling with the theme," he said, "its grandeur and magnificence have been growing upon me, and I had felt more and more doubtful whether I should be able to treat it *conscientiously,*—that is to say, with the extensive research and thorough investigation which it merited."[14]

Irving responded to Prescott's inquiry in a letter dated January 18, 1839. He confirmed that he had planned to write an account of the Spanish conquest of Mexico as a follow-up to his biography of Christopher Columbus, but had completed little more than an outline of what he quickly realized would be a monumental undertaking, and therefore was willing to yield the subject to Prescott, whom he believed, after having read his *History of the Reign of Ferdinand and Isabella, the Catholic,* was more than qualified to do justice to such an important topic. Irving had invested three months researching this subject and outlining the first volume when he abandoned the project. A relieved William Prescott was now free to proceed with his work.

Later, in a letter to his nephew Pierre Irving, Washington Irving expressed his regret over having yielded this project: "I doubt whether Mr. Prescott was aware of the extent of the sacrifice I made. This was a favourite subject which had delighted my imagination ever since I was a boy. I had brought home books from Spain to aid me in it, and looked upon it as the pendant to my Columbus. When I gave it up to him I, in a manner, gave him up my bread; for I depended upon the profits of it to recruit my waning finances. I had no other subject at hand to supply its place. I was dismounted from my *cheval de bataille* and have never been completely mounted since. Had I accomplished that work my whole pecuniary situation would have been altered."[15] Coincidentally, it was Obadiah Rich who had helped Washington Irving procure a number of research books during the celebrated author's time spent in Spain.

In a letter dated November 19, 1843, George Sumner, a lawyer who was a mutual acquaintance of both historians, wrote to his brother Charles about the understanding between William Prescott and Washington Irving: "It is delightful to hear the tones of admiration in which Irving always speaks of Prescott, although the abandonment of the 'Conquest of Mexico' which he had commenced cost him a pang! His steam was just fairly up when he heard that Prescott was at work upon the same subject. For a week after he abandoned it he felt like a fish out of water and took to planting cabbages most desperately."[16]

Washington Irving (1783–1859), American author, essayist, biographer, and historian (courtesy Historical Findings and Library of Congress).

According to Pierre Irving, who later wrote a biography of his famous uncle, Washington Irving destroyed all that he had written on this abandoned topic.

Frequent Interruptions

Voltaire's study of Charles XII, Livy's portrayal of Hannibal, and Irving's depiction of Christopher Columbus all served as models for William Prescott's treatment of Hernán Cortés as the protagonist of his forthcoming *History of the Conquest of Mexico*. Prescott also made a careful study of William Robertson's *History of America*, which provided him with a perspective which contrasted somewhat with the prevailing view of the Spanish chroniclers. The Boston historian would rely heavily on the eyewitness account of Bernal Diaz del Castillo to sketch an outline for his retelling of the Spanish conquest of the Aztec empire. A number of reliable historical accounts were used to embellish and fill in the gaps.

In summarizing his overall plan for *History of the Conquest of Mexico*, Prescott wrote: "Omit no trait which can display the character of Cortés, the *hero* of *the piece*, round whom the interest is to concentrate. The narrative is a beautiful epic. It has all the interests which daring, chivalrous enterprise, stupendous achievements, worthy of an age of knight-errantry, a magical country, the splendors of a rich barbaric court, and extraordinary personal qualities in the hero—can give."[17] He imagined the storyline as being the destiny of Cortés colliding with the fate of Montezuma; the underlying theme being the virtues of Christianity triumphing over the vices of Paganism. Prescott's devout Christian faith helped him to better understand and appreciate the important role that religion played in the daring Spanish expeditions that took place in the New World.

In the preface to his *History of the Conquest of Mexico*, Prescott informed the reader of his approach to writing this epic confrontation that forever altered the course of human events in the New World: "Among the remarkable achievements of the Spaniards in the sixteenth century, there is no one more striking to the imagination than the conquest of Mexico. The subversion of a great empire by a handful of adventurers, taken with all its strange and picturesque accompaniments, has the air of romance rather than of sober history; and it is not easy to treat such a theme according to the severe rules prescribed by historical criticism. But, notwithstanding the seductions of the subject, I have conscientiously endeavored to distinguish fact from fiction, and to establish the narrative on as broad a basis as possible of contemporary evidence; and I have taken occasion to corroborate the text by ample citations from authorities, usually in the original, since few of them can be very accessible to the reader. In these extracts I have scrupulously conformed to the ancient orthography, however obsolete and even barbarous, rather than impair in any degree the integrity of the original document."[18]

Prescott had thoroughly studied Washington Irving's *History of the Life and Voyages of Christopher Columbus* and noticed some pitfalls that he wished to steer clear of in his literary composition. He felt that the various accounts of Columbus sailing from one island to another without finding what he was looking for was monotonous to the reader. More importantly, Prescott believed that the climax of Irving's tale came far too early in the story. The Boston historian endeavored to avoid making the same mistakes in his account of the conquest of Mexico.

In his memorandum dated March 21, 1841, Prescott wrote: "The conquest of Mexico, though very inferior in the leading idea which forms its basis to the story of Columbus is, on the whole, a far better subject; since the event is sufficiently grand, and, as the catastrophe is deferred, the interest is kept up through the whole. Indeed the perilous adventures and crosses with which the enterprise was attended, the desperate chances and reverses and unexpected vicissitudes, all serve to keep the interest alive. On my plan, I go with Cortés to his death. But I must take care not to make this tail-piece too long."[19]

William decided that he would divide his tale of the conquest of Mexico into three distinct categories: A thorough history of the Aztec's ascent to power; the Spanish quest for fortune and glory in the New World, which culminates with the fall of Tenochtitlán; and a chronicle of Cortés's life after the conquest. Prescott felt that the latter topic was anticlimactic but still necessary because of all the new information recently uncovered about the legendary conquistador. He proposed to keep the concluding section short but entertainingly relevant.

Prescott was delighted by the fact that there was now a marked improvement in the use of his eyes, as evidenced by the notation he made in his memorandum in May of 1839: "An industrious week for me. My eyes have done me fair service; and when I do not try them by exposure to light, the hot air of crowded rooms, and the other *et caeteras* of town life, I think I can very generally reckon on them for some hours a day."[20]

However, while working on the *Conquest of Mexico*, Prescott fell victim to his advancing age and suddenly found it necessary to wear spectacles to remedy the inevitable change in his vision. At first he feared that he was beginning to lose sight in his right eye, especially after noticing that his vision had begun to blur while reading. He was greatly relieved to learn that the problem could be remedied with corrective lenses. While the spectacles helped to restore his vision, the lenses tended to exhaust his eyes. The strain on his good eye would often give rise to an acute pain that made reading nearly impossible. Finding that he could tolerate using the spectacles less and less, Prescott became more and more dependent on the eyes of others, particularly those of his secretary, for reading.

Even when his right eye seemed fine, William still found it necessary to limit his reading to around 35 minutes per day, which he portioned out into sessions of five minutes each, with a minimum of a half hour rest between each reading. He always made sure to stop the very moment he felt even the slightest discomfort. William's worst fear was that one day he would no longer be able to recognize familiar faces or places, a loss of vision that would cause him to become a burden to those he held dear. His doctors advised him that his vision would assuredly last much longer if he simply abandoned his literary pursuits. But Prescott could not give up the work that brought him so much satisfaction and provided him with a sense of purpose. Instead, the historian decided to make sure to adhere to the strict precautions he had employed over the years to avoid any undue strain on his good eye.

Prescott would spend an entire year learning everything he could about Mexico—the people, the landscape, and its history. To begin his research on the indigenous tribes, he made extensive notes of Juan de Torquemada's *Monarquía Indiana*, which was written in 1613, and studied an English translation of José de Acosta's *Historia Natural y Moral de las Indias*. In addition to the works of Alexander Humboldt and Antonio de Herrera, Prescott also relied on Fray Bernardino de Sahagún's *General History of the Things of New Spain*, and Lord Kingsborough's *Antiquities of Mexico*, to help him gain a better understanding of the Mexican civilizations. He also listened intently to readings of historical accounts by Fernando de Alva Ixtlilxochitl, Diego Camargo, Fray Toribio de Motolinía, and Alonso de Zuazo to learn more about the history of the Aztecs. Prescott pored over the accounts of foreigners who visited Mexico, beginning with Bernal Diaz del Castillo, and on up through contemporaries such as William Bullock, Henry George Ward, and a young New York adventurer by the name of John Lloyd Stephens.

William wrote of the difficulties and drudgery he faced during his extensive research on the subject of the Mexica, the native tribe he chose to refer to by their earlier name of Aztec, which was derived from their legendary homeland of Aztlán: "Finished notes on the hieroglyphical part of the chapter,—a hard, barren topic. And now on the astronomy—out of the frying-pan into the fire."[21] Because of his struggles with math, Prescott had a hard time assessing many of the astronomical and mathematical accomplishments of the Aztecs. He also studied the historical and travel accounts of Herodotus, Marco Polo, Sir John Mandeville and any other historian or adventurer who wrote about the ancient civilizations of the Old World as a means of providing some measure of comparison to the native cultures of the New World.

The historian felt overwhelmed by the vague and mystical accounts of Mexico's history prior to the arrival of the Spaniards. Prescott stated: "It is impossible to get a firm footing in the quicksands of tradition. The further we are removed from the conquest, the more difficult it becomes to decide what belongs to the primitive Aztec, and what to the Christian convert."[22] Clearly, the section on the history of the Aztec civilization was the most difficult for Prescott to write, as evidenced by the fact that he wrote the remaining two-and-one-half volumes in nearly the equivalent amount of time. Prescott's research on the natives of Mexico and Central America caused him to question why the indigenous tribes of North America had failed to develop equally advanced civilizations.

While studying the writings of Hernán Cortés, Bernal Diaz del Castillio, Antonio de Herrera, Gonzalo Fernández de Oviedo, Bartolomé de Las Casas, and other Spanish chroniclers of the conquest, Prescott had to analyze and evaluate inconsistencies in their various accounts in order to reach a logical determination as to which account was more likely to have occurred. Regarding Bartolomé de Las Casas, the Boston historian found it difficult to reconcile the "gross exaggeration and over-coloring" displayed in the bishop's *Historia General de las Indias*: "His defects as a historian is, that he wrote history, like everything else, under the influence of one dominant idea. He is always pleading the cause of the persecuted native."[23]

Prescott continued his practice of setting stringent writing goals for himself; he would predict at the beginning of each new project an exact date when he planned to finish. Though he often failed to meet these self imposed deadlines, they did serve as an effective means of gauging his progress. In order to stay on schedule, William felt it was necessary to curtail a number of his outside activities. In November 1839, he tendered his resignation as a trustee of the New England Asylum for the Blind, which was in the process of being renamed the Perkins School for the Blind. Not one to take his duties lightly, William felt he could not provide the necessary time and attention required of such an important cause. He knew that others expected him to complete a follow-up book sooner rather than later, and to continue fulfilling his duties as a trustee would interfere with the time needed to work on his chronicle of the Spanish conquest of Mexico. Samuel G. Howe, the director of the institution, tried to persuade him to reconsider this decision but the historian stood his ground. He did, however, continue to provide financial support to the institution he had helped to found.

At home, William maintained a rigid routine that was governed by exactness. He would retire to bed precisely at ten o'clock so that he would be well rested for the next day's work schedule. Even when there were still guests in his home, Prescott would politely excuse himself after telling all that they were welcome to stay as long as they would like, and to freely partake of the wine and food that was in his house. He awoke before sunrise for his daily jaunt to Jamaica Plain to reflect on his work: "As I charge valiantly over hill and dale in my morning rides, I fight over in fancy many a stout battle with the Aztecs."[24]

In May, 1841, Prescott learned that an unsavory publisher planned to poach his work by printing an abridged copy of *History of the Reign of Ferdinand and Isabella, the Catholic.* Ironically, William had thought about working with Little, Brown, and Company on an abridgment of his book but decided not to whittle away at what he had labored so hard to create. He was compelled to revisit this idea after becoming concerned that a pirated abridgment would likely harm his sales as well as the integrity of his writing. His father's status as a lawyer and the fact that he had once studied to enter the field of law made William conscious of the need to vigorously protect his books. A published book priced at $2 might sell for between ten and 25 cents by a publishing pirate. The unauthorized printing of books was the bane of both publishers and authors.

The threat of a pirated abridgment of *Ferdinand & Isabella* in America was taken very seriously by both Prescott and his publisher. To condense three octavo-sized volumes into one duodecimo volume posed a very difficult challenge for the author. Prescott planned to structure an abbreviated rendering as if he were writing for younger readers of school age. The historian promptly put his present work on hold so that he could focus all of his time and effort on completing his own abridged version. The abridgment contract dated May 27, 1841, specified that Prescott was to provide Little, Brown and Company with plates for a book no less than 400 pages in length.

Fearing that the piracy threat extended overseas, William sent instructions to London requesting that Colonel Aspinwall and Richard Bentley make arrangements for an English abridgment of his *Ferdinand and Isabella*. He entered into a contract with Bentley on July 3, 1841. Prescott had his publishers in America and England agree that the abridgment was not to be published unless an unauthorized edition emerged.

In his rush to beat the release of an unauthorized publication, William worked at a feverish pace for three and a half weeks to produce a shortened version of his book, an abridged edition that he managed to complete on the 19th of July. In a letter to Pascual de Gayangos, Prescott wrote of his disdain for having to condense his work: "It is indeed a barbarous process—pruning off the toes and fingers, pecking out the brains, and dwarfing to a child's stature what you have endeavored to make a man of."[25]

It appears that Prescott's preemptive strike compelled the rogue publisher to reconsider his plan, for the bootleg version never appeared and William, much to his delight, was spared from having to publish a butchered copy of his book. Unfortunately, his rushed effort to keep unsavory publishers at bay resulted in his placing a severe strain on his delicate vision.

However, there were interruptions to Prescott's demanding work on *History of the Conquest of Mexico* that were of a much more welcome nature. On April 20, 1838, he received the first of many well-deserved honors with his election as a member of Philadelphia's American Philosophical Society, an organization founded in 1744 by a prominent group that included Benjamin Franklin. Later that year, William was named as a member of both the Massachusetts Historical Society and the Rhode Island Historical Society. The following year saw even more literary honors bestowed upon the Boston historian; he was named an honorary member of the New York Historical Society (March 12, 1839), the New Hampshire Historical Society (June 29, 1839), and the Georgia Historical Society (July 9, 1839). William was also awarded another esteemed Massachusetts honor—membership in the American Antiquities Society.

Prescott was extremely proud of his election in 1839 to two prominent European historical societies, which were Spain's Royal Academy of History and Italy's Royal Academy of Sciences of Naples. Regarding the former, Martín Fernández de Navarrete, the historian who was president of the Royal Academy, wrote to Ángel Calderón de la Barca on May 20, 1839, proclaiming William Prescott's "admission to the Academy of History in the class of Corresponding Members, which is that designated for both Spaniards and foreigners living outside of Madrid who by their learning in Numismatics, Ancient Geography, Diplomacy, etc., are able to contribute to the illustration of our national history in its various civil, ecclesiastical, military, literary, colonial and other branches. In our opinion Mr. Prescott was well worthy of this mark of appreciation, both because of the merit of his work already published on History of the Catholic Kings, and also because of his zeal and industry in illustrating the history of our discoveries and conquests in the New World."[26] In a letter dated August 2, 1839, Ángel Calderón de la Barca complied with this directive by informing William Prescott of his election as a Corresponding Member of History.

William's historical and literary honors continued in 1840 with the awarding of a doctorate of laws from Columbia College of New York as well as recognition from Boston's American Academy of Arts and Sciences and the Literary and Historical Society of Quebec. In July of 1841 the College of William and Mary conferred an LL.D. on him, and this was followed in December by a similar honor from South Carolina College. He was also honored that same year by the Herculaneum Academy in Naples.

This string of accolades continued in 1842 with William's selection as an honorary member of the Kentucky Historical Society. The following year saw cause for the entire Prescott clan to celebrate. The family had been actively involved in the founding of a Bunker Hill monument which paid tribute to Colonel William Prescott and the many brave patriots who fought alongside him. Judge Prescott served for a time as president of the Bunker Hill Monument Association that sought to honor the heroic deeds of his father. The cornerstone for the memorial was laid on June 17,1825, but a lack of capital would bring a halt to the monument's construction on several occasions. Catherine Prescott, who served as Chairwoman of the Executive Committee of the Ladies' Fair at Quincy, helped the organization raise $30,000 for completion of the 221-foot-high granite obelisk commemorating the battle between the British and Colonial armies. William also invested much time and energy in seeing to the construction of this monument that honored his grandfather. The memorial was dedicated on June 17, 1843. A statue of Colonel William Prescott, which was sculpted by William Wetmore Story, was dedicated in 1881.

7

A Sudden Interest in Mexico

> *If I shall have succeeded in giving the reader a just idea of the true nature and extent of the civilization to which the Mexicans had attained, it will not be labor lost.*[1]

Kindred Spirits

While working on his rendition of the Spanish conquest of Mexico, Prescott wrote a letter on December 5, 1840, to Fanny Calderón de la Barca in which he sought her input regarding a particular secondary source: "I have a very beautiful work, containing coloured drawings of the ruins in Yucatan, far superior, to judge from them, to those of Palenque, of which I have the Casteneda drawings, also, in Lord Kingsborough's great work. The Yucatan drawings as well as the descriptions are by Waldeck, whose history you probably know. Now I am really afraid to rely on them: he talks so big, and so dogmatically, and so I don't know how, that I have a *soupcon* he is a good deal of a charlatan. And I should not like to be led into blunders by confidence in him if he does not deserve it. Will you be good enough in your next to let me know whether I am right, that is, whether sensible persons in Mexico place confidence in him."[2]

The questionable artist that Prescott referred to was Jean Frédéric Maximilien, Comte de Waldeck, a French adventurer and artist who was born in Paris in April 1766 to German parents who had migrated to the City of Lights. Waldeck would claim that he was a descendant of a noble German family and therefore anointed himself with a title befitting such high-born lineage. He left Paris at age 14 and joined the African expedition led by the acclaimed French explorer and naturalist François LeVaillant. In 1785, after five years of exploration, Waldeck returned to Paris to study art with Jacques Louis David. He continued his art studies with Pierre-

Paul Prud'hon, and was living in Paris during the volatile era of the French Revolution. Waldeck frequently bragged about his friendship with a number of celebrated individuals: Alexander Humboldt, Lord Byron, Beau Brummell, Marie Antoinette, and Napoleon Bonaparte were among the many names he occasionally dropped to impress others. All that Waldeck claimed to have accomplished during his long life must be viewed with a very skeptical eye.

In 1797, Waldeck enlisted in the French military and served as both a soldier and artist in the Italian campaign. The following year he was a member of the Napoleon expedition to Egypt in which he was part of a group of select antiquarians and artists who were to survey the numerous ancient Egyptian temples resting along the Nile. Waldeck and four others deserted their post after Napoleon's fleet was destroyed at Aboukir. They sailed up the Nile past the rapids of Aswan and then made a foolhardy attempt to cross the vast and barren Sahara in order to reach an outpost in Portuguese North Africa. Waldeck claimed that he was the only one to survive this desert crossing.

Jean Waldeck spent the next 15 years traveling from one grand adventure to another. At age 50 he was at sea with the fleet commanded by Lord Cochrane, the British officer who was aiding the Chileans in their determined struggle to free themselves from Spanish rule. His travels brought him to Mexico City, where he took to introducing himself as Count Waldeck. At some point during 1821, Waldeck found himself in Guatemala where he had an opportunity to see some of the mysterious Mayan ruins. The following year he was in London engraving the illustrations for Captain Antonio del Río's book on the ruins of Palenque, an ancient and abandoned Mayan city buried deep in the forests of Mexico. Waldeck wrote that he was so intrigued by the drawings of Ricardo Armendáriz, the artist who had accompanied Captain del Río on this expedition to explore the forgotten Mayan city, "from the moment I saw the pen-and-ink sketches of that work.... I nourished the secret desire to see the ruins of Palenque for myself and draw the originals."[3] After having studied these sketches, Waldeck determined that Palenque had been built by the Chaldeans of ancient Babylon, but somehow arrived at the conclusion that the time-worn city had been inhabited by Hindus.

It was around this time that Waldeck met Lord Kingsborough, the wealthy Irishman obsessed with the notion that both the Aztec and Maya civilizations were founded by descendants of the Lost Tribes of Israel. Lord Kingsborough, who was busy working on his expensive nine-volume series of tomes on the pre- Columbian antiquities of Mexico, decided to help finance Waldeck's expedition to Mexico to study and make detailed drawings of the ancient ruins.

Waldeck arrived in Mexico shortly after the country had won its independence from Spain. The artist met with Mexican president Anastasio Bustamante, who granted him permission to visit the ruins of Palenque. Waldeck would spend two years at Palenque, during which time he made 90 drawings of the ancient ruins as well as the complex Mayan glyphs that adorned many of the stone monuments. Unfortunately, the artist did not draw the structures or sculptures in their true form, but instead sketched them as he envisioned they might have looked in their complete state. He was also guilty of adding classical touches that were never part of the original Mayan design.

After his return to Paris, Waldeck used his notes and drawings for the publication of his *Voyage Pittoresque et Archéologique dans de la Province d' Yucatan* (A Romantic Archaeological Journey in Yucatan). Released in 1838, Waldeck's book contained 100 pages of text to accompany his 21 engraved plates. But this lavish and expensive work failed to arouse much attention. This was primarily because Europeans were much more interested in the ancient ruins of Egypt, thanks to their exposure by the Napoleon expedition in which Waldeck was a participant. However, Waldeck's book was viewed with great interest by William Prescott, especially while the Boston historian was pursuing his research on the tribes of ancient Mexico. It also captured the attention of John Lloyd Stephens, a New York lawyer and best-selling travel writer, and Frederick Catherwood, a London architect and renowned topographical artist, both of whom were eager to see these magnificent ruins for themselves.

In a letter penned on January 19, 1841, Madame Calderón responded to William Prescott's inquiry of Jean Waldeck: "I must employ in begging you *upon no account* to pin your faith to Waldeck—whose work even by the most Mexicanised of Mexicans is considered a tissue of exaggerations—his sketches very fine, but also painted like a poet. It is a great pity that travelers will so exaggerate—whether in over—or underrating every country that is not well known."[4]

On September 4, 1842, William wrote in his journal: "Company—company—company! It will make me a misanthrope. And yet there is something very interesting and instructive in the conversation of travelers from distant regions. Last week we had Calderón—just from Mexico—Stephens from Central America and Yucatan, General Harlan from Afghanistan, where he commanded the native troops for many years. But what has it all to do with the 'Conquest of Mexico'?"[5] One of these travelers, however, was fated to become a person of great interest to William H. Prescott.

John Lloyd Stephens, the son of a wealthy New York businessman, was an aspiring lawyer who had taken ill shortly after passing the bar. Just like Prescott, Stephens followed the advice of his family and doctor and boarded a ship bound for Europe, where he hoped the salubrious climate of the region would serve him well. Fascinated by the many splendid sights of the Old World, the ailing lawyer, found the strength to set out on a two-year whirlwind tour of France, Italy, Greece, Turkey, Russia, Poland, Germany, Egypt, Arabia, and the Holy Land. The letters he sent home about his adventures found their way into an American periodical. The popularity of these articles about exotic lands he had visited would lead to a book deal for Stephens. His first book, *Incidents of Travel in Egypt, Arabia Petraea, and the Holy Land*, quickly sold 25,000 copies, which was an unprecedented number of sales for an American author. At the urging of his readers, critics, and publisher, Stephens followed up his success by writing *Incidents of Travel in Greece, Turkey, Russia, and Poland*, which proved just as popular and critically acclaimed as his first book. Having discovered a rewarding and appealing niche as a travel writer, Stephens no longer had a desire to resume his career as a lawyer.

During a stopover in London, Stephens forged a lasting friendship with Frederick Catherwood, a well-respected architect and topographical artist who had toured many of the same ancient sites. Intrigued by Stephens mention of opportunities that awaited in America, Catherwood decided to relocate himself and his family to New York City. He quickly found work as an architect, but enjoyed even greater success with the establishment of the first permanent panorama in America, a rotunda where thousands of New Yorkers lined up to see the artists's 10,000-foot detailed *View of Jerusalem*. These instructive and scenic programs were continually changed to attract new audiences. Public interest was also aroused by the fact that many of these panoramic views were described in Stephens' immensely popular *Incidents of Travel in Egypt, Arabia Petraea, and the Holy Land*.

Together, Stephens and Catherwood frequented a popular New York bookshop where the owner showed them books that piqued their interest about mysterious stone cities said to be buried deep in the remote jungles of Mexico and Central America. Eager to learn if these remarkable tales were true, Stephens and Catherwood sailed from New York to the backwater settlement of Belize to begin their search for lost and abandoned cities. From there the two adventurers headed toward the forgotten city of Copán where they saw ancient ruins that removed all doubt about the existence of such spectacular sites. After excavating, exploring, and documenting the magnificent ruins of Copán, the two adventurers set out on a difficult trek to Palenque, where they would spend three weeks clearing and recording the splendid structures of this ancient and long abandoned Mayan city. From there, the explorers visited the ruins of Uxmal, but their exploration of this site was cut short when Catherwood was stricken with a severe case of malaria.

After returning to New York, John Lloyd Stephens immediately went to work on his next manuscript while Frederick Catherwood was busy putting the finishing touches on his detailed drawings that were to be included in *Incidents of Travel in Central America, Chiapas and Yucatan*, which was published in 1841. William Prescott was in the midst of writing his epic *History of the Conquest of Mexico* at the same time that Stephens had begun writing about his and Catherwood's grand adventures and discoveries in Mexico and Central America.

Learning of Prescott's interest in the pre–Columbian civilizations of Mexico, Stephens penned a letter on February 2, 1841, to the Boston historian in which he notes the important discoveries that both he and Catherwood had made during their travels:

> I have drawings taken by Mr. Catherwood of the ruins of Copán, Quiriguá, Tecpán, Santa Cruz del Quiché or Utatlán and Gueguetemango in Guatemala, of Ocosingo and Palenque in Chiapas and of Uxmal in Yucatán, all entirely new except those of Palenque and Uxmal and the former much more complete than Del Río's or Capt. Dupaix.
>
> I wish you could see these drawings and still more that I could have a few hours conversation with you. Robertson [the 18th century Scottish historian] is entirely wrong. Some of the sculptured columns at Copán and Quiriguá are equal to the finest of the Egyptians and the buildings at Palenque and Uxmal are very large and really one can hardly help speaking of them extravagantly, but I am afraid they are not as old as I wish them to be.[6]

This was the first of many correspondences between these two men which helped to forge a mutual admiration that quickly matured into a lasting friendship. A healthier and younger William Prescott surely would have been eager to join them on a search for these Mayan ruins.

William Prescott replied in March of 1841: "You have made a tour over a most interesting ground, the very forum of American ruins, none of which have been given to the public even in descriptions I believe, except Palenque, Uxmal, Mitla, and Copán- and there are no drawings of these latter.... It would help us much if all of the Conquistadores had condescended to give some particulars of the state of the buildings in Yucatán at the time of their arrival. But I have found nothing beyond a general allusion to remarkable buildings of stone and lime and curious architecture scattered over the country. Their eyes were occupied with looking after gold dust. *Your opinion as to the comparatively modern date of these remains agrees entirely with the conclusions I had come to from much more inadequate sources of information, of course, than you possess.*"[7]

Prescott also stated: "I was not aware that the buildings were so well executed as to equal in this respect the Egyptian. Robertson underestimated everything in the New World. It was little understood then, and distrust which had a knowing air at least was the safer side for the historian. The French and Spanish travelers, however, write with such swell of glorification and Waldeck's designs in particular are so little like the pictures of *Ruins*, that I had supposed there was some exaggeration in this respect. No one can be a better judge than yourself, however, who are familiar with the best models in the Old World, to compare them with."[8]

Stephens made sure to send a copy of *Incidents of Travel in Central America, Chiapas, and Yucatán* to his new friend William Prescott, who was currently busy working on his account of the Spanish conquest of Mexico. In a letter dated August 2, 1841, Prescott paid tribute to Stephens: "I cannot well express to you the great satisfaction and delight I have received from your volumes. I suppose few persons will enjoy them more, as very few have been led to pay attention to the subject. You have indeed much exceeded the expectations I had formed, which were not small, and besides throwing much additional light on places and remains before unknown, you have brought others into notice and much widened the ground for general survey and comparison. It is no little result of your labors too that you have shown how accessible many of these places are, and have furnished a sort of *carte du pays* for the future traveller. I have no doubt that your volumes will be the means of stimulating researches into this interesting country, which had been looked on as a kind of enchanted ground guarded by dragons and giants."[9]

Prescott was so impressed with Stephens' book that he arranged to have copies sent to several of the individuals who had helped provide material for his own book. One such copy was sent to Fanny Calderón de la Barca, who had supplied him with a great deal of information about the land and people of Mexico. In a letter thanking Prescott for the book, Fanny wrote from Cuba, where she and her husband now resided. "The Travels are very amusing, and dashed off in a most free and easy style. I hear they are criticized as being very incorrect by those who know the country. One thing is evident—that he could not speak Spanish, which must have caused him many difficulties, but he might have gotten someone to *spell* it for him. I observe that there is not a word of Spanish spelt right, even by chance."[10]

Emanuel von Friedrichsthal, a young Austrian baron, learned of the discoveries of ancient ruins in the Americas by Stephens and Catherwood and decided that he wished to see them for himself. Friedrichsthal, who had done some minor exploring in Greece and Serbia, visited Prescott in Boston to get some perspective on the ancient cities of Mexico. "An Austrian gentleman is here just now," Prescott informed Ángel Calderón de la Barca, "and proposes to visit Palenque which he has been studying in my Lord Kingsborough publications. He may possibly visit Mexico in which case I shall take the liberty to give him a note to you. He is an accomplished man in whose society you and your wife will take pleasure."[11] The baron then headed to New York to prepare for his expedition to explore the ancient and abandoned cities made of stone. At New York he bought a daguerreotype, which he used to take the very first photographs of the Mayan ruins at Chichen Itza, and shortly thereafter he set out on his own archaeological tour of Yucatán. Emanuel von Friedrichsthal contracted a disease in Yucatan that led to his untimely death in 1842.

The popularity of *Incidents of Travel in Central America, Chiapas and Yucatán* sparked interest in Stephens and Catherwood undertaking another expedition to locate the ruins of other ancient and forgotten cities in the Americas. Stephens believed that it might be a good idea to bring along a naturalist on this journey and therefore placed an ad in several papers, including the Boston Courier, for a wildlife expert. The Boston ad was answered by Samuel Cabot, Jr., a graduate of Harvard who had earned a medical degree. The young doctor declared that even though his chosen profession was in the field of medicine, his true passion was ornithology, and expressed his sincere desire to study the many exotic birds known to inhabit the tropics. Cabot stressed that he was an amateur naturalist who had corresponded with many leading European naturalists. Cabot was viewed as the best of the applicants but Stephens was concerned that his youth—he was 26—might be an issue. But after learning that the Cabots were good friends of William Prescott, he decided that age would not be a hindering factor. Stephens also felt it would be a benefit to have a man with medical knowledge on this trip to a region fraught with danger.

On October 9, 1841, Stephens, Catherwood, and Cabot boarded a boat bound for the port of Sisal in Yucatán. To avoid getting caught up in a race with other explorers who might be eager to follow in their footsteps, Stephens made sure that they departed without any fanfare. Stephens had brought a copy of Lopez de Cogolludo's *Historia de Yucatán*, the large folio that William Prescott had loaned him for this adventure. The three explorers spent ten grueling months probing the harsh Yucatán landscape, during which time they visited more than 40 ancient Mayan sites, the majority of which were entirely unknown to the outside world. Uxmal, Kabah, Edzna, Labná, Zahil, Izamal, Chichén Itzá, and Tulum are among the list of abandoned and forgotten stone cities that they explored and documented on their second expedition. Catherwood and Stephens then returned to New York City to begin work on their next book while Samuel Cabot, who was stricken with malaria, went home to Boston to recuperate.

Shortly after returning from his second expedition in search of lost cities, John Lloyd Stephens traveled to Boston to talk with William Prescott about his discoveries and to gain from the historian some additional perspective regarding the ancient civilizations of Mexico. While at Boston, Stephens paid a visit to the Cabot family to check on the condition of young Dr. Samuel Cabot, who was still suffering from his exposure to malaria. Cabot eventually recovered and went on to become a renowned surgeon.

Stephens returned to New York to finish *Incidents of Travel in Yucatán*, which lived up to the expectations of the many fans and critics who were eager to read more about these exotic regions that were home to mysterious ancient ruins. Stephens' articulate descriptions of the landscape, stone monuments, artifacts, and the people of the region were once again enhanced by Catherwood's exceptionally detailed and magnificent drawings of the ruins and the surrounding scenery. Stephens and Catherwood correctly concluded that these splendid cities of stone were built by the ancestors of the people who still dwelled in these lands. Meanwhile, William Prescott had reached the same conclusion, which was contrary to the prevailing views that these abandoned cities of stone had been built by ancient civilizations that came from across the water—a list that included the Egyptians, Greeks, Romans, Atlanteans, Carthaginians, and the Lost Tribe of Israel. It would take a future generation of explorers, archaeologists, and scholars to prove what Stephens, Catherwood, and Prescott had reasoned on their own.

In March of 1843 John Lloyd Stephens made sure to send one of the first copies of his new book to William Prescott: "I sent you yesterday, by Harnden's Express a copy of my Yucatán. Before passing judgment upon it I beg to remind that you committed yourself before I set out on my expedition by saying that if I should make half as good a book as the last, my voyage would not be in vain."[12]

A grateful Prescott promptly replied, "I am truly obliged to you for your welcome present. It opens rich and promising, and I am sure from the sample will be worthy of the elder brother *Incidents of Travel in Central America,* in 1841. I shall read the work through, however, carefully, as it concerns some of the matters to which I shall have occasion to advert, and I shall take occasion to give you my opinion of it in a manner I hope not displeasing to you in my notes in the Conquest."[13]

One month later William Prescott again wrote to John Lloyd Stephens:

> I have accomplished one volume of your work and a part of second. I read slowly, or rather it is read to me, which is a slow process, and I have but little leisure now. It is all interesting to me as the old ruins have ever more attractions than the lively narrative of adventure. Most readers find the adventures told with even more spirit than in your preceding work. You have made a good advertising sheet for our friend the doctor [Samuel Cabot]. I hope he may live to profit by it. He mends very gradually. I know not what to think of the ruins, they leave my mind in a kind of mist, which I shall not attempt to dispel, till I reread the book leisurely when—thanks, no rather no thanks to you—I shall have to tinker on my chapter on American Antiquities, the last of the work.
>
> I believe that there is but one opinion of the work here, and all agree. It is better than its brother.[14]

The Story Unfolds

October 14, 1839, marked the date when William Prescott began the actual process of writing *History of the Conquest of Mexico*. However, after just a few pages into his work, the historian felt utterly displeased with what he had written and decided to begin anew. The author would expend much time and thought into weaving the history, culture, and religious beliefs of the indigenous tribes of Mexico, particularly the Aztecs, into a cohesive narrative that would provide an insightful and interesting analysis of the rise of these remarkable civilizations in and around the Valley of Mexico prior to their fall at the hands of Hernán Cortés and his devoted band of conquistadors.

George Frederick Ware was the new secretary when Prescott began writing his introduction to the history of the indigenous tribes that inhabited the Valley of Mexico. Unfortunately, the historian found this topic far more difficult to write than he had ever imagined. This was because the historical accounts of the pre–Columbian civilizations, most of which had been collected and recorded by Spanish priests after the conquest, blurred the line between myth and history. Prescott had speculated that his introduction would run around 100 pages and take him six months to write, but the wealth of material he received caused the first part of his book to stretch to 250 pages and would take 18 months to complete to his satisfaction. In a letter to Edward Everett dated September 14, 1841, Prescott mentions the effect this had on the length of his work, "I am now in full march over the grand plateau of Mexico, but have still some hard campaigns to fight before I win the capital. The story I find will swell in consequence of the length of the preliminary view of the Aztec civilization into three volumes."[15]

Having to rely on information obtained from others occasionally led to unintended errors. For the measurement of the grand Pyramid of the Sun at the ancient city of Teotihuacan, the historian converted Alexander Humboldt's calculations into English feet, with neither figure being correct. Reflecting on the origin of the imposing city of Teotihuacan, which had been abandoned long before the Aztecs had migrated to the Valley of Mexico, the historian wrote, "It is all a mystery,—over which Time has thrown an impenetrable veil, that no mortal hand may raise. A nation has passed away, powerful, populous, and well advanced in refinement, as attested by their monuments,—but it has perished without a name. It has died and made no sign."[16] Prescott was aware of the fact that it was the Aztecs who had named the ancient site Teotihuacan, which meant The Abode of the Gods.

In explaining his approach toward chronicling the Spanish conquest of Mexico, Prescott wrote: "the true way of conceiving the subject is, not as a philosophical theme, but as an *epic in prose*, a romance of chivalry; as romantic and as chivalrous as any which Boiardo or Ariosto ever fabled." He continued by stating, "The Conquest of Mexico was the greatest miracle in an age of miracles.... It is, without doubt, the most poetic subject ever offered to the pen of the historian."[17]

On May 7, 1842, William wrote the following in his literary journal: "Another long hiatus. Since last entry paid two visits to New York—a marvellous event in my history! First, a visit, about three weeks since, I paid to meet Washington Irving before his departure to Spain. Spent half a day with him at Wainwright's—indeed, till twelve at night. Found him delightful and—what, they say is rare—wide awake. He promises to aid me in all his applications."[18]

The first of these two trips to New York City, which occurred in early April 1842, served a dual purpose: The initial visit was related to his historical studies and the second, as mentioned above, was to see Washington Irving before he departed to assume his duties as the newly-appointed U.S. minister to Spain. Prescott's meeting with Irving took place at the home of the Rev. Jonathan Wainwright, a Harvard graduate, class of 1812—

Reception of Hernán Cortés by the Emperor Montezuma (Library of Congress).

and a former member of the historian's literary club. William knew Wainwright at Harvard and through Susan's Trinity Church where, between 1834 and 1837, he listened to him preach from the pulpit. As for Prescott and Irving, the two acclaimed authors met for six hours, during which time their conversation touched on a variety of topics. Prescott talked at length about his progress on *Conquest of Mexico* while Irving discussed his upcoming plans for a biography of George Washington.

Prescott returned to Boston only to be summoned back to Manhattan by the news that the Reverend Wainwright had been able to arrange a meeting for him with the young Dr. Samuel Mackenzie Elliott, a Scottish oculist who had migrated to New York. Elliott truly believed that he could help relieve the Boston historian's longstanding vision problems. William Prescott arrived in New York aboard the steamboat christened the Massachusetts. On April 26, 1842, William underwent a thorough eye examination by Dr. Elliott, who diagnosed that his injured left eye was hindered by "a paralysis of the nerve which covers much of the retina with a deposit of lymph."[19] The oculist believed that the paralysis could be improved somewhat with a specialized treatment plan tailored expressly for the historian. In order to see any significant results, Prescott would have to follow his explicit instructions for a period of six weeks. The oculist was convinced that strict adherence to this treatment plan could restore a small degree of vision to the damaged eye, but he admitted it would still not be sufficient enough for reading. Since this effort would not help him with his studies, Prescott failed to see that there was any real benefit to undergoing such a treatment.

As for William's right eye, Dr. Elliott concluded that it was afflicted with iritis and retinitis. He warned that over time this condition would likely lead to permanent blindness, which was the same dire warning the historian had heard from Dr. Jackson in Boston and Sir William Adams in London. All of the doctors had agreed that the condition of his right eye was directly dependent upon his general health. Dr. Elliott suggested a one year program that combined medicines and unguents that would help strengthen his vision, but warned that he should not exceed five or six hours of daily reading. Again, Prescott felt that the time and effort involved seemed to offer too little reward. Instead, William decided he would continue to rely on the sight of others, particularly those of his secretary. To further reduce strain to his delicate vision William came to rely even more on his extraordinary memory: "My way has been lately to go over a large mass in my mind—over and over—till ready to throw it on paper—*then* an effort rather of memory than creation."[20] Prescott offered to pay Doctor Elliott for the exams but the oculist refused to take his money.

During his second visit to New York City, the historian was introduced to a number of prominent citizens at a party hosted by the Reverend Wainwright, a gathering which included Henry Brevoort, George Griffen, John C. Hamilton, Henry Carey, and Philip Hone. The latter gentleman, who was the former mayor of New York City and a fervid diarist, described Prescott as "a handsome man ... of intellectual appearance, good manners, agreeable conversation, and much vivacity."[21]

Before returning to Boston, William paid a visit to the 80-year-old Albert Gallatin, a gentleman he had the privilege of first meeting in 1816 when the elder statesman was serving as the American minister to France. Having developed an interest in the language and culture of the Native American tribes, Gallatin published in 1826 *A Table of Indian Languages of the United States*. In 1836 the sprightly diplomat wrote *Synopsis of the Indian Tribes of North America* and six years later he was a founding member of the American Ethnological Society of New York. Gallatin and Prescott touched on a number of topics before the conversation shifted to a shared interest in the Toltecs, Aztecs, and other native tribes of the Americas.

Resuming his writing, Prescott noted on May 17, 1842, that he had just completed the section pertaining to the humiliating defeat of the Spanish officer Pánfilo de Narvaez at the hands of the cunning Hernán Cortés. He recorded in his memorandum on July 11, 1842: "Now for the *Noche triste*—the doleful night. It did not cost me as much to kill Montezuma—as it did Isabella, tho' I rather love the barbarian."[22] A fortnight later he was busy preparing for the Battle of Otumba, the open field engagement which was the Aztec's last best chance to vanquish the quest of Cortés and his battle weary troops.

An unexpected and unfortunate family matter, which occurred in early 1842, suddenly required the historian's full attention; William and Susan's oldest son, William Gardiner Prescott, was suspended from Harvard for poor grades and forced to relocate to the small town of Boylson, near Worcester, to receive private tutoring from a Mr. Sanford. The father was extremely disappointed with his son's failure and promptly cut off his allowance. Prescott then sent a letter in which he chastised his eldest son for his laziness and lectured that he should take this time to reflect on the heartache he had caused his parents. Shortly thereafter, William was glad to hear from Mr. Sanford that his son was making a splendid effort to improve his study habits. Having seen the error of his ways, Will finally began to buckle down and he was soon permitted to return to Harvard.

On December 7, 1842, John Lloyd Stephens, Frederick Catherwood, and a number of other prominent individuals, founded the American Ethnological Society, the first of its kind in America. "The object of this Society shall comprise inquiries into the origin, progress and characteristics of the various races of Man."[23] The highly respected statesman Albert Gallatin was named as president, and John R. Bartlett, the bookseller who piqued Stephens' interest in the ruins of the Americas, served as secretary of the society. In addition to Stephens, Catherwood, Gallatin, and Bartlett, the original members of the American Ethnological Society included Henry R. Schoolcraft, Charles Welford, Dr. Samuel Morton, Dr. Edward Robinson, Caleb Atwater, Daniel Drake, John Pickering, George Ticknor, John Torry, Henry Wheaton, and William H. Prescott.

The recent expeditions of John Lloyd Stephens and Frederick Catherwood had spawned immense interest in the ancient ruins of Mexico and Central America. The two adventurers sought to capitalize on this fascination by publishing a four-volume work tentatively titled *American Antiquities*. Catherwood was to be responsible for between 100 and 120 large and detailed engravings of these ancient and abandoned sites. The writing would once again be the responsibility of Stephens, which were to be bolstered by contributions from a number of other esteemed experts. The list of prospective contributors included the honorable Albert Gallatin; the renowned naturalist and author Alexander von Humboldt; the highly regarded Egyptologist Sir John Wilkinson, and the widely acclaimed historian William H. Prescott.

A meeting of the executive committee of the New York Historical Society was called by Albert Gallatin on May 2, 1843, for the purpose of considering endorsement and sponsorship of Stephens and Catherwood's *American Antiquities* project. Gallatin was 80 years old at the time but still had all his faculties, including his distinctive Swiss accent. The members of the committee agreed to the resolution "that the recent discoveries of ruined cities and the remains of a people and history entirely unknown had given a new aspect to the American continent."[24] Gallatin was confident that this lavish work would be the antiquities' equivalent of John James Audubon's monumental *Birds of America*.

This proposed publication of *American Antiquities*, which was considerably larger in scope and size than Stephens' previous publications, required a minimum of 900 guaranteed subscribers to cover the tremendous costs associated with such an ambitious project. Prescott wrote, "The *American Antiquities* ... is a noble enterprise, and I hope it may find patronage."[25] All of the parties involved were keenly aware of the devastating financial experience of Lord Kingsborough and wished to avoid any possibility of bankrupting themselves. The project had the full support of the New York Historical Society and Harper Brothers, the latter being the firm that had published all four of John Lloyd Stephens' popular travel books.

Unfortunately for Stephens and Catherwood, Harper Brothers soon determined that the project was not financially viable and elected to pull out of the deal. The steep projected price of $100 and the failure to attract even one-third of the necessary subscribers were the factors that caused Harper Brothers to quit the project. The New York booksellers John R. Bartlett and Charles Welford offered to publish the work and tried to stir up interest by displaying some of Catherwood's eye-catching drawings of Mayan ruins in their Astor House store on Broadway. But the efforts of these supportive booksellers was still not enough to attract the needed number of subscribers. When the project fell through, a discouraged John Lloyd Stephens and Frederick Catherwood went their separate ways.

Frederick Catherwood still had designs on publishing a folio of the ruins he had seen in the Americas and even secured a pledge from Stephens, if and when he found a publisher, to produce the text that would accompany his detailed engravings. William Prescott, who was a great admirer of Catherwood's artistic talents, offered to help him in his efforts to produce a scaled down version of the antiquities project. In a letter dated June 15, 1843, to Edward Everett, a close friend of the historian and the current American minister to the Court of St. James, Prescott wrote: "A literary project of some magnitude is set on foot here by Messrs. Stephens and Catherwood. It is the publication of the magnificent drawings made by Mr. Catherwood of the ruins of Central America. The intention is to have them engraved on a scale corresponding to that of the original designs. Mr. Catherwood will embark for Europe in July to confer with the English publishers who have intimated a willingness to be interested in the undertaking. I have taken the liberty to give him a note to you, at his desire.... Mr. Catherwood, who is a truly modest and well-instructed man, desires only to have your approbation of this important undertaking and the interest you take in every liberal enterprise of your countrymen will, I have no doubt, interest you in the success of this."[26] A grateful Catherwood sought to repay Prescott's support by attempting to find a suitable British engraver to illustrate a reprint of *History of the Reign of Ferdinand and Isabella, the Catholic.*

After having been turned down by every publisher he met with in England, a disheartened Catherwood wrote to Prescott: "As regards the large work of Stephens and myself, nothing has finally been agreed on. The booksellers say trade is bad etc., the old story and I fear a very true one.... I delivered your letter to Mr. Everett who received me very cordially but I have not yet attained my object, an audience of the Queen and Prince Albert. It would seem nowadays that nothing is successful here with the rich and aristocratic without the patronage and sanction of royalty which ill accords my *loco foco* notions."[27]

In spite of all the setbacks he encountered, an optimistic Frederick Catherwood penned another letter to William Prescott, in which he elaborated on his alternative plan for publishing his book: "My own work (for Stephens has declined having anything to do with it) is getting on, several of the plates are finished in the best style of lithography and others are in hand. I have no publisher and do not intend to have one on this side at least.... *I shall be my own publisher.*"[28] Catherwood's self-published *Views of Ancient Monuments in Central America* was released in London on April 25, 1844.

A Worthy Tale

On August 2, 1843, five years after having begun his research, William completed work on his *History of the Conquest of Mexico*. The historian noted that he had "tried to write with imperfect *pre-thinking*, i.e. thinking, as Irving said to me with a pen. It won't do for my bad eyes. It requires too much correcting. The correcting in the mind and writing from memory suit my peculiarities bodily, and, I suspect, mental, better than the other process."[29] Revisions for each chapter were worked out as many as six times in his mind before he was ready to commit his words to paper. Prescott managed to find his style while composing this book and from then on he rarely registered any further concerns regarding his manner of writing.

William Prescott's five-year contract with Little, Brown and Company was coming to a close just as he was nearing completion of his second book. While weighing his options, the author seriously considered issuing a serial publication of *History of the Conquest of Mexico*. A single serial usually sold for 25 cents and was generally published weekly or bi-monthly. Such publications were geared toward readers who could not afford the $2 or more cost for a hardbound book. Ironically, an entire serial would very often exceed the hardbound price. A proposed serialization of *History of the Reign of Ferdinand and Isabella, the Catholic* called for 36 installments with each issue slated to have at least one illustration. William Prescott had sought Frederick Catherwood's assistance to produce engravings for this proposed project, but the artist was away from London at the time of this inquiry and therefore the author decided not to pursue the matter any further.

William had contemplated searching for a publishing house that could promote and distribute his work to a much wider audience. With this thought in mind, John Lloyd Stephens would steer Prescott in the direction of Harper Brothers. The travel writer had given the historian a copy of his newly-released two-volume *Incidents of Travel in Yucatán* published by Harpers, which clearly demonstrated the excellent quality of their work. Stephens informed his new friend of the many advantages, especially the monetary benefits, of having the support of a large and distinguished publishing firm such as Harper and Brothers standing behind him.

Stephens stated in a letter that he sent to Prescott in March of 1843, "I have spoken to the Messrs. Harpers about the publication of your next work. They are desirous to undertake it and of course offer their usual best terms i.e. half of the net profits, or they will allow you to have it stereotyped in Boston, and to keep the plates under your own control, they pay the costs, and will allow the same rate per copy that would be allowed by your Boston publisher. They consider that with their capital and business connections they have the means of making larger sales than any other publishing house in the country.... It is my belief that they would sell of such a work as yours at least 2500 copies more than any other house, and I feel persuaded that after a year's trial of them with the new work you will find it to your interest to put Ferdinand and Isabella into their hands."[30]

In responding to Stephens' overture, Prescott indicated that he was receptive to entertaining other offers: "My publishers here have always used me well, and although I have made no agreement with them, they probably expect to have the publication of my work, and I should feel bound in honour and disposed to give them a preference, but it cannot be expected that I should give them the business at a great pecuniary loss to myself."[31]

Stephens recused himself after he arranged a meeting between Prescott and his publisher. Fletcher Harper traveled to Boston to meet with William to pitch his proposal to publish and promote the historian's new work, a favorable offer that Prescott could not refuse. Unfortunately for Little, Brown & Company, they were not in a position to match the generous offer made by the New York publisher. On June 13, 1843, a few months prior to finishing his manuscript, Prescott was in New York City finalizing a book deal with the four Harper brothers; James, John, Joseph, and Fletcher. Prescott might have stayed with Little, Brown and Company if they had shown some interest in his next work, but the publishing firm failed to make any queries about his future writing plans. Towards the end of 1844, Prescott transferred the right to sell *History of the Reign of Ferdinand and Isabella, the Catholic* from Little, Brown & Company to Harper and Brothers.

Prescott was always attentive to the business side of his books, making sure to secure a deal that was fair, profitable, and which permitted him to retain control of the stereotype plates. Harper and Brothers was obligated to print 5000 copies of *History of the Conquest of Mexico*, for which they paid the author the handsome sum of $7500. Prescott was expected to deliver his completed work on stereotype by the 15th of October. Since they had performed such admirable work on *History of the Reign of Ferdinand and Isabella, the Catholic*, the Cambridge firm of Metcalf, Keith, and Nichols was again awarded the contract to make the stereotype plates for Prescott's manuscript.

Charles Folsom, the librarian of the Boston Athenaeum and a good friend of the historian, was paid "fifty dollars per vol. for correcting the printed proofs."[32] Folsom also offered recommendations and criticisms, which Prescott took under consideration and made adjustments that he deemed worthy before delivering the stereotype plates. George Ticknor and his wife also took the time to read Prescott's manuscript and to offer helpful advice and necessary corrections before it was sent to the publisher. They both thought this work was a worthy successor to his *Ferdinand & Isabella*. Prescott appreciated their favorable comments but privately worried that their friendship may have impaired their critical judgment.

William believed it was very important that he should take the time to personally read all revisions before sending them to the printer, a lengthy process considering the poor condition of his eyes. He did take the precaution of limiting his reading time in order to avoid placing too much strain on his good eye. William's relentless pursuit to complete his work enabled him to finish well ahead of the agreed upon deadline to submit his manuscript. The historian managed to have all his work stereotyped by the tenth of September. However, the rush to finish the text, notes, and appendix imposed a heavy burden on his health, particularly upon his good eye. Prescott vowed to never again place so much pressure on himself to meet a deadline; negotiations for all future book deals would have to wait until he had completed his work in its entirety.

Just as he had done with the printing of his first book, William insisted on certain criteria he felt was necessary to ensure a publication of the highest quality. Prescott's ownership of the stereotype plates guaranteed him a measure of control over the size and pattern of the print as well as an assurance that there was no crowding of the lines of his text. He would request Harpers to send him a sample of the paper and print they proposed to use for *History of the Conquest of Mexico*. Prescott followed up by sending the publisher one of the Little, Brown and Company's copies of *History of the Reign of Ferdinand & Isabella, the Catholic* to stress the standards for paper, ink, and print style he considered acceptable. The Boston historian spared no expense in procuring the finest engravings to accompany his text and even suggested to Harpers where each illustration and map should be affixed. William aspired for uniformity of standards for his American and English editions and frequently made corrections to improve subsequent editions.

The London publication of Prescott's *Ferdinand and Isabella*, was in its third edition and still selling briskly by the time the historian had finished his manuscript of *History of the Conquest of Mexico*. Consequently, Richard Bentley was extremely eager to seal a deal to publish Prescott's next book. The British publisher sent him a copy of his newest release, J. S. St. John's *The Manners and Customs of the Ancient Greeks*, to remind the Boston author that he was thinking of him and to inquire about the status of his current writing project. However, William was not quite ready to commit to Bentley, but he did keep the overseas publisher interested with the following reply: "The story is so full of marvels, perilous adventures, curious manners, scenery etc. that it is more like a romance than a history," he declared, "and yet every page is substantiated by abundance of original testimony. If I have not done it in a very bungling style it ought to be taking with children as well as grown people."[33] Prescott would rely on Colonel Aspinwall to negotiate a better deal for the overseas publication of his new book.

Prescott had begun to suspect that Richard Bentley was undercutting his profits for *History of the Reign of Ferdinand & Isabella, the Catholic* by deducting excessive charges for advertising and other services against the net profits. During his visit to America in 1842, Charles Dickens informed Prescott that Richard Bentley could not have spent a fifth of what he claimed for advertising the historian's first book. Dickens had served as an editor at *Bentley's Miscellany* but left after having grown weary of his numerous quarrels with his employer. It was no secret that Dickens and Bentley had an ongoing feud. It was also well known that

Bentley frequently advertised his published books in periodicals that were produced by his agency. William had calculated that his earnings for *Ferdinand and Isabella* should have been $4000 but he had received little more than $1500 from the British publisher.

Unlike his previous efforts to secure a deal with an English publisher, John Murray and his competitor, Longman and Company, would this time make offers to Colonel Aspinwall for the right to publish Prescott's *History of the Conquest of Mexico*. Some 20 letters were exchanged between Aspinwall and Bentley in hopes of negotiating a better deal for Prescott's *History of the Conquest of Mexico*. Despite some initial reservations, the historian decided to retain Richard Bentley after the publisher finally offered a price and terms that were deemed agreeable to both parties. As the London publisher of *Ferdinand and Isabella*, Richard Bentley had significant leverage in these negotiations; Prescott and Aspinwall both feared that he would pull back on promoting his first book if he was not permitted to publish the second book. Bentley released the English edition of *History of Conquest of Mexico* on October 28, 1843.

The title page for both the American and London editions was thus:

> History
> of the Conquest of Mexico,
> With A Preliminary View of
> the Ancient Mexican Civilization,
> and the
> Life of the Conqueror,
> Hernando Cortés

William instructed the London bookseller James Rich to distribute ten author's copies of his English edition of *History of the Conquest of Mexico* to individuals who were in a position to help his book reach a wider audience. Sir Thomas Phillips, Lady Holland, Samuel Rogers, Lord Morpeth, Henry Hallam, P. F. Tytler, Colonel Aspinwall, Charles Dickens, Edward Everett, and Pascual de Gayangos were each recipients of Prescott's new book. The overseas edition of *History of the Conquest of Mexico* sold well enough to prompt the release of a second edition by the following month of May.

Glad to have finished with work on his second book, Prescott made the following notation in his literary memorandum: "On the whole the last two years have been the most industrious of my life. I think—especially the last year, and as I have won the Capitol it entitles me to three months of literary loafing."[34] William retired to his country home at Pepperell to relax amongst the company of family and friends and to enjoy some light reading.

Prescott's much deserved period of rest and relaxation was interrupted on the 28th of October, a day when his father suffered a slight but rather serious paralytic stroke. The facial paralysis severely affected his father's speech and mental faculties, symptoms which were a source of much concern to family and friends. The Judge's recovery was slow but steady. What was most disconcerting to William Prescott was the lingering melancholy mood of his father. The debilitating manifestations of the stroke soon subsided and eventually the patriarch's health was almost fully restored.

Meanwhile, Harper and Brothers fostered interest in William Prescott's new book by issuing 150 review copies. The first volume of the American edition of *History of the Conquest of Mexico* was made available to the public on December 6, 1843. Harper's plan was to release in sequential order the three volumes over a successive three-week period. The author was not pleased with this marketing strategy but understood that he had very little say in this matter. The publisher feared that the hefty price tag for all three volumes would scare off customers; their plan was to hook the reader with the first volume so they would be eager to buy the second and third installments. The second volume was released on the 13th of the month and the third volume was made available on the 22nd of December. The steadily rising sales figures certainly seemed to confirm that this was indeed a wise marketing plan.

On December 24, 1843, Prescott noted in his private journal, "The work goes off briskly as I learn in N. York & Philadelphia, as it does here. My friends seem emulous to swell my sails with all manner of friendly puffs,—and so far at least—the general tone of eulogy has not been broken by a single ill-natured—or caustic criticism."[35]

Spanish translations soon appeared after the American and British release of Prescott's *History of the Conquest of Mexico*; two in Mexico in 1844 and one in Madrid in 1847. A French rendering appeared in 1846 and a German translation was released in 1845. Dr. H. Eberty, a retired physician, voluntarily translated Prescott's first three historical accounts into German. Two years earlier, Eberty had sent Prescott a copy of his German rendering of *History of the Reign of Ferdinand and Isabella, the Catholic*, which came as a welcome surprise to the Boston historian. Dr. H. Eberty worked under the patronage of Friedrich von Raumer, the German historian who had received a copy of Prescott's *Ferdinand and Isabella* from George Ticknor.

Prescott made sure to send a first edition of *History of the Conquest of Mexico* to Baron Alexander Humboldt. A copy was also sent to Washington Irving, who was currently serving as the U.S. minister to Spain. In the preface, Prescott paid tribute to Mr. Irving's generosity in yielding this topic. A gracious Washington Irving made his feelings known by stating: "When I made the sacrifice, it was not with a view to compliments or thanks, but from a warm and sudden impulse. I am not sorry for having made it. Mr. Prescott has justified the opinion I expressed at the time, that he would treat the subject with more close and ample research than I should probably do, and would produce a work more thoroughly worthy of the theme. He has produced a work that does honor to himself and his country, and I wish him the full enjoyment of his laurels."[36]

Prescott was mindful of the fact that interest in his new work benefitted greatly from the public's newfound awareness of ancient civilizations in Mexico and Central America, which had been kindled by the accounts of the two expeditions of John Lloyd Stephens and Frederick Catherwood that had led to the discovery and exploration of nearly 50 long-forgotten Mayan cities. Stephens was among the first to receive a copy of Prescott's new book, who, in turn, showed his admiration for this work by writing a letter of congratulations on December 24, 1843: "I have said behind your back what I shall now dare say to your face and take this to mean to tell you that I have pronounced the '*Conquest*' the best book that was ever issued from the American press. I told the Harpers that it would be so, and I am rejoiced that it has turned out 'all right.'" Really you have done justice to your subject, which is as high praise as I can bestow. Cortez is *used up*. No one will ever mount him again and your names will go down together till octavos are swallowed up by cheap literature. I give you my hearty congratulations."[37]

William Prescott also sent a copy of *History of the Conquest of Mexico* to Frederick Catherwood, who returned the favor by sending the historian some proofs of his nearly completed *Views of Ancient Monuments of Central America, Chiapas, and Yucatan*. Catherwood would spend more than 300 pounds of his own money, a considerable sum at the time, to complete this ambitious project. This limited production of 300 copies was published in London on April 25, 1844. A small print run, which sold at a markedly higher price, were offered with plates that were colored by Catherwood's own hand.

At the encouragement of William Prescott, Frances Calderón de la Barca published in 1843 *Life in Mexico*, a memoir culled from the numerous letters she had sent to her family, which she shared with friends such as Prescott, pertaining to her travels and experiences in that land. Suddenly Mexico was on the lips of nearly every reader in America and abroad.

Prescott served as an unofficial agent to get her book published in America and England. The Boston firm of Little and Brown were quick to offer Fanny Calderón a contract. Chapman and Hall, in Britain, would agree to publish the travel book, thanks to the influential assistance of Charles Dickens. Prescott wrote a 15-page article to help promote Madame Calderón's book, which appeared in the January 1843 edition of the North American Review. *Life in Mexico* was well received by the public, and its description of the land was viewed as being so precise that it served as a guide for American officers engaged in the Mexican War of 1847. Madame Calderón's next book, *The Attaché in Madrid*, was published anonymously in 1856, under the pretense that it was written by an attaché of the German legation.

William Prescott wrote the following preface to Madame Calderón's *Life in Mexico*: "The present work is the result of observations made during a two years' residence in Mexico, by a lady, whose position there made her intimately acquainted with its society, and opened to her the best resources of information in regard to whatever could interest an enlightened foreigner. It consists of letters written to the members of her own family, and, *really*, not intended originally—however incredible the assertion—for publication. Feeling a regret that such rich stories of instruction and amusement, from which I have so much profited, myself, should be reserved for the eyes of a few friends only, I strongly recommended that they should be given to the world. This is now done, with a few such alterations and omissions as were necessary in a private correspondence; and although the work would derive more credit from the author's own name, than from anything which I can say, yet as she declines prefixing it, I feel much pleasure in making this statement by way of introduction to the public."[38]

Meanwhile, Prescott anxiously awaited the opinions of the critics, especially those from overseas, who had reviewed his new book. Edward Everett made sure to send his friend the notices that appeared in the British weeklies. The historian was particularly pleased with a review by the Rev. H.H. Milman's that appeared in the *Quarterly Review* (London, LXXIII 1843–1844) and wrote to him of his sincere appreciation. After a highly favorable review surfaced in the *Edinburgh Review* (LXXXI 1845), William mockingly revised his generally unfavorable opinion of critics: "I begin to have a high opinion of Reviews! The only fault they find with me is, that I deal too hardly with Cortés."[39]

Copies of the American reviews were sent to Prescott as they became available; 130 reviews arrived during the first month of the release of *His-*

tory of the Conquest of Mexico. The vast majority of these commentaries were highly favorable, most believing it was even better than his first book. Joseph G. Cogswell of New York wrote, "It comes up entirely to my idea of a perfect history, uniting all the charms of a beautiful spirited narrative with the authenticity of documenting history."[40]

Counted among the growing legion of fans of William Prescott following the release of *Conquest of Mexico* was Fanny Longfellow, the wife of the poet Henry Wadsworth Longfellow. She wrote in her journal, "It has the fascination of a romance and cannot be left.... Mr. Prescott seems to have seen it all with his own eyes as he makes his reader."[41]

Despite its rather steep price, booksellers found it difficult to keep Prescott's book in stock. Five thousand copies of the three-volume *History of the Conquest of Mexico* sold out in just four months, a quantity the publisher had expected to last an entire year. Its popularity rarely waned and by 1855 the book was already in its 23rd edition.

History of the Conquest of Mexico appealed to a much larger audience than its predecessor. Prescott's new work achieved a degree of literary excellence that was so rare in historical writing. In less capable hands, this epic tale of conquest would have been relegated to a dry rendering of dates, places, and names. The Boston historian had successfully managed to weave an interesting narrative filled with adventure and heroism that seemed to surpass the fictional deeds of Amadis de Gaula, the chivalrous and romantic tales that were a source of inspiration to Hernán Cortés and the many conquistadors who followed him. The numerous and elaborately detailed footnotes not only demonstrated that Prescott had made a thorough investigations of his subject, but also provided valuable additional insight into this awe-inspiring story. For these reasons, the *History of the Conquest of Mexico* is regarded by many as William Prescott's magnum opus.

In addition to being a thorough account of the Spanish conquest of Mexico, Prescott provided a detailed history of the Aztecs and the other tribes that inhabited the fertile Valley of Mexico. He awakened public awareness to the fact that the natives of this region were far more complex than the idyllic image of the noble savage, native lore that had taken root in the 18th century. William noted that these tribes were advanced civilizations that had built cities of stone that equaled or surpassed the greatest contemporary cities of Europe. Prescott is also responsible for reintroducing the name Aztec to the last of the Chichimec tribes to have wandered into the Valley of Anáhuac. This tribe had long ago abandoned the name Aztec in favor of either Mexica or Tenocha. Prescott used the term Aztec to refer to all inhabitants of the Valley of Mexico who spoke the common language of Nahuatl, and the popularity of his book left an indelible mark.

In writing about the fall of the Aztec Empire, Prescott astutely observed: "Its fate may serve as a striking proof, that a government, which does not rest on the sympathies of its subjects, cannot long abide; that human institutions, when not connected with human prosperity and progress, must fall,—and if not before the increasings light of civilization, by the hand of violence; by violence from within, if not from without, And who shall lament their fall?"[42]

There were some who objected to Prescott's interpretations, especially the picture he had painted of a sophisticated and orderly Aztec society. His book described in great detail the magnificent temples and courtyards located in and around the Aztec city of Tenochtitlán. The reports of Cortés and the accompanying conquistadors and priests of the stately stone cities they had seen during the conquest were written off by most contemporary historians and scholars as boastful claims intended to glorify their deeds. Several critics sought to discredit Prescott's rendition by pointing to the fact that such structures did not conform to the known habitats of the Indians of North America, who generally lived in simple villages comprised of crude huts. However, John Lloyd Stephens' account and Frederick Catherwood's drawing of the many splendid Mayan cities they had found during their travels in Mexico and Central America certainly lent credence to reports of grand cities built by ancient cultures. Still, the prevailing thought was that the natives of the New World were savages and therefore not capable of having been the founders of great civilizations. Everyone seemed to have a different theory as to who built the ancient cities explored by Stephens and Catherwood: Egyptians, Norsemen, Chinese, Mongols, Romans, Phoenicians, Carthaginians, Atlanteans, and the Lost Tribe of Israel were promoted as the likely builders of these cities of stone. John Lloyd Stephens, Frederick Catherwood, Alexander Humboldt, and William Prescott were among the few learned men who gave due credit to the ancestors of the indigenous population.

Unlike so many historians before him, Prescott refused to subscribe to the infamous *Black Legend* premise that had been ascribed to the Spaniards by rival European nations that were envious of Spain's newfound wealth. William was a great admirer of the bravery and tenacity exhibited by the Spanish conquistadors. In a letter to Don Pascual de Gayangos dated November 30, 1843, Prescott mentioned his awareness of a reviewer who took issue with the way he presented the conquistadors: "I see I am already criticized by an English periodical for vindicating in too unqualified a manner the deeds of the old Conquerors."[43]

In defense of his portrayal of Cortés, Prescott proclaimed: "The immorality of the act and of the actor seem to me two very different things; and while we judge the one by the immutable principles of right and wrong, we must try the other by the fluctuating standard of the age; the real question is whether a man was sincere, and acted according to the lights of his age."[44]

A highly favorable review by S. M. Phillips of the historian's new book, which appeared in the *Edinburgh Review*, mentioned that "Mr. Prescott has, for many years, been blind." Prescott sought to set the record straight by writing to Macvey Napier, the Scottish editor and historian, regarding the true state of his vision. "But of late years," he wrote, "my eye has acquired sufficient vigor to enable me, most of the time, to use it reasonably during the day in study, though in writing I am still obliged to make use of a Secretary, who deciphers a very illegible manuscript made by means of a writing-case used by the Blind."[45] This explanation did little to change the British perception of his visual impairment.

One of Prescott's most cherished compliments came to his attention from John Lloyd Stephens following the well-known adventurer's 1847 visit with Alexander Humboldt, which took place at the renowned naturalist's residence in Germany. During this more than one hour meeting, the two celebrated explorers discussed a variety of topics. Stephens wrote, "Outside of Europe, Mexico seemed to be the country which interested him most; perhaps from the connection with those countries which had brought me to his acquaintance, or, more probably because it was the foundation of his own early fame. He spoke of Mr. Prescott's History of the Conquest [of Mexico] and said that I might, when the opportunity offered, to say to that gentleman, as from himself, there was no historian of the age, in England or Germany, equal to him."[46]

8

The Conquest of Peru

"Breaking ground on a new subject is always a dreary business."[1]

Literary Loafing

Following the success of his new book, an admirer offered William Prescott his opinion as to what should be the author's next historical undertaking. Benjamin F. French of New Orleans wrote a letter to the Boston historian suggesting that he should consider writing a history of Louisiana, which he felt would make for a most interesting and popular subject. Mr. French even offered to provide Prescott with his own extensive collection of historical manuscripts pertaining to this very topic. William politely declined Benjamin French's proposition. The historian firmly believed that the achievements of individuals was vastly more interesting than that of nations, or in this case a state: "Instead of a mere abstraction, at once we see a being like ourselves…. We place ourselves in his position, and see the passing current of events with the same eyes."[2]

On February 3, 1844, Prescott made note of his plan to "break ground" on his follow-up book, which was the *History of the Conquest of Peru*. However, the historian had concerns about the choice of the Spanish explorer and conquistador Francisco Pizarro as the central character of his book: "A hero that could not even write his own signature!"[3] He went on to declare, "I must look into some popular stories of highwaymen."[4]

Starting work on a new writing project was generally a difficult period of transition for Prescott; he knew all too well that there would be numerous doubts, concerns, and interruptions to confront. Therefore, William decided to enjoy some pleasurable pursuits before plunging into his next project. Per Susan's request, he made use of this free time by posing for an oil painting by the Boston artist Joseph A. Ames. He also honored the request of the sculptor Richard S. Greenough to capture his likeness in a marble bust. These sittings stretched from mid–February to the end of March, a period of idleness which the historian greatly cherished.

Prescott paid another visit to New York City in mid April to attend to some minor affairs with his publisher and to enjoy the company of friends, both old and new. On May 5, 1844, following his return to Boston, William made the following notation in his journal: "I went to New York, thinking I might pass a couple of days. It turned out twelve, and then I found it no easy matter to break away from friends who, during my stay there, feasted and feted me to the top of my constitution. Not a day in which I rose before nine, dined before five or six, went to bed before twelve. Two years ago I did not know half a dozen New Yorkers; I have now made the acquaintance of two hundred at least and the friendship, I trust of many. The cordiality with which I was greeted is one of the most gratifying tributes I have received from my country men, coming as it did from all classes and professions."[5]

Numerous accolades continued to pour in from admirers during Prescott's extended and well deserved period of literary loafing. John Quincy Adams remarked to Edward B. Otis, William's secretary at the time, "Mr. Prescott possessed the two great qualifications of an historian, who should be apparently without country and without religion. This," Mr. Otis goes on to say, "he explained by saying that the history should not show the political or religious bias of the historian. It would be difficult, Mr. Adams thought, to tell whether Mr. Prescott were a Protestant or a Catholic, a monarchist or a republican."[6]

More honors were bestowed upon William Prescott following the tremendous success of his first two historical accounts. In the fall of 1843, Prescott, along with his friends George Bancroft and Jared Sparks, was awarded an honorary Doctor of Laws degree from Harvard, his alma mater. The celebrated historian was also accorded honorary membership in the Indiana Historical Society. The following year William was the recipient of honorary memberships in the Maryland Historical Society and the National Institute in Washington, D.C.

In February of 1845 an unexpected honor was conferred upon him, recognition which he waited until April 23, 1845, to note in his literary memorandum:

> In my laziness I forgot to record the greatest academic honor I have received—the greatest I shall ever receive—my election as Corresponding Member of the French Institute, as one of the Academy of Moral and Political Science. I was chosen to fill

the vacancy occasioned by the death of the illustrious Navarrete. This circumstance, together with the fact, that I did not canvas for the election, as is very usual with the candidates, makes the compliment the more grateful to me.

By the last steamer I received a diploma from the Royal Society of Berlin also as Corresponding Member of the Class of Philosophy and History. This body, over which Humboldt presides, and which has been made famous by the learned labors of Niebuhr, Von Raumer, Ranke, & c., ranks next to the Institute among the great Academies of the Continent.[7]

Following the death of the Spanish historian Martín Fernández de Navarrete, William Prescott received 18 of 20 ballots to be named as a member of the Academy of Moral and Political Science of the French Institute. As for the other two ballots, one was cast for George Bancroft and the other was left blank. William always considered this the highest honor ever bestowed upon him.

During William Prescott's writing hiatus there arrived the tragic news of the death of his brother Edward, which occurred during a voyage to the Azores. The youngest child of William and Catherine Prescott had long lived in the shadow of his older brother. After earning his degree at Harvard, Edward studied law under the watchful eye of his father. Additionally, Ned served in the militia, where he attained the rank of Colonel, and was also a representative in the Boston legislature. But seven years later Edward grew weary of life as a lawyer and decided to enroll in the ministry.

In 1837 the 33-year-old Edward Prescott was admitted to the Order of Deacons of the Protestant Episcopal Church. He left Boston to study for the clergy at a New Jersey parish, where he was tutored by Bishop George Washington Doane. Unfortunately, failing health interfered with his religious duties and he decided to travel to the Azores, just as his older brother had done many years earlier, to seek comfort in the favorable climate of St.

The bust of Prescott by Ball (from *Complete Works of William H. Prescott* published in 1912 by DeFau & Co.).

Michael's Island and the company of the Hickling clan. On his second day at sea Edward suffered an unexpected attack, perhaps apoplectic, and passed away early the next morning. The date was April 11, 1844. The body of the 40-year-old Edward was committed to the sea. He left behind a wife who lived but a few years longer, and a mountain of debt. Much time passed before the Prescott family received the sorrowful news of Edward's death.

Prescott wrote of his brother's passing in a memo dated June 9, 1844: "It is dreary and mournful to the imagination, that he should have passed away, on the desolate waters, without a friend near to close his eyes.—He has left with me the remembrance of many kindly virtues, and of a liberal nature, free from all jealousy and ungenerous feeling." William concludes by praying, "May the Almighty in his infinite mercy, pardon his frailties and transgressions, to receive him into his mansion of everlasting rest."[8] To save the family name from financial embarrassment, the Prescotts quietly settled all of Edward's outstanding monetary obligations.

In mid–June of 1844, William's 16-year-old daughter Elizabeth was stricken with an illness that she could not seem to shake. The concerned father decided to take her to Niagara Falls, where he believed the climate would prove much healthier for her delicate condition. The 14-year-old William Amory would accompany his father and sister on this journey. The eldest child, William Gardiner, was unable to join them because of academic studies necessary for his upcoming graduation in August. The Prescotts were joined on this trip by Martha Endicott Peabody, the teenage daughter of Francis Peabody of Salem.

On the 18th of June, the historian and his three young companions departed by train for a 15-day excursion that covered more than 1100 miles of the Empire State. They passed over the Hudson and continued on to the Mohawk Valley, a scenic region nestled between the majestic Adirondack and Catskill mountains. At Utica they boarded a stagecoach for a side trip to Trenton Falls. There the cautious William Prescott had to restrain the girls from venturing too far along the ridge, where one slip would easily have sent them plummeting to their death among the rocks and water below. After viewing this place of interest the gratified sightseers returned to their train, which passed through Auburn and Rochester before reaching its intended destination.

Once at Niagara Falls, William and the children visited Goat Island, situated between the American and Canadian sides of the cascading waters. Prescott complained that a flare up of rheumatism reminded him he was much too old and far too frail to keep up with his young and adventurous companions: "The sun and water blind me, the dampness gives me rheumatism, the half baked biscuit gives me the dyspepsia. Such poor devils as myself should never migrate further than Pepperell.[9] William and his young companions stayed on the American side of the majestic Falls the first day and crossed to the Canadian side the following morning."

William wrote of the magnificent view of the Falls from the Canadian side in letter to his wife, "I assure you it filled me with solemn feelings to be thus lying on the brink of the vast abyss with the ceaseless hum of breakers in my ear. A column of spray rises up perpetually in a sort of misty veil, which in this morning's sun takes all the gay colors of the rainbow, while the huge volume of water rolls over the fall in a deep emerald green, which is soon broken up into sheets of pearly foam. Ragged trees 70 and 80 feet high, torn up by the roots, lie prostrated on the river banks and add to the savage grandeur of the scenery. Is there any spot in the world calculated to give such an idea of the might of the Creator?"[10]

The return journey saw William Prescott and company pass through the cities of Buffalo and Rochester before making a scheduled stop at Auburn. Their train then passed through Syracuse on its route to Utica. From there they passed by Schenectady on their journey to Albany. The last stop was Springfield before they disembarked at Boston. William and his children had returned just in time to prepare for their seasonal stay at Nahant.

William Prescott's scheduled three months of literary loafing had managed to stretch all the way to nine, after which the historian wholeheartedly devoted his efforts to the completion of his next book. William, however, was not quite as idle as he let on: He had spent many long sessions listening intently as his secretary read Garcilaso de la Vega's commentaries on the early history and culture of Peru, as well as other noted historians who had written about this little known topic. He also studied a rare manuscript written by Don Juan Sarmiento, President of the Royal Council of the Indies, who had traveled throughout the region shortly after the Spanish conquest of the Inca empire.

Prescott continued to correspond with both John Lloyd Stephens and Frederick Catherwood even after the explorers had gone their separate ways. The historian was elated to learn that Stephens and Catherwood were considering a possible expedition to Peru to explore and document the ruins of the Incas and other native civilizations of the region. Prescott, who was now working on the *History of the Conquest of Peru*, wrote to Catherwood in the hope of encouraging him to undertake such an expedition: "Stephens tells me that you have talked to him of a trip to Peru. This is 'my ground' but I suppose it will not be the worse for your mousing into architectural antiquities, and I wish I could see the fruits of such a voyage in your beautiful illustrations."[11] Prescott thought that the findings of Stephens and Catherwood amongst the lands conquered by Francisco Pizarro and his small band of conquistadors would prove extremely beneficial to his work. Unfortunately, this expedition never materialized.

Breaking Ground

On August 12, 1844, while vacationing at the family seashore home in Nahant, William Prescott began to draft an outline of his *History of the Conquest of Peru*. Barely more than a year had passed since he had finished writing *History of the Conquest of Mexico*, which was to serve as the template for his proposed third historical account. The historian was eager to get started on this undertaking, especially after he had received 800 folio pages dispatched from the German cities of Berlin and Gotha, for which he owed thanks to the valuable connections of Alexander Humboldt and the committed efforts of the diplomat Theodore Sedgwick Fay. Prescott felt in excellent health to pursue his work, an improvement he attributed to his recent trip to Niagara.

Prescott was fortunate that the previous batch of research materials that were collected and sent to him for his *History of the Spanish Conquest of Mexico* also contained many essential articles and records related to the Spanish subjugation of Peru, particularly those materials obtained from the vast collection of the Spanish historian Juan Bautista Muñoz. Consequently, this enabled him to begin his research almost at once, which greatly contributed to William's ability to complete his studies and composition at a pace that vastly exceeded his previous works. However, as he delved into the material on hand the historian soon realized, "The subject is by no means so rich a one, so poetical and picturesque as Mexico."[12]

Other difficulties which William had to overcome was the realization that this tale lacked a worthy hero and that the conquest of Peru occurred with relative ease and quickness. The latter realization meant that for the reminder of his book he would have to focus on the bitter feud that erupted between the conquistadors over claims to titles and riches, and the failed efforts of the Incas to reclaim their realm. In a letter to Pascual de Gayangos dated September 14, 1844, William stated: "I am at work on Peru, trying to pick some gold out of the Andes.—I Hope you will be able to get

Francisco Pizarro (Library of Congress).

for me a sketch of the arms of the Pizarros. My hero will need all the illusion of chivalry to recommend him."[13]

William left no source unturned in his search for original material related to the Spanish conquest of Peru. He would later note in the preface of his book, "the collection of manuscript materials in reference to Peru is fuller and more complete than that which relates to Mexico, so that there is scarcely a nook or corner so obscure, in the path of the adventurer, that some light has not been thrown on it by the written correspondence of the period."[14]

Sources for Prescott's *History of the Conquest of Peru* included Inca Garcilaso de la Vega's *Commentarios Reales de los Incas,* Pedro Cieza de León's *Crónicas del Perú,* José de Acosta's *Historia Natural y Moral de las Indias,* and Diego Fernández's *Primera y segunda parti de la Historia del Perú.* However, Prescott had serious concerns about the accuracy of Garcilaso de la Vega's account, reservations that Albert Gallatin shared in a letter to Prescott (June 2, 1845): "I have no faith in Garcilasso de la Vega, who in his account of Soto's expedition to Florida, is both a plagiarist and a romancer."[15] A mestizo who was the illegitimate son of the Spanish officer Sebastian Garcilaso de la Vega and the Inca princess Palla Chimpu Occlo, Garcilaso de la Vega recorded the remembered tales of his Inca ancestors in *The Royal Commentaries of the Incas,* an informative but overly subjective and somewhat imaginative historical account written nearly 70 years after the Spanish conquest of Peru.

Prescott also studied the writings of Fernando de Montesinos, Pedro Sarmiento de Gamboa, and a number of other Spanish historians who had written about the Spanish subjugation of the Inca empire. The historian had to rely heavily on the chronicles of the Spaniards because the tribes of this region did not leave behind records of their own history. The dominant Incas, who never developed a written language, relied on mnemonic aids, such as the quipa, and the remembrance of stories handed down through the generations. It was the Spanish priests who sedulously pieced together their history. The works of Manuel José Quintana, William Robertson, and Washington Irving were employed by Prescott to form an outline for his *Conquest of Peru.*

Once again, the pre–Columbian studies presented a rather troublesome topic for Prescott; he feared getting bogged down in this subject as he had with his introduction of the Aztec culture. Regarding this concern, Prescott noted: "the astonishing contrast presented by the Mexican in the extremes of civilization and barbarism produced a striking and picturesque effect, which I shall not get from the uniform, tame and *mould-like* character and institutions of the Incas. How many pages shall I allow for the Introduction? A hundred?"[16] The 90-plus pages that comprise book one of *History of the Conquest of Peru* provides a very detailed historical sketch of the rise of the Inca Empire. When taking into account that archaeological and ethnological research into pre-Hispanic civilizations were in their infancy, the Boston historian had pieced together a rather impressive study of Inca history and culture.

Unfortunately, Prescott did not have a source in Peru who could supply him with useful information on the topography, flora and fauna, and unique customs of the people as Madame Calderón had done for him in Mexico. Because of this lack of insight, many of his descriptions of the land, historic sites, and rituals suffered somewhat in their detail and accuracy.

On May 17, 1844, Pascual de Gayangos, the Spanish scholar who freely offered his services to locate research material for the Boston historian, wrote Prescott that he and his wife Frances were grief-stricken over the death of their three-year-old son. In a letter dated June 30, 1844, William sought to console his dear friend. "I most sincerely sympathize with you both. A similar calamity befell me, excepting that mine was a daughter, some years since. It was my favorite child, taken away at the age of four, when all the loveliness and vivacity of the character is just opening on us. I can never suffer again as I then did. It was my first heavy sorrow, and I suppose that we cannot feel twice so bitterly. It recalls a most painful period of my existence in thus alluding to it."[17] Even though the two scholars never met, the frequent correspondence and similar literary interests of Prescott and Gayangos had quickly evolved into a sincere and lasting friendship. Don Pascual de Gayangos could write eloquently in both English and Spanish, but preferred to write his letters to the American historian in Castilian.

On July 14, 1844, William wrote of being stung by a review in the Baltimore Catholic Magazine which labeled him a "bigot" for his allusions to some of the Catholic dogmas. He also complained that the *Dublin Quarterly Review* wrote that it "breathes a prayer for my conversion from spiritual error."[18] Prescott felt that neither critique was justified.

In late August of 1844, the family made a special trip to Cambridge to attend William Gardiner Prescott's graduation ceremony, which marked the third generation of Prescotts, each of whom were named William, to graduate from Harvard College. On September 1, 1844, a proud William H. Prescott noted in his memorandum: "Attended Commencement last Wednesday when Will took his degree.... It is just 30 years since I quitted

Alma Mater.... It is worth remembering that Will occupied the same room in old Hollis, which I occupied 30 years ago, and which his grandfather occupied about 30 years before me; three William Prescotts in three generations, and all alive to meet together in the same scene of boyish recollections."[19] Hollis 11 was the room that all three William Prescotts occupied at Harvard. The newest family graduate went on to study law but never did practice this profession.

A Family Tragedy

Sunday, December 8, 1844, would prove to be a day of immeasurable sadness for the entire Prescott family. Judge Prescott was relaxing in the library when Nathan Webster, the household servant of 30 years, noticed that the patriarch of the family appeared somewhat unsteady, and rushed to his aid the instant he saw him start to collapse. The Judge made a momentary recovery but his condition quickly took a turn for the worse. The elder Prescott lay prone on the floor as the rest of the family gathered by his side; everyone believed this was a relapse of the paralytic attack he had suffered in October of the previous year.

The 82-year-old head of the family had complained for nearly a fortnight that he did not feel well and was greatly bothered by nagging pains on his left side, which the doctors believed was a rheumatic affliction. The Judge rested on the floor while the family doctor was summoned. The physician arrived quickly and instructed that the elder Prescott should be carried at once to his upstairs bedroom, where he breathed his last just shy of 15 minutes after having been placed upon his bed.

The 76-year-old Catherine Prescott was inconsolable over the loss of her husband of 51 years. As for the historian, he lost not only a father but a friend and confident. William would record in his journal: "I have lost my father, my counsellor, companion, and friend from boyhood to the hour of his death. The event took place on Sunday morning, about eight o'clock, December 8th, 1844. I had the sad comfort of being with him in his last moments, and of witnessing his tranquil and beautiful death.²"[0]

Having retired from his chosen profession, the Judge had spent the last 16 years of his life enjoying time to read and study topics of interest found in his vast collection of books; taking long walks, often in the company of his eldest son; and tending to the gardens at his three houses. He found immense pleasure in the company of his family, time which was divided at his homes in Boston, Pepperell, and Nahant. The Judge had made it known to all that he was extremely proud of his son's success as an historian. Three days after his passing, William Prescott, Esq. was laid to rest in the crypt of St. Paul's Church.

As the appointed executor, William Prescott suddenly found much of his valued time consumed with handling responsibilities that had previously been attended to by his father. The complex affairs of the Judge's numerous holdings was taxing on both the time and emotions of the historian. At the time of his passing, the Judge had stock holdings in six railroads, 12 manufacturing firms, four banks, four insurance firms, as well as shares in eight other profitable businesses. He was also the holder of ten promissory notes. Other assets included his three homes and a number of properties valued at $343,736.85. Fortunately, William was ably assisted by the lawyer Franklin Dexter, his brother-in-law and co-executor of his father's will. William H. Gardiner, his long time friend and an accomplished lawyer, was co-trustee of his sister's trust.

For the next several weeks William was unable to concentrate on his work—his thoughts were constantly drawn to fond memories of his dear departed father. William wrote of his father's lasting influence, "He has always been a part of myself; to whom I have confided every matter of any moment; on whose superior judgment I have relied in all affairs of the least consequence; and in whose breast I have been sure to find ready sympathy in every joy and sorrow. I have never read any book of merit without discussing it with him, and his noble example has been a light to my steps in all the chances and perplexities of life."[21]

In response to the request of a friend who desired to know more about the character of his father, William wrote: "As he had great sagacity, extensive learning, high principle, chivalrous honor, love of truth, reverence for the Deity most unaffected and remarkable, he had the equalities which command reverence without forfeiting love. There are some whom we venerate for high talents or principles, who have not the attractions that secure our affections. But none approached him,—however intimately,—without mingled feelings of reverence and love. How much and tenderly he was beloved can be known only to those who have seen him round his own hearth."[22]

Two months would pass before William felt the desire to return to work on his book. This was around the time he had received an encouraging letter dated October 26, 1844, from Alexander Humboldt, but which did not arrive until after the death of his father. Prescott recorded in his literary journal: "Received a letter from Baron Humboldt,—a gratifying testimonial of his approval of my Mexican labors. He says he has gone over the book, line by line, with a critical eye,—& professes his intention to have translated it, but was anticipated. May be so—may be not."[23]

To be thought so highly of by a man he so greatly admired inspired Prescott to resume work on *History of the Conquest of Peru*. In all likelihood, Humboldt played a pivotal role in the Boston historian's appointment as a member of the Royal Academy of Berlin. The renowned naturalist and philosopher was president of the Academy and a great admirer of the American historian. "Such testimonies—from a distant land," the Boston historian recorded in his literary journal, "are the real rewards of the scholar. What pleasure would they have given to my dear Father!"[24]

A Collection of Essays

Another suspension of work on *History of the Conquest of Peru* occurred during the winter season, which stretched between late 1844 and early 1845, after William consented to Richard Bentley's proposal to publish a collection of his writings that had previously appeared in the *North American Review*. It was actually Prescott who had conceived the idea of releasing such a compilation. Knowing that his books were fairly popular in England, and since few British readers were familiar with his writings that had appeared in the *Old North*, William convinced himself that a compendium of his best essays would be of tremendous interest to English readers.

Prescott dashed off a letter to Colonel Aspinwall to inquire about the prospects of publishing in England a book composed entirely of his old articles. Aspinwall responded, "the publication of the Essays shall have my best attention in conformity with your wishes and instructions."[25] The historian then informed his New York publisher of his plan and Harper Brothers, without even inquiring about the contents of this proposed anthology of essays, immediately replied that they would be delighted to publish such a work in America.

On March 8, 1845, William Prescott posted in his journal: "Finished doctoring my old articles in the N. A. for Bentley. Have run them over very superficially. If they prove as hard reading to the public as to me, I pity them. But to me they are an old tale."[26] This compilation was published in England under the title *Critical and Historical Essays* while a similar version was published in America by Harper Brothers, which was titled as *Biographical and Critical Miscellanies*.

As the date neared for the release of this publication Prescott began to fear that perhaps he had made a terrible mistake. In a letter to Edward Everett, the former editor of the *North American Review*, William confessed his reservations about this project: "I am about to commit a folly, which you will think savors of mental blindness; that is, the publication of some of my periodical trumpery, whose value, or rather little value you know."[27]

Prescott's *Critical and Historical Essays* was released in England on August 16, 1845. The book was comprised of 13 previously published articles reflecting the author's varied literary interests over the preceding 20 years. The contents were as follows:

1. Charles Brockden Brown, the American Novelist
2. Asylum for the Blind
3. Historical Composition (aka Irving's Conquest of Granada)
4. Cervantes
5. Sir Walter Scott
6. Chateaubriand's English Literature
7. Bancroft's United States
8. Madame Caledron's Life in Mexico
9. Molière
10. Italian Narrative Poetry
11. Poetry and Romances of the Italians
12. Scottish Song
13. Da Ponte's Observations

The British publication included an engraved portrait that failed to meet with Prescott's approval. On September 15, 1845, the historian noted in his journal: "As to the portrait of the author, it shows more imagination, I suspect, than anything in the book."[28] *Biographical and Critical Miscellanies* was released in early December 1845 by Harper & Brothers, just a few months after the publication of its British counterpart. A second London edition was brought to market in 1850. Prescott's review of George Ticknor's *History of Spanish Literature*, which was published on January 1, 1850, was added as the 14th entry in Richard Bentley's edition of *Critical and Historical Essays*.

Though sales were lackluster, especially when compared to his previous releases, the book managed to achieve a modicum of success—selling 13,000 copies by the end of 1860. However, sales were mostly generated by the celebrity of the author rather than the quality of content. Prescott had expected there would be limited interest in these essays, which helped cushion the disappointment. But he was dismayed to learn from Harpers that a significant number of his *Miscellanies* taken on consignment by booksellers had been returned to the publisher. The few critics who bothered to review the book were, in general, kind; there was little to say because there was so little to write about. Its fair to say that the *Miscellanies* did little to enhance the reputation of the historian.

A Change of Address

Because there were so many tender memories of Judge Prescott haunting nearly every turn of their Bedford Street home, the family agreed that after the New Year it would be best to find a new Boston residence. In mid–February of 1845, William Prescott purchased from Augustus Thorndike a four-story brick house painted white that was located at 55 Beacon Street, which he planned to remodel to suit the particular needs and tastes of his family. In a letter to George Ticknor about his new home

Prescott's study in his home in Bedford Street, Boston, where "Ferdinand and Isabella" was written (from *Complete Works of William H. Prescott* published in 1912 by DeFau & Co.).

in the fashionable district of the city, the historian could not resist his fondness for play on words: "The truth is I have three places of residence, among which I contrive to distribute my year. Six months I pass in town, where my home is in Beacon Street, looking on the Common, which, as you recollect, is an uncommonly fine situation, commanding a noble view of land and water."[29] The new address placed the historian in the neighborhood of several good friends; next door was the home of William Appleton and he was in walking distance of the estate of David Sears II. He was also very near the residence of his long-time friend George Ticknor. The Prescotts' old Bedford Street house was eventually torn down.

Painful remembrances of the Judge were even more prevalent at the ancestral Pepperell home. On June 15, 1845, William wrote in his journal: "Every where I see the evidences of his care—the trees which he planted—& in whose shadow I am now to sit—without him—My morning rides and evening walks—the quiet scenery, never more lovely than now—yet with a melancholy beauty—the Sabbath meeting—where I fill his seat—every thing recalls him—& I almost expect to meet him in my rambles—or as I enter the house to receive his kindly greeting. Never more."[30]

Pepperell, however, was the one family residence that William Prescott would never abandon. Prescott had previously declared his fondness for this scenic location. "How sweet the mountain air —the green fields—how sweet the solitude. Can I ever be weary of it?"[31] The historian later added that this country estate was "dearer to me than any other spot I call my own."[32]

In a letter to Mr. Putnam, the publisher of *Homes of American Authors*, which was released in 1852 and featured an article about the residences of the Boston historian, Prescott wrote, "The place at Pepperell has been in the family for more than a century and a half, an uncommon event among our locomotive people. The house is about a century old, the original building having been greatly enlarged by my father first, and since by me. It is here that my grandfather, Col. Wm. Prescott, who commanded at Bunker Hill, was born and died, and in the village church-yard he lies under a simple slab, containing only a record of his name and age. My father, Wm. Prescott, the best and wisest of his name, was born and passed his earlier days here, and from my own infancy, not a year has passed that I have not spent more or less of in these shades, now hallowed to me by the recollection of happy hours and friends that are gone."[33]

The extensive remodeling of the Beacon Street home was overseen by Catherine Prescott while William, Susan and their offspring remained behind at Pepperell. Settling into the new house proved a major interruption to just about every aspect of William's daily routine, especially regarding his work on *History of the Conquest of Peru*. He wrote that it was "a month of Pandemonium; an unfurnished house coming to order; parlors without furniture; a library without books; books without time to open them. Old faces, new faces, but not the sweet face of Nature."[34]

By early December the Beacon Street house had been arranged in a manner suitable to the wishes of the family. The extensive restorations to the new house cost them the princely sum of $13,973.25. The library and study, located at the rear of the house, were designed to the historian's explicit specifications. The library was home to the numerous and treasured novels and historical works that William had acquired over the years. The spacious library also served as a family room and a comfortable place to converse with guests. As expected, the large windows were adorned with drapes to protect William's sensitive eyes from the bright light of the sun. The oak paneled ceiling showcased a luxurious chandelier that hung from the very center of the room. The library also displayed the busts of

Prescott's library in his home at No. 55 Beacon Street, Boston (from *Complete Works of William H. Prescott* published in 1912 by DeFau & Co.).

Sir Walter Scott and Washington Irving, two writers that Prescott held in the highest esteem. A decorative fireplace provided warmth during Boston's many long winter nights. Above the marble fireplace there hung the crossed swords of his paternal grandfather Colonel William Prescott and Susan's maternal grandfather Captain John Linzee.

William's library and study were adorned with oil paintings of Ferdinand and Isabella, Gonsalvo de Córdoba, and Hernán Cortés, portraits that William had commissioned from Spanish artists. In a letter to Pascual de Gayangos, Prescott stated that these copies of original paintings were "the size of life; and as they hang on the walls around me, I feel myself transported to the glorious land of chivalry."[35]

William Prescott was quite pleased with William Makepeace Thackery's small tribute to him at the beginning of his book *The Virginians*: "On the library wall of one of the most famous writers of America, there hang two crossed swords, which his relatives wore in the great War of Independence. The one sword was gallantly drawn in the service of the king; the other was the weapon of a brave and honored republican soldier. The possessor of the harmless trophy has earned for himself a name alike honored in his ancestors' country and his own, where genius such as his has always a peaceful welcome."[36] The acclaimed English novelist had visited Prescott's house during his American lecture tour. These distinguished crossed swords were gifted to the Historical Society of Massachusetts shortly after William passed away.

Most of the walls of the library were lined with bookcases and shelves made of rich and polished oak that showcased William's large and impressive collection of books, which the historian proudly referred to as his "literary treasures." The bookcases with wooden doors were waist high. Recessed shelving above these bookcases rose up to the molding in place around the 14-foot-high ceiling, an expanse which allowed for seven levels of shelving. William took pleasure in perusing the numerous books in his library, making sure each was in its proper place. He often spoke to them as he gently caressed their binding, almost as if he were carrying on an intimate conversation with an old and dear friend. Edmund Otis, a former secretary of the historian, recalled, "Mr. Prescott loved his books almost as he loved his children; he liked to see them well dressed, in rich, substantial bindings; and if one, by any accident, was dropped, it annoyed him almost as much as if a baby fell."[37]

Over the years, Prescott had managed to amass a unique and magnificent collection of books numbering between 4000 and 5000 titles. He dedicated a great deal of time and thought to organizing his library: "The great point is to have a particular place for each work, and to know where that place is. I shall master this by degrees, and I shall not change,—and I trust I shall never have occasion to pull down and set up again."[38]

In regard to his vast collection of books, which reflected his wide range of literary interests, Prescott complained in a letter to Pascual de Gayangos: "when I survey my present treasures, and my means of coping with them without eyes, they fill me with almost as much uneasiness as pleasure." William goes on to complain: "I am like a poor devil with a rich armoury around him, but with only one hand, and that in a sling, to profit by it. But Fate cannot rob me of the historical bantlings I have already begot—that is a comfort."[39]

The study was located directly above the library, which was accessed by a spiral staircase hidden behind a spring lock door built into the bookcase. Books and manuscripts relevant to the Spanish project that the historian was currently working on were removed from the library and carried to the study—a chore usually performed by the secretary. This atelier, which Prescott thought of as his sanctuary, measured approximately 25 square feet. A large picture window, which was constructed in a bay style consisting of successive windows, was installed with shades that allowed him to control the amount of light that passed through the glass. A screen near the fireplace helped to dull the brightness of the fire.

Two desks were positioned in the middle of the study. The noctograph rested atop the desk where Prescott did most of his composing. The historian sat comfortably in a large leather chair and near the desk there rested a cozy red velvet sofa that was ideal for lounging. The secretary made use of the other desk, which was positioned near the window, where he executed such daily duties for his employer as reading aloud relevant research materials, copying letters, and transcribing the drafts of new chapters.

After he had settled into the Beacon Street residence, the first entry that William posted in his memorandum occurred on the one year anniversary of his father's passing. "How rapidly," he states, "has it flitted. How soon will the little [remaining] space be over for me and mine! His death has given me a new position in life, a new way of life altogether,— and a different view of it from what I had before. I have many, many blessings left; family, friends, fortune. May I be sensible of them, and may I so live that I may be permitted to join *him* again in the long hereafter."[40] Prescott was ready to resume work on his book once everything had been arranged to his satisfaction in his new home.

Return to Writing

The opening section on Incan history and culture was nearly as difficult for Prescott to piece together as were the preliminary chapters on the Aztecs of Mexico. On May 11, 1845, William made the following entry regarding these complications: "I never found it *so hard to come to the starting-point. The first chapter was a perfectly painful task*, as painful as I have ever performed at school." But a week later he noted that his efforts had been worthwhile: "The two chapters required a good deal of correction; yet, on the whole, read pretty well. I now find that it only needed a little courage at the outset to break the ice which had formed over my ideas, and the current, set loose runs on naturally enough. I feel a return to my old literary interest; am satisfied that this is the secret of contentment, of happiness, for me."[41]

William had fair use of his good eye while working on his *Conquest of Peru* but somewhat less than he had during his previous writing project. The arrival of the new year saw Prescott sidelined by a cold of such severity that Dr. Jackson, the family physician of 30 years, insisted that the historian discontinue work on his book until he had fully regained his health. A compliant Prescott passed the time listening to his secretary read Lord Henry Brougham's treatise on English life during the reign of King George III.

Once he had sufficiently recovered, Prescott worked at a feverish pace to complete the *History of the Conquest of Peru*. Unfortunately, he placed too much stress on himself to make up for lost time and on March 10, 1846, he suffered a strain of the nerve in his right eye while reading manuscripts pertaining to his current subject. A sharp recurring pain served as a warning that he needed to strictly limit the use of his good eye. Forced to temporarily refrain from work, William decided to use this time to engage in a week-long visit to Washington D. C. He was accompanied by the lawyer Charles Sumner on this journey to the nation's capital. Prescott and Sumner would travel by both train and boat to reach their intended destination. The two travelers stopped in New York City just long enough for a hearty breakfast. The historian had spent enough time at New York to judge that it was "the nosiest, filthiest and most crowded city that was ever built."[42]

Prescott and Sumner boarded a train at New York City which pulled into Philadelphia that very afternoon. The next morning they made their way to the nation's capital where, thanks to prior arrangements made by Madame Calderón, they enjoyed a comfortable stay at Coleman's Hotel on

Pennsylvania Avenue. Prescott was very pleased to receive an invitation to attend a dinner hosted by President James K. Polk. In a letter to Susan, William wrote, "In the evening we went to a soirée at the President's, a mean looking individual enough, who gapes and chaws tobacco. Madame is much the more of a President in air and conversation."[43]

Prescott was an honored guest at a party arranged by his good friend and fellow historian George Bancroft, who in 1845 had been appointed by President Polk as the new secretary of the navy. William was delighted to make the acquaintance of John Y. Mason, the former secretary of the navy. During their chat, Mason informed him that sailors aboard the USS *Delaware* had signed a petition requesting that a copy of *History of the Conquest of Mexico* be added to the ship's library, and soon thereafter it was decided that Prescott's book would be included in the library of every warship in the American fleet—news that was a source of tremendous pride for the Boston historian. During this visit to the nation's capital, William found the time to sit for a portrait by George P. A. Healy, an artist who had recently been commissioned to paint a likeness of President James K. Polk.

At the end of their week-long stay, the two gentlemen from Boston departed the District of Columbia and returned to New York City. Once there, both Prescott and Sumner made an appointment to see Dr. Samuel Elliott, the noted oculist who also counted Henry Wadsworth Longfellow as a patient. Sumner felt it was necessary to see the doctor because of a recent and annoying inflammation of his eyelids. The oculist once again treated Prescott's afflicted eye by means of bloodletting and the application of soothing salves. After nearly a week of treatments William felt that Dr. Elliott's remedies had significantly improved the condition of his right eye.

Prescott remained a good friend of Charles Sumner and stood by him when "all blue-blooded Boston turned its very cold shoulder upon the man whose radicalism, Ticknor said, had placed him outside the *pale of society*."[44] Though at different ends of the political spectrum, William refused to abandon his friend, a kindness that Sumner never forgot. In 1856, while serving as a U.S. senator of Massachusetts, Sumner was severely beaten by a cane wielded by South Carolina congressman Preston S. Brooks over remarks that he considered were an attack upon the character of his uncle, Senator Andrew P. Butler.

Concerned by this assault on Sumner's stance against slavery, William Prescott wrote to his friend, "You have escaped the crown of martyrdom by a narrow chance, and have got all the honors, which are almost as dangerous to one's head as a gutta-percha cane. There are few in old Massachusetts, I can assure you, who do not feel that every blow on your cranium was a blow on them."[45] Three years would pass before Charles Sumner sufficiently recovered from the physical and psychological scars he had suffered from this brutal beating.

Feeling rejuvenated and confident that his right eye was now strong enough to handle three hours of use per day, William recommenced work the moment he returned to Boston. Prescott continued to treat himself with the remedies provided by Dr. Elliott, but the best medicine seemed to be the invigorating ocean air at his Nahant residence. William described his seashore retreat in a letter to Fanny Calderón: "It is a wild spot and the winds at this moment whistle an accompaniment to the breakers that might fill a poet's cranium with the sublime. But I am no poet. I imagine myself however in some such place as the bold headland in the Algarve, on which Prince Henry of Portugal established his residence when he sent out his voyages of discovery."[46]

Taking care not to add undue stress to his good eye, the historian divided his reading time into brief intervals with adequate periods of rest between each work session. Despite these precautions, he soon discovered that his right eye was limited to just a half hour of use per day, and this soon faded to but a mere ten minutes. He fell into a melancholy mood after realizing that his eyesight was weakening because of advancing years. To take his mind off this troubling matter, William decided to follow through on a friends suggestion to pose for a portrait by the artist William Edward West.

There were many friends, acquaintances, and admirers who had clung to the erroneous belief that William Prescott was completely blind in his injured eye. But the truth is that the historian still retained a limited amount of vision in his left eye. Shortly after finishing *History of the Conquest of Peru*, William stated in a letter to George Bancroft, "My eye grows so dim that I think of putting myself under Elliott, the New York oculist's care before long. It is my last hope, and that is faint, for my faith is weak, and faith you know is essential to the miracle-working efficacy. Yet I do not fear blindness as my other eye will answer for all purposes but reading."[47] At best, Prescott's vision was poor but rarely was his sight left totally in the dark. Though there is no denying that his eyesight was always limited, perhaps the term purblind is a better word to describe the historian's visual impairment.

On May 4, 1846, William paused to meditate on having attained a milestone in his life: "My 50th birthday—a half century. This is getting on with a vengeance. It is one of those frightful halting places in a man's life that may make him reflect a little."[48]

Once Prescott felt strong enough to resume work on *History of the Conquest of Peru* he found that his pace was slowed considerably by having to rely primarily on the vision of others as part of his determined effort to avoid causing any further damage that might lead to permanent blindness, which was one of his greatest fears. When the time came to correct the proofs, William discovered that he could only rely on his vision for around 90 minutes a day, which had to be broken into short intervals. However, he was still able to continue to write with his noctograph, a device which did not require the use of his eyes. From this point on, the historian strictly limited the use of his right eye to no more than 30 minutes of reading per day.

In August of 1846, William received another box of rare books and manuscripts that had been collected for him by Don Pascual de Gayangos. Included in this collection was a four-volume translation of his *History of the Reign of Ferdinand and Isabella, the Catholic*. An elated Prescott wrote to Gayangos: "I prize a translation into the noble Castilian, more than any other tongue. For if my volumes are worthy of translation into it, it is the best proof that I have not wasted my time, and that I have contributed something in reference to the institutions and history of the country which the Spaniards themselves would not willingly let die."[49] Soon thereafter, William was also pleased to learn that *Ferdinand and Isabella* had been translated into Italian. Volumes one and two were dated 1847 and volume three was marked with the year 1848.

The remainder of *History of the Conquest of Peru* proceeded at a pace so rapid that it surprised even Prescott. At one point he was able to write 51 pages in a mere four days, a feat which caused him to note, "I never did up so much yarn in the same time. At this rate Peru will not hold out six months. Can I finish it in a year? Alas for the reader!"[50]

Since the majority of his research material was already at hand, Prescott was able to finish this book much faster than either of his previous historical accounts. Taking pride in a job well done, Prescott wrote, "I have, in the composition of the work, availed myself freely of my manuscript materials, allowed the actors to speak as much as possible for themselves, and especially made frequent use of their letters; for nowhere is the heart more likely to disclose itself, than in the freedom of private correspondence."[51]

William completed work on *History of the Conquest of Peru* during his seasonal stay at Pepperell, which had provided a pleasant atmosphere for his constitution. Prescott was particularly fond of a secluded spot on a hill at the rear of the house that overlooked Mount Monadnock and the sprawling Nashua Valley. He enjoyed this site so much that he had a seat built on this hill so he could spend as much time as he liked for contemplating and composing. It was toward the end of October that the historian was able to finish the mental composition of the final chapter while riding his horse through the woods. William managed to complete all of his writing on November 7, 1846, but the hurried pace had done considerable harm to his health, especially his delicate vision.

Another Bestseller

Prior to the publication of *History of the Conquest of Peru* there occurred an interesting encounter, one which was reminiscent of the time when William Prescott had sought approval from Washington Irving to continue his work on *History of the Conquest of Mexico*. John Lothrop Motley, a young scholar who would emerge as a prominent historian in his own right, was beginning work on a history of the Dutch Republic when he learned that Prescott had future plans of writing a biography of Philip II, a topic that covered a portion of the same ground.

Fearing to proceed without letting Prescott know of his intentions, Motley paid a visit to the distinguished historian. Twelve years later, shortly after learning of Prescott's passing, Motley wrote a letter to his friend William Amory, who was Prescott's brother-in-law, about this encounter: "I remember the interview as if it had taken place yesterday. It was in his father's house, in his own library, looking on the garden. House and garden, honored father and illustrious son,—alas! All numbered with the things that were! He assured me that he had not the slightest objection whatever to my plan, that he wished me every success, and that, if there were any books in his library bearing on my subject that I liked to use, they were entirely at my service."[52]

Motley was greatly moved by Prescott's approval and support of his project: "Had the result of that interview been different—had he distinctly stated, or even vaguely hinted, that it would be as well if I should select some other topic, or had he only sprinkled me with the cold water of conventional and commonplace encouragement,—I should have gone from him with a chill upon my mind, and, no doubt, have laid down the pen at once; for, as I have already said, it was not that I cared about writing a history, but that I have felt an inevitable impulse to write *one particular his-*

tory."⁵³ John Lothrop Motley's *The Rise of the Dutch Republic* was published in 1856.

In a contract that was signed on December 18, 1846, Harper & Brothers once again agreed to serve as William Prescott's publisher. The arrangement called for 7500 copies of *History of the Conquest of Peru* to be printed by Harpers, for which the historian was to receive $1 per copy. Colonel Aspinwall again acted as his overseas agent for negotiating a suitable deal with a British publisher. An accord was once again reached with Richard Bentley, who agreed to pay 800 pounds, the equivalent of $4000, for the British copyright. The contract that was signed on January 19, 1847, was very similar to the previous arrangement for the London publication of *History of the Conquest of Mexico*.

The Boston historian made several emendations to his work, some of which were constructive suggestions provided by his friend Charles Folsom, before sending the proofs to the Cambridge printers. Thirty-four boxes of stereotype plates were sent to Harpers at New York City, which included plates for the maps and illustrations that were to accompany the text. Prescott held back two boxes of plates to ensure that the American edition was not released before the agreed upon date for publication of the British edition. William dispatched a corrected manuscript to Colonel Aspinwall by way of a diplomatic pouch.

After having completed all that was required for the midyear publication of *History of the Conquest of Peru*, both at home and abroad, Prescott decided to reward himself by taking another trip to New York City. He traveled in the company of his daughter Lizzie and her good friend Cora Lyman. For the nearly-19-year-old Elizabeth this visit was to serve as her formal introduction to society. William and his young female companions would attend a great number of dinners, parties, and balls during their whirlwind tour of social engagements. The historian managed to find the time to journey to Tarrytown, New York, to visit Washington Irving at his Sunnyside residence located at a scenic spot overlooking the North River. Irving had recently returned from service as minister to Spain.

An additional trip was taken by Prescott in June of 1846 to Albany to attend the wedding of his friend Nathaniel Thayer to Miss Van Rensselaer. William traveled in the company of his daughter Elizabeth and son William Amory Prescott. The three made their way by boat down the North River, a section of the Hudson, which passed along the scenic views of the Catskills and West Point. Prescott and his children arrived at their summer residence in Nahant on the 25th of June.

In the spring of 1847, George Ware, who had returned to serve as Prescott's secretary in the autumn of 1846, tendered his resignation. Ware recommended Robert Carter as his replacement. The 28-year-old Irish-American came with excellent references: he had been a writer for the *Pioneer*, a short-lived periodical, and had worked at several Boston publishing firms. Prescott hired Carter and paid for a month-long course which would instruct him in the proper pronunciation of Spanish. Robert Carter began his duties as the historian's new secretary in May of 1847, a service for which he received an annual salary of $400 as well as daily meals. As for George Ware, who had first worked for the historian during the period of 1840 to 1842, the former secretary suffered an untimely death in 1849.

The English edition of *History of the Conquest of Peru* was released on May 17, 1847, and the American printing was made available to the public on June 22, 1847. The title page read:

History
of the
Conquest of Peru,
With A Preliminary View
of
The Civilization of the Incas

Prescott secretly feared that this historical account did not rise to the caliber realized in his two previous works. He worried that the subject of this conquest was not nearly as interesting as that of Mexico and that this cast of conquistadors were not worthy of comparison to Hernán Cortés and the brave lot who faithfully followed him. Of even greater concern to the writer was that he had completed this work too quickly and that critics would surely pick up on this fact to point out any errors.

Once again, Prescott's concerns about his book were laid to rest after numerous critics, both at home and abroad, heaped praise on his new book. This outpouring of critical acclaim was exceeded by overwhelming public demand; the American edition sold 5000 copies in the first five months of its release, and in England 2500 copies sold during the same period. His new work was soon translated into French, German, Spanish, and Dutch. It went on to amass combined sales totals of 16,965 for the American and English editions by January 1, 1860.

In his preface to *History of the Conquest of Peru*, Prescott again felt the need to address the inaccurate reports about his visual impairment: "Before closing these remarks, I may be permitted to add a few of a personal nature. In several foreign notices of my writings, the author has been said to be blind; and more than once I have had the credit of having lost my sight in the composition of my first history. When I have met with such erroneous accounts, I have hastened to correct them. But the present occasion affords me the best means of doing so; and I am the more desirous of this, as I fear some of my own remarks, in the Prefaces of my former histories, have led to the mistake."[54]

More literary and academic honors were bestowed upon William Prescott; In 1846 he was named a member of the New Jersey Historical Society. In 1847, following the success of *History of the Conquest of Peru*, Prescott was elected to the Royal English Society of Literature, and he received an invitation to join the Royal Society of Antiquaries, the latter an honor never before extended to an American. He was also named a member of the New England Historic—Genealogical Society.

"Now that I have discharged Peru," William wrote to Lady Lyell in 1847, "I feel like an ordinary tar whose ship is laid up in ordinary. But time is a bitter drug, and I feel I shall soon be afloat again, probably on board the good ship 'Philip the Second,' of which you have heard me speak, though I am but a blind pilot, and have not half an eye to steer with."[55]

9

Philip II

> *It is no easy matter to extract a probability from many improbabilities.*[1]

Failing Health

Prescott chose to delay the start of his next project, which was slated to be a biography of Philip II, King of Spain. His hesitation was partly in response to the need to take a well deserved break, but mostly because of concerns regarding the deteriorating condition of his vision. At this point, William could read with his good eye for no more than an hour a day, which he divided into two equal sessions, with a very long interval between each use. The frustrated historian wrote, "Here I am with the richest collection that ever fell to a history-monger, scarce old books and manuscripts without end, all lying around me, and alas! Without an eye to look at the title pages. The physicians agree that if I would save it for the vulgar purpose of life, I must wholly abstain from using it in books. So I do nothing but lounge about like any loafer. I may come to it, but I can't make up my mind yet to sit in my un-easy chair, and be read to in outlandish gibberish at the rate of an octavo a week. Were I well entered, I could go on, I suppose. But I can't make up my mind to undertake such a huge subject as Philip II blindfold."[2]

Following a first consultation with an oculist who was visiting Boston, William Prescott had renewed hope that his condition might improve. The doctor determined that a small deposit of lymph was obscuring his retina and that there were signs of amaurosis, a decaying of the nerve. The oculist felt that relief, to an uncertain degree, could be achieved with the proper treatment. Prescott, however, had his doubts. He knew full well that the strain of one eye having to do the work of two over a period of 34 years had done irreparable damage to his good eye. He consulted with prominent physicians, none of whom were oculists, about his disorder and all reached the same conclusion that Prescott had made on his own; he would have to discontinue the use of his good eye for reading in order to avoid any further damage to his vision. This was a difficult decision but Prescott feared becoming totally blind, a condition he felt would place a far too heavy burden on his family and friends.

It was during this troubling period that William Prescott, in accordance with his doctor's recommendation, was compelled to give up horse riding. He substituted these solitary morning outings with long walks or carriage rides. Two glasses of sherry and a Havana cigar would continue to serve as part of William's daily routine for relaxing. Prescott was always well stocked with Havana cigars, which were generously supplied by his Cuban admirers. A note in his literary memorandum dated November 25, 1849, sums up his positive attitude toward coping with his problems: "whining about my troubles unmans me, and is of itself the worst augury. Making light of these—quiet energy, justifiable self-reliance, cheerful views of life are the best guarantees of success as I have hitherto succeeded. I will."[3]

While William had assumed the role as the head of the family after the passing of his father, the duties of the household, however, remained in the capable hands of his dear mother. On September 24, 1847, the 80-year-old Catherine Prescott submitted a letter addressed to both Susan and William in which she formally notified them of her immediate resignation as head of the Beacon Street household. She validated this decision by stating, "It is proper, my dear son, that your wife should be the mistress of your family. Your children should consider her the head to guide and direct in every thing."[4] Not wishing to be a burden to anyone, Catherine insisted that she would pay her board and any medical expenses. William had been married for 27 years by the time his mother decided that his wife should be mistress of the house.

Despite having signed a two year contract to serve as Prescott's secretary, Robert Carter tendered his resignation a mere nine months after being hired. Mr. Carter claimed that the main reason for quitting was that his eyesight had begun to suffer terribly from the lengthy readings he was required to perform in such a dimly lit room. He also had probably grown weary of the routine, which required him to work six days a week with each day split into two shifts. Carter recommended John Foster Kirk as his replacement. Prescott agreed with the choice and on June 9, 1848, Kirk signed a five-year contract as his new secretary.

In March of 1848, William temporarily strayed from his next historical project to write a memoir of John Pickering, a noted scholar who was also a good friend. The Massachusetts Historical Society had commissioned him to write this memoir: "It will not be long," he wrote of this task, "but, long or short, it will be a labor of love; for there is no man whom I honored more.... He was a true and kind friend to me; and, from the first moment of my entering on my historic career down to the close of his life, he watched over my literary attempts with the deepest interest. It will be a sad pleasure for me to pay an honest tribute to the good man's worth."[5] This touching *Memoir of the Honorable John Pickering L.L.D.*, which Prescott completed before the end of the year, was the first and only time he did not compose a published work on his noctograph. Instead, he dictated the entire piece to his secretary, a process which he felt very uncomfortable doing. However, William always felt comfortable dictating personal letters to his secretary.

In 1848, William was elated to learn that he was the recipient of an honorary Doctor of Laws degree from Columbian College in Washington, D.C. Prescott also devoted a portion of his time during the spring of 1848 to review and offer opinions on George Ticknor's manuscript *History of Spanish Literature* before it went to press. In a letter to Pascual de Gayangos, Prescott wrote, "I have just finished the perusal of Ticknor's MS. It will make three stout octavos. It is a most elaborate and scholar like production; minutely entering into hidden recesses of the Castilian literature; boldly grappling with the most doubtful topics, and displaying an accurate map of the whole country, in which every writer of any note has his proper place, and is subjected to a critical analysis. I am sure it will be read by the Spaniards with the greatest interest. It will, I do not hesitate to say, be *the work* to which the student must hereafter resort for the fullest development of the treasures & resources of a literature so imperfectly comprehended by foreigners."[6] This epic three-volume study of Spanish literature, which took the Boston scholar two decades to complete, was published in 1849. John Murray served as the London publisher of Ticknor's book. Pascual de Gayangos would provide necessary emendations and helpful notes to the Spanish translation of Ticknor's *History of Spanish Literature.*

Prescott took a nearly-six-month-long break before beginning work on *Philip the Second*, a book he had contemplated writing as far back as 1833. He listened intently to lengthy readings of William Robertson's *Charles the Fifth*, Robert Watson's *Philip the Second*, Leopold von Ranke's *Popes*, and chapters of Samuel Astley Dunham's *Spain and Portugal* that were related to this specific time frame. He debated for the longest time as to whether he should style this work in the confined manner of a memoir or as a much broader historical account.

Prescott briefly considered putting his *Philip the Second* on hold following an intriguing proposal put forth in a letter from Charles King, a New York lawyer, who urged him to consider writing an account of the recent conquest of Mexico by General Winfield Scott. King made it clear that General Scott, who had plans to run for president, was willing to provide him with all of his personal papers for this project. Taking a page from Prescott's *History of the Conquest of Mexico*, General Scott landed his troops at Vera Cruz and followed a near identical route taken by Hernán Cortés and his band of conquistadors in order to defeat the Mexican army commanded by General López de Santa Anna. Nevertheless, William politely declined this offer after deciding that his efforts would be better served pursuing the subject he had already begun. The historian noted in his journal: "The theme would be taking; but I had rather not meddle with heroes who have not been underground two centuries at least."[7]

Another Difficult Start

Once again, Prescott issued requests to a number of friends and acquaintances abroad to seek out documents and books relating to the subject he proposed to write about, which this time was an account of the lengthy reign of Spain's Philip II. These investigations were conducted in a number of public and private libraries located in Paris, London, and Madrid. The collection of these research materials would prove more difficult than Prescott ever envisioned. To begin with, the Boston historian had lost the valuable assistance of Arthur Middleton, who was no longer associated with the Spanish legation. These difficulties were compounded when Dr. Friederich Wilhelm Lembke, his principal contact at Madrid, had unexpectedly worn out his welcome with the Spanish government. The German scholar was suspected of leaking confidential material and was accordingly instructed to leave the country at once. Dr. Lembke took up residence in Paris where he was permitted to peruse and copy relevant material discovered in the collections of M. Mignet and M. Ternaux-Compans. Regrettably, Friederich Lembke remained in Paris for only a few months.

Don Pascual de Gayangos, the Spanish scholar and avid supporter of

Prescott's work, admirably filled the void caused by Dr. Lembke's departure. While In London, Don Pascual was granted access to the numerous documents stored in the archives of the British Museum and the State-Paper Office, from which he arranged for 1800 relevant pages of manuscripts to be copied for Prescott's benefit. Sadly, Pascual Gayangos found the State-Paper Office to be an utterly disorganized mess, a disturbing find which he characterized as "a disgrace."

Pascual de Gayangos also obtained for William Prescott a number of valuable papers that he had been permitted to copy from the vast private collection of Sir Thomas J. Phillips, in Worcestershire. Gayangos later traveled to Brussels armed with letters of permission from Sylvain Van de Weyer, Minister of Belgium in London, to make copies of any papers in the archives he felt might be useful to the Boston historian. The Spanish scholar and Orientalist then made his way to Paris, where, with the help of the French historian François M. Mignet, he discovered additional papers of importance at the Royal Library of Paris as well as the Archives of the Kingdom, in the Hôtel Soubise, which were copied for the benefit of his American friend. Don Gayangos even loaned the Boston historian a number of books and manuscripts from his personal library, many of which were quite rare. By 1842, a considerable amount of pertinent papers, manuscripts, and books had been collected and forwarded to William Prescott.

In 1842, Don Pascual de Gayangos returned to Spain where, towards the end of the year, he was appointed Professor of Arabic Literature at the University of Madrid. There he was able to use both his position and the well-respected name of William Prescott to gain access to germane material stored in the National Library, the Archives of Simancas, and a number of personal libraries belonging to some of Spain's most illustrious families. Initially, Gayangos encountered difficulties trying to gather documents related to Philip II. There were a few authorities who feared that these manuscripts might be used to assail the character of the monarch and impugn the deeds of the Spanish Crown. Once these suspicions were allayed, Don Pascual was permitted in 1844 to spend two months at the archives in Simancas, where he located a treasure trove of beneficial material that was transcribed for the Boston historian's research. The scholar also perused the family archives of the Marquis of Santa Cruz and Medina Sidonia, both of which yielded a vast amount of useful information.

Don Gayangos wrote of the trouble he encountered buying books in Spain, "You cannot conceive of the difficulty of collecting books on any given subject, especially if they are rather rare. The booksellers here publish no catalogue of their books, nor do they even have private lists of what they own, trusting for the most part to their memories. If you add that they are totally ignorant of bibliography, you may imagine that it may be a matter of eight or ten years before one can meet with some essential book."[8] The Spanish scholar also conducted extensive research for George Ticknor. Don Gayangos often combined shipments of books and manuscripts for Prescott and Ticknor, a shipping method approved by both American authors. Ticknor and Prescott would share equally in the shipping costs for books sent by Pascual de Gayangos. Letters, manuscripts, and books crossed the Atlantic by either sail or steam ships.

In the preface to *Philip the Second*, William paid tribute to the untiring effort that Don Pascual de Gayangos exhibited on his behalf: "This eminent scholar was admirably qualified for the task which he so kindly undertook; since, with a remarkable facility—such as long practice only can give—in deciphering the mysterious handwritings of the sixteenth century, he combined such a thorough acquaintance with the history of his country as enabled him to detect, amidst the ocean of manuscripts which he inspected, such portions as were essential to my purpose."[9]

Prescott also received valuable assistance on Spanish history from his good friend and distinguished statesman Edward Everett, Dr. Ferdinand Wolf of Vienna, as well as Alexander Humboldt and Leopold von Ranke of Berlin. These influential gentlemen helped to provide him with highly beneficial materials stored in the libraries and public offices located in Tuscany, Austria, Prussia, and Gotha.

William found Leopold von Ranke's *The Ottoman and Spanish Empires in the Sixteenth and Seventeenth Centuries* a useful guide for his account of the reign of Philip II. The historian stated, "His book contains inestimable materials for a more minute and expanded history." He added, "It is a sort of skeleton—this bone-work of the monarchy. It must be studied."[10] William heeded his own advice by selecting relevant portions of the German historian's work, which was compiled into nearly 200 pages and reprinted in typeface large enough for him to read and review.

By mid 1848, Prescott had received from his foreign correspondents 370 volumes pertaining to the life and times of the Spanish monarch Phillip the Second. As for the hand copied manuscripts he had received, William had all of them handsomely bound into 38 large folios. These works occupied a special spot in his library, a collection which he fondly referred to as his *Seraglio*. An outline of *History of the Reign of Philip the Second, King of Spain* was firmly in place by February of 1849, and in late July of that year he was ready to attempt a synthesis of his assembled notes to begin writing the first chapter.

The historic events that William Prescott sought to focus on to enrich his *History of the Reign of Phillip the Second* included Spain's war with France, the infamous Spanish Inquisition, the bitter conflicts with the Turks and the epic Battle of Lepanto, the rebellion of the Moriscos, the subjugation of neighboring Portugal, the disastrous defeat of the Spanish Armada, and the War of the Netherlands.

Though a fervent patriot and conservative Whig by conviction, William Prescott generally shied away from the politics of the day, a profession which he considered a "dirty trade." In a letter dated September 15, 1844, to Angel Calderón de la Barca, the Boston historian noted, "A Conservative of our day is as much of a Liberal in his politics as a Democrat of the time of Jefferson, while a Democrat of the present day—Lord help us!"[11]

William's primary political interests were those related to the specific period of history he was currently researching: "I belong to the sixteenth century," William declared, "and am quite out of place when I sleep elsewhere." Another example of his lack of interest in such matters is noted in a letter dated November 30, 1844, to Lord Morpeth: "I take refuge from these political squabbles among the Andes, where I am trying to dig out a few grains of Peruvian gold."[12]

One of the few times that William Prescott felt compelled to embroil himself in a political affair occurred in July of 1849, a circumstance which pertained to a matter involving another author. The Boston historian voiced his strong objection to the politically motivated removal of Nathaniel Hawthorne, a Democrat, from his post at the port of Salem. He wrote to Daniel Webster, who was currently serving as a senator from Massachusetts, "Many respectable Whigs here do not see any good grounds for the removal.... Will you allow me, therefore, to request your interest in his behalf?"[13]

Daniel Webster handed William Prescott's letter to Secretary of the Treasury William M. Meredith along with his own notation:

> This letter is from Mr. Prescott, the Historian; a man, not more distinguished for learning and ability as a writer, than for amiable manner, generous affections, true friendships—in fact, "For every virtue under Heaven." I hope you know him.
> I suppose it will be best to leave Mr. Hawthorne where he is, for the present.[14]

In spite of the best efforts of William Prescott and a number of other prominent citizens of Boston and Salem, the dismissal of Nathaniel Hawthorne was never rescinded. Shortly thereafter the struggling author lost his dear mother. A number of admirers took up a collection for Hawthorne; a compassionate Prescott made a generous donation to this worthy cause. Fortunately for Hawthorne, his termination turned out to be a blessing in disguise. The despondent writer buried his sorrows in writing *The Scarlet Letter*, a masterly work which brought him the fame and fortune he so greatly deserved.

Prescott was quite generous with donations to charities for the poor and was always willing to lend a helping hand to those in need without ever expecting anything in return. Mr. Robert Carter, who served as his secretary during the period of 1847 to 1848, recalled that on one particular day he explained to his boss that the reason he was late to work was because he had encountered an old friend named Michael Sullivan, who had recently lost his job. Because of this turn of events, Mr. Sullivan and his family was now forced to occupy a building which had very little coal to provide much needed warmth during the frigid winter season. After hearing this tale of woe, Prescott immediately arranged for a ton of coal to be delivered to their building and also provided some money for the family to live on. Every day the historian would inquire about the condition of Michael Sullivan and his family. These inquiries ended once Robert Carter informed him that Mr. Sullivan had found employment and the family was doing well. The subject was never again mentioned. The benevolent William Prescott regularly contributed one tenth of his annual income to charities, a tithing instilled by his religious convictions.

A Murder in Harvard

On Friday November 23, 1849, right around noontime, the highly respected and affluent Dr. George Parkman left his house on Walnut Street, situated in the prestigious Beacon Hill district, to attend a hastily scheduled appointment with Dr. John White Webster at Harvard's Massachusetts Medical College, located on North Grove Street. Webster and Parkman had known one another for a very long time. This spur of the moment meeting had been called to resolve an outstanding debt that Webster owed to Parkman. It was the last time that the 59-year-old George Parkman was ever seen in public.

Elizabeth Parkman became concerned when her husband failed to show for their two o'clock dinner, for this was the first time in 33 years of marriage that he had failed to join her for a meal without giving prior notice. Two days after George Parkman had gone missing, troubled members of his family confronted John Webster about their hastily scheduled meeting. Dr. Webster claimed that he had paid George Parkman the nearly $500 he owed him when they briefly met in his office at around half past one o'clock, after which Dr. Parkman departed, but not before stating that he was on his way to see the city clerk to record that this monetary obligation had been paid in full. Dr. Webster, however, seemed more concerned about whether or not his outstanding debt had been cleared than he was about what might have happened to the gentleman who had lent him the money.

With the whereabouts of George Parkman still in question, Robert G. Shaw posted a $3000 reward for any information that would lead to finding his missing brother-in-law alive. Later, when it was feared that Dr. Parkman was very likely dead, an additional $1000 reward was offered for any news that would lead to the recovery of the missing doctor's body. Search parties were quickly formed by Francis Tukey, the City Marshal of Boston, whose men spent much of their time following up a number of unsubstantiated sightings of George Parkman. Various sections of the river and harbor were even dredged in an attempt to locate Dr. Parkman's body. The sudden and mysterious disappearance of George Parkman quickly became the talk of all Boston.

John Webster, a professor of chemistry at Harvard College for 25 years, had very close ties to the Prescott family; his wife was Harriet Hickling, the half-sister of Catherine Prescott—the mother of William Hickling Prescott. She was the same Harriet Hickling who showered William Prescott with attention and kindness during his visit to St. Michaels. John had courted and married Harriet during his year-long visit to the Azores to collect mineral specimens that he proposed to write about in an upcoming published book on geology. The wedding ceremony took place at the home of Webster's new father-in-law, which was the same house where the young and ailing Prescott had stayed while visiting his maternal grandfather.

Upon his return to Boston, Dr. George Parkman would help the newly-married John Webster secure a teaching post at Harvard. The Reverend Francis Parkman, the brother of George Parkman, would baptize John and Harriet Webster's four daughters, as well as a son who died very young. The minister would later perform the wedding service for the marriage of Sarah, the Webster's oldest daughter, to Charles Dabney.

Professor Webster had long enjoyed a lavish lifestyle that he simply could not afford on his meager $1200 annual salary. Webster had exhausted the more than $50,000 he inherited after the death of his father, a large sum of money which was mostly spent furnishing and maintaining an elegant and expensive mansion that was specially constructed in Cambridge. The remainder was squandered on entertaining, travels abroad, and making sure that his wife and children enjoyed all the trappings of wealth. Once the funds dried up, the Websters were compelled to move to a modest house in Cambridge that they leased from Jonas Wyeth. To keep himself afloat, Webster had to borrow money from a number of Boston socialites, a list that included Catherine G. Prescott, William H. Prescott, Robert Gould Shaw, and George Parkman.

Over time, Dr. Webster realized just how difficult it was to keep up with even the interest payments on his borrowings, and eventually the professor found himself in such dire financial straits that he had to offer his furniture as collateral in order to secure new loans to keep himself afloat. In fact, it was this sort of mortgage issue that served as a point of contention between Dr. Webster and Dr. Parkman. John Webster had recently pledged his mineral cabinet as collateral for a loan from Mr. Robert Shaw, an asset that George Parkman viewed as having already been used to secure a loan he had made to the Harvard instructor. It was at this point that George Parkman decided that he needed to pay a visit to John Webster.

Professor Webster owed the Prescott family a total of $437.50, which amounted to more than a third of his annual income. But the Boston police were primarily interested in his over due debt in the amount of $483.64 to Dr. George Parkman, especially after learning that the missing physician had gone to Harvard to confront the professor about his attempt to secure a loan from another lender with collateral he had already pledged to him. William Prescott knew full well that Webster owed Parkman a considerable sum of money and privately feared that a demand for payment may have led to raised voices, which easily could have escalated into a violent encounter. Nearly everyone who knew George Parkman, including Prescott, were aware of the fact that he had a volatile temper.

On the 27th of November, Ephraim Littlefield, the college janitor, who harbored his own suspicions about John Webster, spied on the activities of the Harvard professor of chemistry by peering from under the door of an adjoining room. From this position, Littlefield quietly watched as the professor made a total of eight trips between the furnace and the fuel closet. The furnace burned so hot that the janitor could feel the heat on the wall from where he was observing. Littlefield patiently waited for Professor Webster to leave so that he could search the room. The janitor noticed that the recently filled kindling barrels were almost empty and saw unusual spots on the floor, which he discovered to have a peculiar acidic aroma and taste.

On Thanksgiving Day, Ephraim Littlefield took it upon himself to investigate further. He used a hammer, chisel, and a borrowed crowbar to break through a brick wall that led to a vault directly beneath Professor Webster's coal pen. After he had successfully tunneled into the vault, the college janitor soon found that he was wholly unprepared for the grisly sight of human remains he was about to uncover; within the vault he found a "man's pelvis, a thigh from hip to knee, and the lower part of a leg."[15] Littlefield also discovered a significant amount of blood mixed in with the dirt. The shocked janitor rushed to find his wife to inform her of his gruesome discovery. Dr. Bigelow, a Harvard professor, was immediately notified, after which Marshal Tukey was quickly summoned.

The human remains were carefully removed from the vault so that they could be thoroughly examined by the coroner. When questioned about these findings, Professor Webster claimed he knew nothing about these bones, and then quickly attempted to shift the blame to Littlefield by pointing out that the janitor was the only other person who had full access to his private work area. A further search of the scene led to the discovery of a chest which emitted a powerful and disgusting stench. Stored inside was a torso missing its head and both arms. It was also noticed that there had been an unsuccessful attempt to burn the torso. The investigators determined that the head had been sawed off below the Adam's apple, a logical conclusion after the offending saw was found nearby. The heart and other vital organs had been removed and replaced with a severed leg of the victim.

Mrs. Parkman was called in to examine the torso after the coroner, Jabez Pratt, determined that the discovered remains did not belong to any discarded cadaver used by the school for medical dissections. She was able to identify some distinguishing marks which left little doubt that the remains were those of her dear husband. Further investigation led to the discovery of blood stained clothes that belonged to the chemistry professor. The newly-discovered and incriminating physical evidence led to the immediate arrest of Professor John Webster.

In a letter dated December 2, 1849, to his son Will, who was traveling abroad, William Prescott stated, "You have most probably learnt, by rumor at least, of the mysterious disappearance of Dr. George Parkman—the father of your late traveling companion. The last accounts of him were of an appointment with Dr. Webster at the Medical College in Boston. This was between one and two, on Friday the 23rd of November—ten days since. A large reward was offered for his discovery, by Mr. Shaw, but ineffectually till, day before yesterday, a small portion of a dead body was found in a vault of the College, which had connection only with Dr. Webster's laboratory. This and some other suspicious circumstances led to Dr. Webster's arrest as the probable murderer! This occurred on Friday evening, the 30th of November. Some bones of the head, &c. were also found in the furnace, nearly destroyed by fire. Since then a still larger fragment of the body, on which some wounds appear, has been discovered in the laboratory, covered up with tan and with minerals in a box."[16]

Prescott also made mention of the demeanor of the incarcerated Professor Webster and his distraught family: "I have seen him twice in prison—the first time, much overcome; the second, tranquil—protesting his innocence. I was today at Cambridge with his distressed family—distressed, indeed, though firmly believing his innocence—their only comfort. Their friends are all most ready to show their sympathy. They have great need of it"[17] Because of his close and recent association with George Parkman, Jr., who was Dr. Parkman's son, the circumstances surrounding this curious case were of particular interest to William Gardiner Prescott.

The Prescott family canceled all of their social engagements during this unsettling period. William attempted to return to work on *History of the Reign of Philip the Second, King of Spain*, but found it very difficult to concentrate on anything other than the events surrounding this bizarre murder case. The unseemly revelations of this investigation were particularly stressful for Professor Webster's wife and four daughters; Catherine, Harriet, Marianne, and Sarah. Catherine Webster had been named after her aunt Catherine G. Prescott. Meanwhile, the coroner's report confirmed to the grand jury that there was sufficient evidence to charge Dr. John Webster with murder. The Harvard chemistry professor would remain confined to his jail cell for the duration of the legal proceedings.

Professor Webster's trial, which was to gain both national and international attention, began on March 19, 1850, and lasted for 12 days. Franklin Dexter, a distinguished lawyer who had an aversion to handling murder cases, agreed to be Webster's acting attorney until another could be hired. Dexter had made it very clear to all that he was not interested in serving as Webster's trial lawyer. William Prescott met with Franklin Dexter, his brother-in-law, to discuss whether or not there was a case against Webster. Dexter told Prescott that he did not believe Professor Webster would be found guilty, but cautioned that he had not yet seen the findings of the coroner's jury. They also discussed who might be a good choice to defend John Webster. The name of Edward Sohier was mentioned as a possible candidate.

The acclaimed Daniel Webster, who was not related to the defendant, was asked to serve as Professor Webster's defense lawyer, but he respectfully declined. William Prescott volunteered to pay the fees for Pliny Merrick and Edward D. Sohier, the two lawyers who would finally agree to defend John Webster. Mr. Merrick was a classmate at Harvard and Mr. Sohier was Susan Prescott's brother-in-law. Judge Lemuel Shaw presided over the trial and a courtroom which was filled to capacity by onlookers who fought over a spot to hear the lurid details of the case involving members of Boston's gentry. Spectators admitted to the gallery were permitted to watch the trial for only ten minutes, after which they were ushered out so another group could have a chance to view the proceedings. An estimated 60,000 people managed to catch a glimpse of the trial from the courtroom and gallery over this 12-day period. Conspicuously absent from the trial was Professor Webster's wife, who was too distressed to view the proceedings.

Clouds of suspicion began to swirl around Ephraim Littlefield after it became public knowledge that he had been paid to dig up corpses for Harvard's medical studies, a requisite service which the janitor was paid $25 for each useable cadaver he furnished for the school. Jared Sparks, President of Harvard and a friend of William Prescott, testified as a character witness for the defense. However, damning evidence against Professor John Webster was provided by Dr. Nathan Keep, George Parkman's dentist, who was able to identify the recovered set of false teeth as the dentures he had specially fitted for Dr. Parkman.

William Appleton, Prescott's neighbor. was one of the many Boston citizens who regularly attended the trial. After the second day of the judicial proceedings, the optimistic Appleton noted in his diary, "They will not convict him I think; so it looks now." However, he would soon have to revise his opinion: "The trial of Dr. Webster brought to a close; after hearing the Charge of the Judge, I went to prepare Mrs. Prescott for the news of the sad event."[18] The jury reached a unanimous verdict of guilty the very afternoon that the lawyer's completed their closing arguments. Professor Webster was sentenced to hang for the murder of Dr. George Parkman. After the guilty verdict was rendered, Catherine Prescott rode in a carriage to the Webster house at Garden Street to console her distraught half-sister.

Even after he had been found guilty of murder, William Prescott would continue to visit Dr. Webster in his jail cell. They discussed a variety of topics, including their fond remembrances of time spent in the Azores. Knowing that the food served at the jail was of a questionable quality, the historian arranged for more suitable meals to be delivered to John Webster. At his last meeting with Dr. Webster, Prescott informed him that he was leaving on the 22nd of May for a visit to England and would not return until autumn. Both understood that this was to be the very last time they would see one another.

After all of his appeals were denied, Professor Webster decided to admit to killing Dr. George Parkman, emphasizing in his written statement that the murder was not premeditated. He confessed that he picked up a stick and beat George Parkman to death after the physician kept demanding immediate payment of the debt, a sum which he could not pay. Webster had hoped that this confession would spare him from being executed, but it was to no avail. Meanwhile, Mrs. Webster would plead for clemency from the governor, but her request was denied. On August 30, 1850, John Webster swung from the gallows until he was pronounced dead. Fearing that his gravesite would become a target for grave robbers, John Webster's body was interred in an undisclosed plot in the cemetery at Copp's Hill, which brought a sense of closure to this scandalous affair. Edward Everett, the former editor of the North American Review, distinguished statesman, and president of Harvard University, would refer to the murder of Dr. George Parkman as "the most disgraceful event in our domestic history."[19]

A Need to Get Away

A number of health issues were suddenly starting to interfere with Prescott's ability to concentrate on his work. His sensitive eyes continued to worsen, and soon he was plagued by uncomfortable bouts of dyspepsia. William was also bothered by complications of the urethra, which made it extremely painful for him to write in a sitting position, a disability he managed to work around by writing on his knees. He also noticed a slightly diminished capacity for memorization and that his hearing was starting to fail him. In February 1850 he noted: "Increasing interest in the work is hardly to be expected, considering it has to depend so much on the ear. As I shall have to depend more and more on this one of my senses, as I grow older, it is to be hoped that Providence will spare me my hearing. It would be a fearful thing to doubt it."[20]

Wishing to take his mind off his mounting health concerns and the disturbing events surrounding the murder trial of the convicted Dr. John Webster, Prescott decided to take another trip to Washington D. C. He left Boston on the eighth of April in the company of his youngest son, William Amory Prescott, who was now 19 years old, and his nearly-21-year-old daughter Elizabeth. The historian was also accompanied by Mrs.

Charles Amory, Mrs. Howland Shaw, and his brother-in-law, Mr. William Amory. As usual, Susan Prescott, who had no interest in such adventures, remained at home.

On their first night in the nation's capital the tourists from Boston were welcome guests at the residence of Sir Henry Bulwer, the British ambassador to the United States. This was followed by dinner invitations from Daniel Webster and numerous other friends and admirers of the historian. Finding that he sorely missed the comforts of home, William decided to make this a brief visit. His last dinner at the nation's capital was as a guest at the White House. Zachary Taylor was the third president that William Prescott had the honor of dining with; the previous two being John Quincy Adams and James Polk. On the return trip, William visited New York City for four days, during which time he dined with George Bancroft, who had recently returned from England. He also had an opportunity to break bread with Washington Irving.

William Prescott returned to Boston on the 24th of April feeling physically rejuvenated, but his mind was still clouded with melancholy thoughts. He decided, after much reflection on the matter, that a lengthy visit to England—a trip he had long wished to undertake—would help improve his spirits. Such a visit had been urged by Richard Bentley and motivated by the historian's desire to meet up with his oldest son, William Gardiner Prescott, who was currently traveling in Europe. Prescott thought that it was a good idea that his son should "kick up his heels" before settling into his intended field of law and therefore financed his journey to the Old World.

The Boston historian journeyed to New York where, on May 22, 1850, he boarded the British ship *Niagara* for a voyage to England. William was accompanied by John Foster Kirk, his devoted secretary, and armed with letters of introduction to Thomas MacCaulay, Lord Ashburton, Lord John Russell, and the Duke of Northumberland. These letters of introduction were supplied by his good friends Edward Everett and George Bancroft.

William was quickly reminded of why he had been so hesitant to make another voyage across the Atlantic. He complained of suffering so terribly from sea sickness that he was unable to eat many of the foods he normally enjoyed, and was compelled to chew chamomile to help combat his symptoms of nausea. In a letter to his wife, the historian declared, "Nothing can redeem the utter wretchedness of a sea life—and never will I again put my foot in a steamer, except for Yankee land, and, if I were not ashamed, should reembark in the Saturday steamer from Liverpool, and settle the wager in another fortnight."[21]

The *Niagara* docked at Liverpool shortly after midnight on June 3, 1850. William was met by Alexander Smith, an old friend he had not seen in 33 years. While at Liverpool he also met Sir Charles Lyell, the eminent Scottish geologist, and his lovely wife, Lady Mary Lyell, both of whom he had become acquainted with during their visit to America. Prescott stayed at Alexander Smith's home for two days before boarding a train headed to London. He was accompanied on this journey by Mr. and Mrs. Charles Lyell. The train reached the city in the afternoon, after which Prescott and his traveling companions settled into their respective apartments at Mivart's Hotel, located along Brook Street and very near Grosvenor Square. Abbott Lawrence, a good friend and the current American minister at the Court of St. James, procured for William the services of a manservant named Penn, and a brougham complete with horses for his transportation needs. The minister was the father of James Lawrence, a young man who would later wed William's daughter Elizabeth.

Prescott's arrival at London had been greatly anticipated. Mr. Lawrence invited William to a diplomatic dinner he was hosting that very evening, which was intended to be his formal introduction to London society. Still weary from his long journey, the historian politely declined this dinner invitation. However, he did feel strong enough to have tea with Lady Lyell, and afterwards accompanied her to the evening party at the minister's residence, a gala event which followed the dinner he had earlier turned down. Still feeling exhausted, William kept his visit brief. But he did stay long enough to make several interesting contacts, which soon led to invitations from a number of prominent members of the British upper class.

While in England, Prescott met two future prime ministers of the United Kingdom, Benjamin Disraeli and William Gladstone. He wrote of his awkward introduction to Disraeli at a London reception: "Pray," said he, "are you related to the great American author—the author of the Spanish Histories? I squeezed his arm, telling him that I could not answer for the greatness, but I was the man himself; and though at first he was a little confused—as one or two near smiled at the blunder—we had a merry chat."[22]

William also had an opportunity to make the acquaintance of John Gibson Lockhart, the son-in-law and biographer of Sir Walter Scott who was one of the historian's favorite authors. Prescott also met the 87-year-old poet Samuel Rogers, and was introduced to the historian Archibald Alison. He also had the pleasure of meeting Lord Thomas Babington Macaulay, Henry Hallam, Connop Thirwall, and Henry Hart Milman. Prescott had the honor of dining with Harry Temple, who was the current foreign secretary and later the prime minister. He also met Arthur Wellesley, the Duke of Wellington, and had an opportunity to dine with Robert Peel, the former prime minister, a week before the elder statesman passed away. While in the company of the American and Swedish ministers, Prescott viewed the popular horse races held at the village of Ascot.

A highlight of William's visit occurred on the twentieth of June, for this was the day when he was presented to Queen Victoria at St. James Place. The gracious Lady Mahon instructed Prescott on the proper etiquette expected of him during his royal introduction. The American historian was regally attired in a blue coat trimmed with gold lace, white pants, silk hose, gold-buckled patent leather boots, and a sword, the latter of which he feared might cause him to embarrassingly loose his footing. He wrote of his introduction at court to Queen Victoria and Prince Albert, "I was presented by our Minister, according to the directions of the Chamberlain, as the historian of Ferdinand and Isabella, in due form—and made my profound obeisance to her Majesty, who made a very dignified curtsey, as she made to some two hundred others who were presented in like manner. I made the same low bow to his Princeship to whom I was also presented, and so bowed myself out of the royal circle, without my sword tripping up the heels of my nobility."[23] At the conclusion of his royal introduction, Lord Carlisle kept Prescott close by his side while he pointed out the various lords and ladies who paid their respects to the Queen. Following this royal reception, William was a guest at a grand luncheon at the Stafford House hosted by the Duchess of Sutherland. A few days later William Prescott was at Buckingham Palace attending the Queen's ball.

Prescott also had the pleasure of meeting Richard Ford and William Stirling, two authors who shared a similar admiration of Spanish history and culture. After visiting with Ford, the same Richard Ford who had previously criticized his *History of the Reign of Ferdinand and Isabella, the Catholic*, William wrote, "the lunch was all Spanish—Spanish wines—delicious, Spanish dishes, which good breeding forced me to taste, but no power could force me to eat—for they were hotter than the Inquisition."[24] William Stirling had him over for a lunch that offered food which was more to his liking. Prescott greatly admired the unique collection of Spanish art that Stirling had on display.

At the urging of Lord Carlisle and William Stirling, Prescott posed for a portrait by the accomplished English artist George Richmond during his stay in London. Later, when instructed that his portrait commissioned by Lord Carlisle was completed, William requested that Lady Lyell send a copy to Richard Bentley. The British publisher greatly appreciated this gift and in thanking Prescott he inquired if a bust of the historian had been made with his approval, and if so, would it be possible to get a copy. A flattered Prescott replied in a letter dated April 26, 1853: "A few years since a bust was made of me by Richard Greenough, an American artist, now in Florence. He is a man of real genius, and this bust is executed with great delicacy. I have the original in marble, from which casts have been taken; and I have had the pleasure to order one to be put up for you. It will go by the steamer that takes this, and I trust will reach you in good condition. I have directed that all charges be paid. Should there be any blunder in this particular, you will please let me know it, as I would not have the outside of my head put you out of pocket, any more than I would the inside."[25] Bentley received the gift and informed Prescott that it would be a prized ornament in his library.

William was invited to Oxford, where he was a guest of the bishop. On June 24, 1850, the University honored him with a degree of D. C. L. (Doctor of Civil Law). Prescott was quite proud of his honorary degree from Oxford University: "Now," said the Boston historian, "I am a *real* Doctor."[26] He received his honorary degree attired in the scarlet robes that all Academic candidates were expected to wear. This was the only honorary ceremony that William ever attended.

Prescott would later learn that the vice-chancellor of the University of Oxford had reservations about granting an honorary degree to the American historian, concerns that centered around William's religious convictions. In a note to George Ticknor, Prescott wrote of an unspoken bias toward Unitarians: "The term [Unitarian] is absolutely synonymous in a large party here with Infidel, Jew, Mohammedan; worse even, because regarded as a wolf in sheep's clothing."[27] There were also a few narrow-minded individuals who thought that the historian's writings were anti–Catholic, which seemed to suggest that the author was a nonbeliever. The dean of St. Paul's came to Prescott's defense by telling the administration officials that if they bothered to read *Ferdinand & Isabella* they would see that it more than qualified him for an honorary degree from Oxford. A special convocation ruled in William's favor. As the land of his ancestors, the Boston author was instilled with a sincere admiration of English society and was extremely gratified to earn acceptance in England for his literary achievements.

Of all the tributes paid to William Prescott by members of British society, none touched his heart as much as the one paid by a member of the working class: "I do not know any compliment that pleased me more than the wish expressed by the foreman of my shoemaker to bring the shoes to me that he might see me, for the pleasure he had had in reading my books. The man was a Scotchman."[28]

On the Fourth of July, Prescott had the great pleasure of receiving his eldest son, William Gardiner Prescott, who had just arrived in Southampton following an extensive tour of Africa and Southern Spain. He wrote to his wife that their adventurous son looked well, but was "as black as a Moor from the African sun."[29] In February 1850, Will had traveled to Spain and paid a friendly visit to Pascual de Gayangos, the scholar who had greatly aided his father's research.

William made time for a brief visit to his British publisher Richard Bentley to discuss the sales of his books. Bentley presented his celebrated American client with a new edition of the letters of Horace Walpole, fourth earl of Orford. Prescott appreciated the gift, a gesture that helped to soothe business related tensions between them. Not wishing to get too friendly with Bentley, Prescott respectfully declined his invitation for a social get-together. He did, however, accept an invitation from John Murray, the founder of the *Quarterly Review* and a publisher he held in the highest esteem, to dine with him at his home in Greenwich. This Fourth of July dinner hosted by Murray was attended by Richard Ford, William Stirling, Henry Hallam, John Lockhart, an unnamed diplomat, an unidentified big game hunter (most likely Roualeyn George Gordon-Cumming, who was known as the *lion hunter*), and William Prescott, who was accompanied by his son Will. The lively guests dined on whitebait, a seafood delicacy, and vintage wine as they conversed on a vast array of topics. Cigars were passed around and enjoyed prior to William and his son returning to London by coach.

While overseas, William wrote the following passage to his beloved wife: "Contrary to the assertions of La Bruyere—who somewhere says that the most fortunate husband finds reason to regret his condition at least once in twenty-four hours—I may truly say that I have found no such day in the quarter of a century that Providence has spared us to each other."[30]

After deciding to embark on a tour of the European Continent, William Prescott traveled to Paris in the company of his secretary, John Foster Kirk, and his manservant, Penn. Will had gone ahead of his father and they were soon reunited at the City of Lights. Two days later, on the 22nd of July, Prescott set out for Brussels, the capital of Belgium, in the companionship of his secretary and manservant for a tour of the Low Countries, a region rich in history that was relevant to his unfinished work. Belgium was the home of the young prince Charles, the future king of Spain, Holy Roman emperor, and father of Phillip the Second.

William Prescott and his two assistants proceeded to travel through the beautiful countryside that stretched between Brussels and Antwerp. From Antwerp the trio journeyed to Rotterdam, a location ideal for tours of Delft, the Hague, Haarlem, and Amsterdam. The trip to Belgium and the Netherlands was the only time that Prescott made an effort to visit a region that figured in his historical accounts. It is rather curious that the historian did not take this opportunity to visit Spain, the nation that figured so prominently in his histories, and to pay his respects to Pascual de Gayangos, the Spanish scholar whose tireless efforts to procure research material for Prescott's benefit had proved to be an invaluable service. A likely possibility is that William admired both the country and scholar so greatly that he did not want to destroy any illusions he might of formed about either Spain or Gayangos. After ten days of exploring the Continent, William Prescott and his companions returned to the Mivart's Hotel in London.

Shortly after his return, William and his son set out on an extensive tour of the English countryside. The British gentry graciously opened their extravagant homes to the venerable American historian. Just like at London, Prescott was the recipient of so many invitations that he had to politely decline a number of offers. He visited Abbotsford, Melrose Abbey, and Dryburgh Abbey on his way to the Scottish Highlands.

Prescott particularly enjoyed spending a day at Abbotsford, the country mansion of the late Sir Walter Scott. Since the Scottish novelist was one of his favorite authors William therefore took the time to fully acquaint himself with Scott's choice collection of books that lined his library, the cozy study where he wrote, and the many mementos that he had acquired over the years. William noted that the gothic style of "Abbotsford is a disappointment to those who examine it architecturally. But I thought of it only historically, in the light of its association with its author. And it is a most characteristic work in all its detail—as well as in its books, furniture, old knick-knackery, rusty jackets, &c.—the very type of the national feeling of the poet and antiquarian, whose spirit seems still to linger around the scene he so fondly created."[31] Considered to be the founder of the historical novel following the release of *Waverly* in 1814, Scott went on to write such classic tales as *Rob Roy*, *Ivanhoe*, and *The Talisman* before his death in 1832 at Abbotsford.

Both father and son continued on to Stirling and Loch Katrine, after which they penetrated the legendary Scottish Highlands. William's whirlwind tour and visitations continued as a welcome house guest of the Duke of Sutherland at Trentham Hall, a majestic country estate with vast and spectacular gardens fashioned in the Italian style. There were seven miles of gravel path that wended through sublime gardens that were maintained with the utmost care. William and his son stayed in rooms called the chambers of birds, where everything, according to Prescott, had an "ornithological significance." The estate had accommodations for a variety of domesticated birds; peacocks and many other splendidly feathered crea-

Abbotsford, residence of Sir Walter Scott, Scotland, Library (courtesy Historical Findings and Library of Congress).

tures freely roamed the grounds. William was accorded the honor of planting an evergreen cypress in the garden, which was the same variety of tree that Queen Victoria had ceremoniously planted at Castle Howard. The Duchess told him that this evergreen would forever be remembered by her and her children as Prescott's tree, so that all who had the pleasure of viewing it would recall his visit to Trentham.

William Prescott and his son were also guests at the lavish residences of Lord Lansdowne, the Duke of Northumberland, the Duke of Argyle, and Lord Grey. The young Duke and Duchess of Argyll would take William and Will on a tour of Loch Awe, the largest lake in Scotland. Prescott enjoyed the company of his gracious hosts so much that he remained at Inveraray Castle for an entire week before resuming his journey. Each day of this extended visit was filled with social gatherings that revolved around bountiful feasts, entertaining music, and graceful dancing, all of which Prescott found most delightful. But these activities eventually grew tiresome and the historian soon began to long for home.

William and Will Prescott's next visit was with Lord Carlisle at Naworth Castle, which is located near Hadrian's Wall and the ruins of Lanercost Abbey. The next day Lord Carlisle escorted his guests to Castle Howard, some 17 miles outside the city of York. Both father and son could not help but admire the stately Yorkshire castle, which was made all the more charming by a landscape of sprawling, well-cared lawns and majestic woods where herds of deer freely grazed. The historian thoroughly enjoyed browsing Castle Howard's 150-foot-long gallery adorned with many magnificent works of art as well as the castle's equally impressive library. William and Will Prescott could not help but notice that everyone was hurriedly preparing for an upcoming royal visit.

William and his son were still at Castle Howard when Queen Victoria, Prince Albert, and their royal entourage made their grand entrance on the 27th of August. Prescott wrote to Susan about having dinner with Queen Victoria: "I was as near the Queen as at our own family table. She had a good appetite, and laughs merrily. She is very plain, with fine eyes and teeth, but short and dumpy, with a skin that reddens easily with the heat of the room. She was dressed in black, silk and lace, with the blue scarf of the Order of the Garter across her bosom. [After dinner] ... she did me the honor to come and talk with me, asking me about my coming here, my stay in the castle, what I was doing now in the historic line, how Everett was and where he was, for 10 minutes or so, and Prince Albert afterwards a long while, talking about the houses and ruins in England and the churches in Belgium and the pictures in the room and I don't know what. I found myself now and then trenching on the rules by interrupting &c; but I contrived to make it up by a respectful 'Your Royal Highness' 'Your Majesty' &c."[32] Prescott truly enjoyed his ten-day visit at Castle Howard.

Having already booked passage for his return to New York, William realized the time had come to conclude his six-week-long tour of the English countryside. On the way back he had an opportunity to see Lord Clarendon's home, Baron Parkes estate at Ampthill, and the residence of the Marquis of Lansdowne before arriving at Liverpool. On the 14th of September, William and his son boarded the *Niagara* at the Liverpool dock for their return voyage to America. The *Niagara* docked in New York City on September 27, 1850. Prescott felt that this trip had helped to rejuvenate his spirits, restore his health, and improve the strength of his eyes. The visit also helped boost his royalties: William's engaging wit and personality had won the affection of many British citizens which, in turn, translated into a substantial increase in his London book sales. George Ticknor would declare that Prescott's trip to England was "the most brilliant visit ever made to England by an American citizen not clothed with the *prestige* of official station."[33]

Finishing What He Started

Once back home, Prescott found it rather difficult to resume his normal writing routine. Much of his time was occupied with writing letters to friends about his trip overseas and pondering over the continued lack of copyright protection abroad for his books. He also made an effort to help a young and promising historian get his work published in England. Francis Parkman, Jr., the son of the Rev. Francis Parkman, a prominent and affluent Unitarian minister of Boston, and the nephew of Dr. George Parkman, the recently murdered physician, had just completed a work titled *History of the Conspiracy of Pontiac*.

The young Francis Parkman suffered from a number of serious health issues, including partial blindness—a deprivation of vision that forced him to follow Prescott's method of employing copyists to search libraries and archives for materials related to his work. This 28-year-old former student of Jared Sparks at Harvard had already made a favorable impression in literary circles with his first publication, *The Oregon Trail*. Seeking to help this fellow historian find an overseas publisher, Prescott wrote to Bentley, "My friend Mr. Parkman, of this city, proposes to send out by this steamer the proof sheets of a new work of his relating to the occupation of this country by the French, and their intercourse with the Indians."[34] Eager to please his favorite American client, Bentley agreed to publish Parkman's new manuscript. Unfortunately, *History of the Conspiracy of Pontiac* failed to attract much attention; only 153 copies were sold during the first year of its release.

Prescott also recommended two other Boston authors to Richard Bentley; the historian Samuel Eliot, who had written *The Liberty of Rome*, and Thomas Bulfinch, the author of *The Age of Fable*. Samuel Eliot was the grandfather of the distinguished historian Samuel Eliot Morison. Prescott also brought to Bentley's attention another book he felt would command the interest of a large British audience—Harriet Beecher Stowe's *Uncle Tom's Cabin*. Unfortunately, this book was already published in America and its popularity had quickly caught the attention of English publishers who released pirated copies before Bentley even had a chance to contact the author. This did not deter Bentley from publishing his own inexpensive edition of *Uncle Tom's Cabin*. Unable to secure a deal for Stowe's next work, Bentley tried to hide his disappointment in a letter to Prescott: "The success of Uncle Tom has indeed been marvelous; but it is not cheering to sound literature to see immense successes follow productions, one of whose chief merits, in my very humble judgment, is that they strike a particular chord at a moment when the public mind is in a sort of furore. So it is with us in regard to Slavery, and the most extravagant stories are eagerly swallowed."[35]

Finding himself still in a literary funk, Prescott hoped to brighten his mood by embarking on another scenic trip to Niagara Falls. This excursion, however, did little to rejuvenate his desire to write, which is evident by the fact that during his following seasonal stay at Nahant he accomplished nothing related to his work on *Philip the Second*. Part of the problem was that he still could not decide if this work should be styled in the manner of a memoir or treated as an historical account. While at Pepperell, William finally found inspiration to write the final chapter to part one of his book. It was after starting work on the section pertaining to the rebellion of the Netherlands that Prescott finally realized this work should be treated as an historical account. Prescott was elated to learn that in 1851 he was named an honorary member of the Mexican Society of Geography and Statistics, Mexico.

A little more than a year after his return to America, William and his wife were delighted to celebrate the marriages of their two oldest children. Such joyous occasions served as a temporary interruption to work on the second section of his book. Ever since the announcement of the engagement of Josephine Augusta Peabody and William Gardiner Prescott, both families were consumed with preparations for their nuptial vows, a marriage which took place on November 6, 1851. William and Susan Prescott would lovingly refer to their daughter-in-law as Augusta. The newly-married couple moved into a house on Chestnut Street, which was close enough for the historian to see from his study.

William and Susan Prescott had barely recovered from the frenzied wedding preparations of Will and Augusta when they suddenly found themselves thrust into making arrangements for the marriage of Elizabeth Prescott, their beloved daughter, to James Lawrence, the eldest son of Abbott Lawrence, a ceremony which took place on March 6, 1852. James was a graduate of the Harvard class of 1840 and had already made a name for himself at his father's firm.

Once these blessed events had passed, Prescott was free to concentrate on his work, and by mid–April he had managed to complete the first volume of *History of the Reign of Philip the Second, King of Spain*. But William's work on the second volume came to an abrupt halt on May 17, 1852, a mournful day when his dear mother passed away.

The first sign that William's 84-year-old mother's health was beginning to fail was when she complained a few days before Elizabeth's wedding of suffering sporadic and debilitating pains in her chest and back. Despite these problems, she managed to summon enough strength to attend the marriage ceremony of her granddaughter and even displayed plenty of vigor by dancing at Elizabeth's reception. But Catherine Prescott was soon weakened by additional painful attacks, which were severe enough to confine her to bed. On the 17th of May, Catherine's condition began to grow graver with each passing hour and her mortal life came to a close that very afternoon. William, who never left her side, wept bitterly over the loss of his much loved mother. The funeral services for Catherine Greene Hickling Prescott were presided over by the Rev. Dr. Alexander Young at the New South Church. She was buried next to her beloved husband in a crypt in St. Paul's Episcopal Church.

A few days after this family tragedy, Prescott wrote a letter to a friend in which he describes the truly honorable character of his late mother: "My mother had a warm and sympathetic nature, a heart full of love, a hand open to charity. And her charity was not limited to the purse. It showed itself in a great indulgence to the frailties of others, as well as in sorrow for their distresses. She had, indeed, a generous nature, wishing ever to do good and to make those around her better."[36]

After having spent several weeks mourning the loss of his mother, William and the rest of the family set out for Nahant. On July 4, 1852, he noted in his journal, "Nahant, where we came on the first,—cold, dreary and desolate. I miss the accustomed faces. All around me how changed, yet not the scene. There all is as it always has been. The sea makes its accustomed music on the rocks below. But it sounds like a dirge to me. Yet I will not waste my time in idle lament. It will not bring back the dead,—the dead who still live, and in a happier world than this."[37]

William soon felt that there were too many painful memories haunting the family home at Nahant and decided to relocate to a newly-built cottage at Lynn Bay, which was approximately six miles from their house at Nahant. The *villa*, as the new residence was originally referred to, was far more luxurious than their *Fitful Head* home, and offered an even more spectacular view of the ocean. Another advantage to this location was that It was very near the country home of his daughter and new son-in-law. Since there was but one large cherry tree to provide much needed shade for the sensitive eyes of the historian, a great many young trees were immediately planted. William would frequently walk beneath the shade of the mature cherry tree while carrying a light umbrella to shield his eyes from the sunlight that managed to penetrate its thick canopy of leaves. The historian wore a deep path that encircled the trunk of this tree, a trail that remained visible for many years after his death. The Nahant home was not sold, just deserted in favor of their new residence at Lynn, which soon came to be known as *Red Rock*.

During the first quarter of 1853, a proud William and Susan Prescott were twice blessed as grandparents. March 23, 1853, marked the birth of their grandson James Lawrence, and on April 20, 1853, their granddaughter Edith Prescott was welcomed into the world. Having admirably fulfilled the roles of loving son, brother, husband, father, William Prescott now had the opportunity to add the role of adoring grandfather.

Prescott retired to his new house in Lynn on June 21, 1853, in the hope that the scenic surroundings of the countryside and the ocean would be conducive to his health, mood, and work. However, William had a hard time settling into his new residence, a period of adjustment which proved unsatisfactory for his literary pursuits. Pleasurable visits from Sir Charles and Lady Lyell, and the Earl and Countess of Ellesmere during his stay at Red Rock helped to take his mind off the lack of progress he had made on the second volume of his book.

William had hoped to complete the second volume of *History of the Reign of Philip the Second, King of Spain* by the autumn of 1853, but the loss of his mother had clearly dampened his enthusiasm toward work. His health was also an issue. During the year-long period that had begun in 1852 and extended into 1853, Prescott suffered terribly from a recurrence of acute rheumatism, an affliction that had not bothered him for quite some time.

In July of 1852, William Prescott received a letter from Richard Bentley asking him to provide an expected time frame for the completion of *Philip the Second*. But William, who had previously vowed to never again write under such time constraints, could not comply with the British publisher's request. He did, however, write to Bentley regarding the ongoing legislative debate to implement an international copyright agreement: "There will be an effort here to introduce an international copyright law in the next session of Congress. It will be presented in the form of a treaty to the Senate—and will have a better chance of passing than if laid before the House of Representatives, as it has hitherto been. Mr. Webster has applied to me to give my views to him on the subject which I shall do. If this effort fails, I should fear that some retaliatory measure would be taken by your government."[38]

It wasn't until Prescott returned to Pepperell that he finally felt the urge to resume his work. But even then his progress was painfully slow. He acknowledged concerns over his sluggish pace by stating. "Dull sailing—I fear dull writing."[39]

During the winter season of 1852–53, William managed to make some excellent strides in his writing and appeared to have finally rekindled his desire to complete this grand work. On July 30, 1853, the author made light of his writing by noting in his literary memorandum, "Yesterday fell asleep while Kirk read it to me for the corrections; a good omen for my readers!"[40]

On December 10, 1853, the Harper and Brothers Publishing firm suffered a devastating setback after a massive fire destroyed their warehouse that stored thousands of books

Philip II (1527–1598), King of Spain (courtesy Historical Findings and Library of Congress).

in their inventory. It was later determined that the disastrous fire was started by a negligent plumber who dropped a lit match into a pot of highly volatile camphene. The firm lost all 34 of their large presses and all of the stereotype plates that were currently in use. Included in these losses were a multitude of Prescott's works, printed copies which the firm had already made payment for to the author. Prescott feared that his future royalties would be affected by this disaster, but luckily his four sets of stereotype plates were not in use at the time and thus were spared from the raging inferno. In a letter penned on December 28, 1853, Harpers told Prescott, "The plates to all your works, we are happy to inform you, are *safe*; and we intend to reprint from them as soon as we can possibly find presses & paper."[41] The relieved author granted the publisher permission to reprint as many copies as had been consumed in the fire.

The writing of *History of the Reign of Philip the Second, King of Spain* had begun in July 1849, during Prescott's stay at Nahant, and was concluded five years later on August 22, 1854, while the author was vacationing at Lynn. Harper and Brothers, which was still trying to recover financially from their devastating fire, had assumed that they would continue to serve as William's publisher, but the historian was eager to negotiate a more favorable deal for his new book.

Upon learning that William Prescott and Harper Brothers were having difficulty reaching an agreement, Francis H. Underwood, an assistant editor at the publishing firm of Phillips, Sampson & Company, suggested to his superiors that this might be a good opportunity to reach out to the Boston historian. Moses Dresser Phillips arranged a meeting with William Prescott at his Red Rock residence. He was able to reach an accord with the author and soon drew up a lengthy contract that was signed on August 4, 1854. The historian wrote of this new publishing deal in his memorandum: "I have quitted the Harpers, and entered into a contract with the house of Phillips, Sampson & Co. of Boston. I have left the Harpers not from any dissatisfaction with them, for they have dealt well by me from the first to the last, but because they were not prepared to come up with the liberal offer made by the other party. We part, therefore, with some good understanding in which we have always kept together."[42] The six-year contract executed between Prescott and Phillips, Sampson and Company extended beyond the life of both the author and the publishing house.

After reaching an accord with Phillips, Sampson & Company, Prescott turned his attention to attaining a favorable deal with his British publisher. Colonel Aspinwall was retired from his overseas service and had returned to Massachusetts when William Prescott opened negotiations for the publication of an English edition of *History of the Reign of Philip the Second, King of Spain*. An agreement was eventually reached with Richard Bentley, but due to various concerns, it was agreed that the English edition would be delayed until autumn of 1855.

Shortly after dispatching his manuscript to Bentley, news came to Prescott's attention that his longtime London publisher was on the verge of bankruptcy. The historian immediately made it clear to Bentley that he wished to terminate their contract and wanted his manuscript of *Philip the Second* returned at once. When Bentley failed to comply with his demands, William sought the help of Russell Sturgis, an agent at the house of Baring Brothers & Company. A reluctant Richard Bentley finally agreed in August to cancel their deal. Sturgis then set out to find a new publisher for Prescott's work. The Routledge house, which had previously expressed an interest in publishing *Philip the Second*, made a monetary offer that was significantly below what they had originally indicated. In the open bidding for the rights to publish the two volumes of *History of the Reign of Philip the Second, King of Spain* it was Richard Bentley who submitted the highest offer, which was still well below what Prescott had expected to receive. William was hesitant to agree to Bentley's offer, but accepted it after realizing that this was the best deal he was going to receive. Believing that he had been manipulated by Bentley, this ignoble affair further deepened the mistrust that Prescott harbored toward his British publisher. Russell Sturgis would continue to serve as Prescott's second and final literary agent in London.

After making the final corrections to his manuscript during his stay at Pepperell, William returned to Boston and entered into a contract with Metcalf and Company of Cambridge to produce the stereotype plates for his *Philip the Second*. This painstaking process was begun in November of 1854 and completed in May of 1855. His good friend Charles Folsom once again proofread the work and his secretary John Foster Kirk performed a number of essential duties to help Prescott complete the finishing touches to his book. The first volume was finalized by mid–February 1855, and the second volume was finished two months later on the 27th of April. The preface, illustrations, and final proofs took another four weeks of polishing before both volumes were ready for the publisher.

Prescott's *History of the Reign of Philip the Second, King of Spain* was released first in London on October 30, 1855, and then in America on December 10, 1855. As expected, advance sales were quite robust and the reviews were highly favorable. The elated author wrote, "From the tone of the foreign journals and those of my own country, it would seem that the work has found quite as much favor as any of its predecessors, and, as the sales have been much greater than of any other of them in the same space of time, I may be considered to have as favorable a breeze to carry me forward on my long voyage as I could desire."[43] More than 8000 copies were sold in the United States within the first six months of its release and these sales figures were nearly matched in England, the latter result partially due to the favorable impression he had made during his recent visit. The historian's new work also stimulated much interest in his previous books.

In a letter penned on August 6, 1855, to Pascual de Gayangos, George Ticknor bragged about his good friends newest release: "Vols I and II of Prescott's Philip II are out and every body is reading them. It is a grand work, quite worthy of all he has done before. The opening is very brilliant; the conclusion very touching; & the list of Netherlands (in parts at least) is more acute and profound than anything in Ferdinand & Isabella, which, I think is the most solid of his previous works. Wise men will be satisfied with its estimate of Philip in Spain, fanaticks will be satisfied with it nowhere."[44]

There was, however, a quietly held belief that Prescott's newest work did not quite measure up to his previous literary efforts. This composition marked the first time that the historian had released a work that still required at least another volume to complete, which was a point of contention for a number of critics and readers. There were also complaints that William had failed to breathe life into Philip II in the same eloquent and deft manner as he had done in his character studies of Ferdinand and Isabella, Hernán Cortés, and Francisco Pizarro.

Prescott was extremely disappointed that the *North American Review* waited more than six months to review his new book, a delay that failed to generate the awareness and interest that would have further boosted his initial sales. The journal had previously reviewed his titles once they were released and in much greater length and depth. In a letter to Charles Folsom dated April 9, 1856, Prescott complained, "It, however, is not very creditable to a journal of the pretensions always maintained by the *North American* to overlook the literature which springs up under its own nose, especially when coming from one who has been one of the most copious contributors to its pages."[45]

William was very grateful for the many fans who took the time to write of their appreciation for his work. There were so many individuals who requested his autograph that the historian had form letters drafted, to which he applied his signature. Prescott was particularly moved by an appeal submitted by R. Augustus Wright: "Will you favor one of your younger readers with your autograph? And will you allow him to return you his most hearty thanks and acknowledgments for having cured him of novel reading? I was a most desperate and determined peruser of the 'yellow-covered' until my good sister Agnes gave me all your histories (superbly bound) and I confessed I wanted no better 'novels.' Dear Sir, you are a magician; again and again I go back and put myself under your delightful spell. Allow me to thank you and to love you for the good you have done me."[46]

In 1855, a very appreciative John L. Motley, who was currently in Italy visiting the historic city of Florence, penned a letter to William Prescott: "I thank you very much for your very handsome allusion [in the Preface to Philip II] to my forthcoming work which I am sure in America at least will be of much value to me. I hope you will take the trouble to read the work when it appears (a copy will of course be sent to you) and that you will not be ashamed afterwards of having complimented me on trust. It is so much the fashion for literary men and artists generally to look upon any man in the street who is trying to get into the omnibus as an intruder, and to bully him with assurance that there is no room for him, that I feel most sensibly your courtesy in trying to make a place for me at your side, however, unable or unworthy I may be of your kindness."[47] Motley's *Rise of the Dutch Republic*, which enjoyed tremendous critical and financial success, was released in the spring of 1856, just a few months after the release of Prescott's first two volumes of *Philip the Second*.

Richard Bentley wrote to William Prescott during the winter of 1855 to inquire as to when he might expect to see the third volume of *History of the Reign of Philip the Second, King of Spain*. The historian respectfully replied, "I write to please myself, and because I love labor. But then it must be a labor of love, or I could not write at all. I am at present tolerably industrious, and propose to continue so, if my health serves me."[48]

10

Growing Health Concerns

My pen is my good lance with which I may fight the battles of humanity—for the diffusions of truth, & virtue, & civilization.[1]

An Addendum

In February of 1855, William and Susan Prescott warmly welcomed the arrival of two more grandchildren. Elizabeth gave birth to a daughter on the 19th, who was christened Gertrude Lawrence, and three days later Augusta gave birth to a son who was baptized with the name of his celebrated grandfather, William Hickling Prescott. Meanwhile, the historian used this break between writing projects to catch up on his private correspondences. On March 15, 1855, William penned a letter to Lady Mary Lyell in which he informs her of his deep admiration for Alexander Humboldt: "I have had some very kind letters from Humboldt, who has always taken a friendly interest in my historical career; and, as this has lain in his path, it has enabled me to appreciate the immense services he has done to science and letters by his curious researches and his beautiful manner of exhibiting the results of them to the reader."[2]

After the release of *History of the Reign of Philip the Second, King of Spain*, William revisited the idea of writing an account of the reign of Philip's father and the reclusive life he purportedly led after choosing to abdicate the throne. Prescott had toyed with the idea of writing a new history of Charles V, king of Spain and Holy Roman emperor, as early as 1842. But believing the reign of the monarch had already been adequately reported by William Robertson in his three-volume history of the monarch, which was published in 1769, the Boston historian decided not to tread over ground already covered by the Scottish historian.

George Ticknor, Edward Everett and several other friends and admirers urged Prescott to reconsider his decision; they reminded him that he had access to numerous German and Spanish documents that were never made available to Robertson. William began to have a change of heart on this matter after receiving from William Stirling, the Scottish writer he had enjoyed the company of during his recent visit to England, a copy of his *Cloister Life of Charles V*, an informative work which forced him to admit that William Robertson's conclusions regarding the cloistered life of Charles V were not an accurate representation of the monarch's final years.

New information obtained from the archives of Simancas also dispelled the accepted notion that Charles V had little to do with affairs of state following his abdication. While searching through historical collections for Prescott's research into the reign of Philip II, Pascual de Gayangos happened upon documents that clearly showed the abdicated Emperor Charles had been more involved in the affairs of government than previously thought, a discovery that provided fresh impetus for a need to amend the Scottish historian's account. Appreciating all that the Spanish scholar had done for him, Prescott communicated his feelings in a letter to Gayangos, "How fortunate I am in having a friend like yourself interested in my literary projects!"[3]

William was deeply saddened to learn of the passing of Mrs. Gayangos and expressed his deepest sympathies in a letter dated June 17, 1855, to his good friend Don Pascual. "It was with sincere sorrow that I received your letter informing me of the great affliction that has lately befallen you. I have never been called to endure it; but I can well comprehend how great it must be, and especially after a union so long as yours has been. I had not the pleasure of knowing your wife personally, any more than yourself. But I have long felt as if I knew you both—I have so long communicated with you, and with her sometimes as well as you. There is no relief that a

Charles V (1500–1558), King of Spain and Holy Roman emperor (courtesy Historical Findings and Library of Congress).

friend can afford under such a bereavement. The only consolation is to be found in time, and in the sweet though sad memory of the past."[4]

In May of 1855, Prescott decided to set aside work on his third volume of *Philip the Second* so that he could turn his full attention toward producing an updated rendering of Charles V. He proposed to write a brief but thorough account that focused on the life of the king of Spain and Holy Roman emperor following his abdication, which he regarded as a continuation of William Robertson's history. Since he already had most of the research material close at hand and the topic was rather familiar to him, William was able to complete his writing by January 1856. Prescott's addendum amounted to less than 200 pages. A good deal of this material was gleaned from book one of his *History of the Reign of Philip the Second, King of Spain*.

Phillips, Sampson and Company would once again serve as William Prescott's publisher. The cost of converting Robertson's nearly 1700 pages of text to stereotype plates was evenly shared between William and the publisher while the cost of stereotyping the supplemental material was the sole responsibility of the historian. To avoid competing with his *Philip the Second*, the release of Prescott's account of Charles V was postponed until December 8, 1856.

In a letter to Richard Bentley dated August 4, 1856, Prescott informed his longtime British publisher that he was getting ready to issue an addendum to William Robertson's *History of the Reign of Charles the Fifth*. He let Bentley know that if he wished to publish this work he would have to compete with two other publishing houses. When Bentley failed to match a competing offer, Prescott replied, "I am sorry you did not give me a better bid than £100 for the continuation of Robertson's Charles V, as it falls considerably below the offer of the Messrs. Routledge, to whom of course I have been obliged to deliver the book."[5]

The Routledge offer exceeded Bentley's bid by a mere ten pounds, but Prescott viewed this as an excellent excuse to sever his business ties with the British publisher. William had met George Routledge during the publisher's visit to America in 1854, a meeting that left a favorable impression on both men. In October of that year, George Routledge, who was known for producing inexpensive editions of classics, published a two-volume pirated edition of Prescott's *History of the Reign of Ferdinand and Isabella, the Catholic*. In spite of their professional differences, Richard Bentley and William Prescott continued to correspond with one another even after the American historian had switched his British publishing rights to George Routledge.

The title page of the Phillips, Sampson, and Company edition read:

> The History of the Reign
> of the
> Emperor Charles the Fifth
> by William Robertson, D.D.
> with
> An Account of the Emperor's Life After His
> Abdication,
> by
> William Prescott

In a letter to George Ticknor dated December 8, 1856, Prescott declared, "My 'Charles the Fifth,' or rather Robertson's, with my Continuation, made his bow to the public today, like a strapping giant with a little urchin holding on to the tail of his coat. I can't say I expect much from it, as the best and biggest part is somewhat of the oldest. But people who like a complete series will need it to fill up the gap betwixt "Ferdinand" and "Philip."[6] Sales of the American and English editions of *History of the Reign of the Emperor Charles the Fifth* exceeded Prescott's expectations but failed to achieve anywhere near the sales success of his previous histories.

The Panic of 1857, the financial crisis that had severe international implications, was a contributing factor to lackluster sales figures for William's latest release. In a letter to Phillips and Sampson dated December 10, 1857, Prescott wrote of the effects of the economic downturn on his book, "The account you present is on the whole a pretty fair one considering the horrid times. It is a pity to see a book that opened so brilliantly as Charles V thus nipped in the bud. But sunshine will come sooner or later."[7]

After finishing the epilogue to William Robertson's historical account, Prescott prepared a 19-page testimonial for the private distribution of the National Portrait Gallery which paid tribute to the Honorable Abbott Lawrence, a good friend and father of his son-in-law, who had passed away on August 18, 1855. The following year Prescott was delighted to learn that he was the recipient of literary honors from the Historical Society of Florida, St. Augustine and the Historical Society of Iowa, Burlington. A year later the Boston historian was named an honorary member of the Historical Society of Tennessee, Nashville.

Third Volume of *Philip the Second*

Prescott began work on the third volume of *Philip the Second* once he had completed his *Memoir of the Honorable Abbott Lawrence*. Unfortunately, William's progress was stalled by the realization that he now suffered from a lack of enthusiasm for continuing with this topic. Physical manifestations also contributed to an abrupt sense of apathy. In December of 1856, the historian began to exhibit signs that his health was steadily deteriorating. Over the next three months he suffered severe headaches, which, on some days, were much too painful for him to concentrate on his work. William avoided making notations in his journal during this prolonged period of suffering, which seems to indicate either a lack of will to write or that such efforts were simply too painful—or very likely a combination of these factors. Dr. James Jackson, the long-time family physician, was convinced that this new affliction was symptomatic of his rheumatic condition. The doctor felt that rest was the best medicine that he could prescribe for his long-suffering patient.

In spite of these pounding headaches, Prescott still retained his desire to engage in social activities. Many years earlier, Professor Theophilus Parsons had made mention of the gracious and charming manner that William always exhibited at social gatherings: "He came, always bringing the gift of cheerfulness, and always offering it with such genuine cordiality, that it was sure to be accepted, and returned with increase. No wonder that he was just as welcome everywhere as sunshine. If I were asked to name the man whom I have known, whose coming was most sure to be hailed as a pleasant event by all whom he approached, I should not only place Prescott at the head of the list, but I could not place any other man near him."[8] During his seemingly inescapable period of writing doldrums, William kept his spirits afloat by continuing his normal routine of attending dinners, entertaining guests, spending time with his family, and relaxing while listening to appealing stories that were read to him.

In the spring of 1857, there came an unexpected assault on William Prescott's literary integrity. A lawyer by the name of Robert Anderson Wilson, an Englishman who had relocated to Rochester, New York, would momentarily win the confidence and empathy of Prescott by mentioning in a letter that he had developed an interest in history while recovering from a protracted illness and now wished to try his hand at writing an historical account. However, any thoughts of making available material from his personal library were cast aside after Wilson had the audacity to state that it was his intention to write about "the Conquest of Mexico, without the fable." The arrogant lawyer added, "I took it for granted that you had fought your Mexican battle, and that the market for your book had been supplied—and that your Mexican library had become cast-off lumber."[9] Refusing to be drawn into a war of words over these unwarranted aspersions cast by Wilson, the ever-gracious William Prescott recommended specific books that might aid the aspiring historian and even indicated that he would help him find a publisher.

Seeking evidence to support his contention that the conquistadors had greatly exaggerated the degree of civilization achieved by the Aztecs, Wilson drew upon the conclusions of Jean-Jaques Rousseau, St. Hilaire, and Albert Gallatin that the native tribes of North America had much in common with the indigenous tribes of Mexico. He also relied heavily on the distorted account provided by the controversial Bartolomé de Las Casas, the zealous Spanish priest who had been anointed with the title Defender and Apostle to the Indians.

The eyewitness accounts of Hernán Cortés and other Spanish soldiers pertaining to the many magnificent stone cities of Mexico, which they declared were grander than any in Spain, were dismissed by many historians and scholars as simply the boastful claims of brutal conquerors seeking to justify and glorify their deeds. Many of the cities seen by Cortés and his men had been leveled either during or shortly after the conquest of Mexico. The Aztec capital of Tenochtitlán was demolished during a long siege by the conquistadors, and the Spaniards used the battered stones to build Mexico City atop the ruins, which served as the capital of New Spain.

During their search for ancient cities buried deep in the forests of Mexico and Central America, John Lloyd Stephens and Frederick Catherwood learned that many of the ruins had been further degraded by Spanish priests who had ordered the removal of the stones from the Mayan temples and pyramids to use for the construction of new churches and homes. Prior to the explorations of Stephens and Catherwood, and the scholarly account written by Prescott, most historians made reference to the fact that the indigenous people of Mexico, especially those of Yucatan, lived in small villages as being undeniable proof that these reports of sprawling stone cities were simply not true.

The historian William Robertson had added fuel to this fiery debate by writing in his *History of America*, "Neither the Mexicans nor the Peruvians were entitled to rank with those nations which merit the name of civilized." Their homes were "more fit to be the habitation of men just emerging from barbarity ... low straggling huts ... scattered about irregularly."[10]

Robert Wilson was convinced that the Aztecs were an offshoot tribe of the North American Indians, native societies which embraced a relatively simple lifestyle. Using the Iroquois nation as his model, this amateur ethnologist concluded that the Spanish tales of large and magnificent cities inhabited by tens of thousands of natives living in complex societies was simply not realistic. However, Wilson's credibility suffered from his Eurocentric bias, as he firmly believed that the native Indians were descendants of the Phoenicians. He also deliberately ignored the findings of the two expeditions by John Lloyd Stephens and Frederick Catherwood which had uncovered in Honduras, Guatemala, Chiapas, and Yucatan numerous stone cities built on a grand scale; discoveries that clearly supported the Spanish accounts of magnificent native cities built of stone.

Wilson's *A New History of the Conquest of Mexico* was published in 1859, shortly after William H. Prescott had passed away. His account was an extremely biased view of this epic event; the author seemed to take tremendous delight in bashing the Catholic Church, the Spanish Crown, and Hernán Cortés and every conquistador who followed him. He was also critical of Prescott's sources as well as the conclusions he had derived from them. Wilson even went so far as to capitalize on the letters that William Prescott was kind enough to write to him, which he shamelessly used to imply that his work had the endorsement of the eminent Boston historian.

Both John Foster Kirk and George Ticknor took up their pens to fiercely defend the good name of their dear departed friend. An anonymous writer came to Prescott's defense with an article in the *Atlantic Monthly* that pointed out Robert Wilson's faulty research and biased conclusions. The column also exposed that Wilson's benchmark for his native studies was the nation of the Iroquois, a native society that did not build temples or offer human sacrifices, to wrongly conclude that the Aztecs could never have performed such deeds. That same year, William Prescott's *History of the Conquest of Peru* come under attack from Lambert A. Wilmer, the author of *The Life, Travels and Adventures of Ferdinand de Soto, Discoverer of the Mississippi*. Wilmer, like Wilson, favored the Black legend accounts that arose from the partisan views of Bartolomé de Las Casas.

In a report presented before the Massachusetts Historical Society in 1861, George Ticknor declared that Robert Anderson Wilson "does not deserve the name of an historian." The Boston scholar took exception with Wilson's ideas regarding Bernal Diaz del Castillo, the conquistador who penned *The True History of the Conquest of Mexico*. Ticknor wrote, "Such a work, of course, stood directly in the way of a person like Mr. Wilson, who, in order to maintain his theories about Mexico, was obliged to deny all the received accounts of that extraordinary event, and especially those of Bernal Diaz. After some consideration, he seems to have made up his mind that the cheapest and shortest way was to declare boldly that no such man ever existed; or, to use his own words, he 'with much deliberation concluded to denounce Bernal Diaz as a myth.'[11]

By denying the evidence of Bernal Diaz del Castillo that appears in numerous records during his lifetime, especially in Guatemala, where the grizzled veteran lived after the conquest and where he wrote his classic account of the events surrounding the fall of Mexico, Robert Wilson had undermined the integrity of his work. In response to his critics, Wilson stated that he had sought to "denounce the authorities, on which Prescott had relied, as physically impossible; as more intensely fabulous than the Arabian Nights or Munchausen's Tales, as the religious romance and pious frauds of Spanish priests."[12] Wilson's rebuttal failed to dissuade a growing list of skeptics, and consequently his book quickly sank into obscurity.

In April of 1876, Lewis Henry Morgan, a pioneer ethnologist, sought to debunk Prescott's characterization of Aztec society, which he perceived as being overly imaginative. Morgan did not intend to assail Prescott's character, a man he held in the highest esteem, but he did criticize the Spanish sources that the Boston historian relied upon for his conclusions about the advanced state of Aztec society. Morgan had spent a great deal of time living and working with the Iroquois, and just like Robert Wilson, whose book he had read, he used this tribe as his model for all Native American cultures. In an article for the *North American Review* titled "Montezuma's Dinner," he rebuked the notion of Montezuma's grand palace—claiming it was merely a "joint-tenement house of the aboriginal American model, owned by a large number of related families, and occupied by them as joint proprietors." Morgan claimed that the sumptuous dinner of Montezuma was nothing more than "the usual single daily meal of a communal household, prepared in a common cook-house from common stores, and divided, Indian fashion, from the kettle." He added that the multitude of natives tribes that Hernán Cortés and his small army of conquistadors had encountered in the Valley of Mexico was nothing more than a "simple confederacy of three Indian tribes, the counterpart of which was found in all parts of America."[13] Morgan was convinced that Prescott had romanticized the Spanish conquest of Mexico by relying too heavily on the tales told by the conquistadors. Like Robert Wilson and Lambert Wilmer, Lewis Morgan was guilty of twisting facts to support his thesis.

Franklin Dexter, the loving husband of William's sister and beloved father of four sons, passed away on August 14, 1857, after losing his battle with a long, drawn-out illness. In the latter months of that year, Phillips,

Sampson and Company launched *The Atlantic Monthly*. Prescott would contribute a brief article for the second issue of the magazine titled *The Battle of Lepanto*, a piece that he would incorporate in his third volume of *History of the Reign of Philip the Second, King of Spain*.

Unfortunately, Phillips, Sampson, and Company, like so many other businesses throughout the nation, was struggling to stay afloat during the harsh economic downturn of 1857. The publishing firm had fallen behind on its payment of royalties, which amounted to several thousand dollars owed to the Boston historian. Sympathizing with their financial plight, Prescott graciously extended the terms of their outstanding obligation. The Boston firm managed to tread water a bit longer but was finally forced to declare bankruptcy in 1859, the same year that William Prescott passed away.

During the night of February 3, 1858, William Prescott complained that he was suffering from a pounding headache and was experiencing numbness in his right leg. He also felt sluggish and overly tired. Susan tried to entertain him with some light reading but William felt much too sleepy to even pay attention. He tried to write a note but became very confused and therefore gave up. The next morning William Prescott recalled that his mind had been somewhat bewildered and that he had much difficulty remembering names. He felt rather glum after confessing these symptoms but managed to cheer himself up enough to resume his normal routine.

The following day William Prescott was out for his usual morning walk when he experienced a sudden loss of muscular control. He managed, after much effort, to make his way back home. The housemaid noticed that her employer seemed terribly troubled that his wife was not at home. The servant also noted that she had "to render him unusual attentions." As he was making his way up the stairs to the library, William felt an increasing weakness in his legs and found it nearly impossible to ascend the last few steps. When the maid entered the room the historian complained that he was not feeling very well and asked her to retrieve Mrs. Prescott, who was visiting the home of their neighbor. Susan rushed home and saw that her husband appeared to be very ill; she helped him to the couch and then summoned Dr. Jackson, which was right around two o'clock in the afternoon. Susan was at his side when William, who truly believed he was near death, whispered to her: "My poor wife! I am so sorry for you, that this has come upon you so soon!"[14]

The 80-year-old Dr. James Jackson arrived to find his patient slumped on the couch. He observed that William's mind was in a very confused state but noticed that he was still fully aware of his surroundings. Prescott attempted to speak but his speech was quite feeble and somewhat incomprehensible. He felt nauseous and had already vomited. The historian also complained that he was feeling extremely weak and had experienced some uncontrollable twitching of his limbs. William was helped to his bed, at which point the doctor prescribed three doses of ipecac powder, which caused the patient to heave profusely. Purging seemed to help, for he soon experienced a slight return of his speech and his mind began to clear. William rested quite comfortably for the rest of that evening and night.

The following morning William's health appeared to have greatly improved. His mobility was restored but several other senses remained impaired, most noticeably a pronounced slurring of speech and blurred vision. Prescott complained of noticing some unusual "spectra" that continued to appear for several days. These phantoms occurred during the light of day and often while receiving visitors—recurring ghostly images that frequently involved a gathering of gentlemen all dressed in black, marching orderly about the room until they gradually faded from view. Prescott was heard to declare, "There go my gentlemen."[15]

There was a lingering fear that the historian had suffered irreparable damage to his brain. But after Dr. Jackson had been able to determine that none of the vessels in the brain had ruptured the physician was certain that Prescott's injury was slight. The family physician felt confident that William would make a full recovery, a diagnosis that provided great relief to both family and friends, as well as William Prescott. As for those previous headaches that had affected the historian's sleep and work, they had been an unheeded warning of an ensuing apoplectic shock.

When Prescott inquired about his condition, Dr. Jackson informed him that he was afflicted with a mild case of apoplexy. The doctor stressed to his celebrated patient that he must adhere to a strict diet—one that avoided meats if he wished to avoid another attack, which would surely be more acute. The family doctor also ordered Prescott to rest and forbade him from continuing work on his upcoming book until his health had returned to normal. The only writing that William indulged in during this period of convalescence involved dictating letters to his many friends and acquaintances.

William was confined to his bed for the next two days. On the third day he was visited by his good friend George Ticknor, who was delighted to see that Prescott's health had improved significantly, but observed that he still had some difficulty with his speech. The historian's movements were a bit shaky and his vision was still out of focus, the latter of which kept him from reading because the printed lines tended to blur with one another. He also had trouble recalling proper names and certain words, which was a source of frustration to one who prided himself in his ability to memorize lengthy passages. As always, Prescott bore his affliction with quiet dignity, refusing to give into feelings of melancholy.

Prescott followed his doctor's advice to the letter and within a week he felt strong enough to walk without assistance. Dr. Jackson still enforced a strict vegetable diet but did permit him to partake of a daily glass of wine. Acquaintances who came to visit William believed that he had made a full recovery, but family and friends who saw him regularly noticed that he was still not his former self. His strength improved with each passing day and very soon he was able to resume his daily walks, though he was still not strong enough to venture as far as he had in the past. William Prescott was a man accustomed to overcoming physical adversities and therefore was confident that he would eventually make a full recovery. After three months had passed, the historian's health had improved enough that the doctor allowed him to resume his literary pursuits, but in moderation.

On April 18 1858, Prescott made note of the effects of his ailment in his literary memorandum: "Much reason have I to be grateful that the effects have gradually disappeared, and left no traces now, except a slight obscurity in the vision, and a certain degree of weakness, which may perhaps be imputable to my change of diet. For I have been obliged to exchange my carnivorous propensities for those of a more innocent and primitive nature, picking up my fare as our good parents did before the fall. In this way it is thought I may defy the foul fiend for the future. But I must not make too heavy or long demands on the cranium, and if I can get three or four hours' work on my historic ground in a day, I must be content.... With Prudence and the blessing of Heaven I may hope still to be in at the death of Philip, though it may be some years later than I had expected."[16] William's impaired vision, which was worse than usual, and a general state of weakness persisted for longer than he cared to admit.

Health issues prevented William Prescott from accepting an invitation to attend the dedication of "Plummer Hall," a Salem library which promoted literary and scientific research. Funding for the hall, which was erected at the very site where the Prescott house formerly stood, was provided by the estate of Miss Caroline Plummer, who had been a dear friend of the Prescott family. William noted in his RSVP to Salem officials, "I need not assure you that I take a sincere interest in the ceremonies of the day, and I have a particular interest in the spot which is to be covered by the new edifice, from its having been that on which I first saw the light. It is a pleasant thought to me, that, through the enlightened liberality of my deceased friend, Miss Plummer, it is now to be consecrated to so noble a purpose."[17]

The arrival of spring was accompanied by a significant improvement in William Prescott's general health. The return of his youngest son, William Amory Prescott, from travels abroad helped lift the historian's spirits. Meanwhile, Will Prescott and his family were still traveling in Europe but were scheduled to return in the summer, which the author looked forward to with great pleasure. William now felt well enough to resume work on the third volume of *Philip the Second*, though at a considerably slower pace. He already had 470 completed pages, to which he planned to add an additional 50 pages but, sadly, he never did get around to writing them. Prescott kept the Cambridge printers informed of his progress and the expected date of completion. Charles Folsom would once again proofread his manuscript and offer insightful editorial suggestions.

Prescott's latest health issues had compelled him to make a number of changes to *History of the Reign of Philip the Second, King of Spain*. The third volume, which he had been working on prior to his attack, was condensed, and he concluded the last chapter from what he had committed to memory. His third volume of *Philip the Second* was finished in April of 1858, and the stereotyping was completed over the ensuing summer. Prescott had originally planned on covering the reign of Philip II over the course of five volumes, but decided not to proceed with a proposed fourth volume for fear that he would not be able to finish what he started, a concern that would ring true.

Work was temporarily set aside on the 19th of July, for this was the long-awaited day that Will, Augusta, Edith, and little William Hickling Prescott returned from their travels abroad. The only writing that Prescott did during this period were a number of letters in which he stated the overwhelming joy he felt now that his family had been reunited, and a supplemental clause to his will. His good friends George Ticknor and William Amory were to oversee the trust he had established for his wife and children. The historian had named William Howard Gardiner, his oldest and dearest friend, as the sole executor of his estate. James Lawrence was later named as a third trustee. A fourth and final codicil was executed on August 21, 1858, which terminated the trust for his eldest child, thereby allowing William Gardiner Prescott to receive and manage his inheritance. The retired Nathan Webster, the family's faithful and long-time manservant, was remembered in Prescott's will—he was originally bequeathed $50 but the amount was later amended to $100.

As expected, Phillips, Sampson and Company were to publish the American edition of his third volume of *History of the Reign* of *Philip the Second, King of Spain*. Plans for publishing in London were negotiated with both Richard Bentley and George Routledge, the latter once again winning the publishing rights with a more favorable offer. Bentley, who had tried to woo his former client with gifts of books, was deeply disappointed over losing the right to publish the third volume of Philip II, which now left him with an incomplete set of the Spanish monarch to sell. Feeling he had been betrayed, Bentley sought to exact revenge by capitalizing on his past relationship with the Boston historian. The British publisher assembled a number of letters he had received from the American author and released them in book form under the title *Correspondence of William H. Prescott, Esq. with Richard Bentley, from August 1856, to November, 1858*, which was published in 1859.

Prescott continued to suffer during the summer and fall seasons of 1858, a time when he was plagued by periodic headaches, many of which were painfully severe. Consequently, the historian's mood turned melancholy during the latter weeks of the year. News from England that Richard Ford, the writer and critic he had befriended in London, and who was of similar age, had passed away gave much cause for William to ponder his own mortality.

11

The Final Chapter

Family, friends, fortune—these have furnished me materials for enjoyment, greater & more constant than is granted to most men.[1]

A Valiant Effort

While the third volume of *Philip the Second* was being prepared for publication, Prescott began work on expanding and incorporating additional notes he wished to have included in a brand new English edition of *History of the Conquest of Mexico*. He had been inspired to perform this task after having read the numerous and insightful notes made by the scholars Don José F. Ramírez and Don Lucas Alamán to their respective Mexican translations of his book. He was even motivated to proceed with work on a fourth volume of *History of the Reign of Philip the Second, King of Spain* but only got as far as drawing up an outline of the first chapter.

Meanwhile, the publisher George Routledge sent William Prescott the royalty payment for the third London edition of *Philip the Second* along with a note inquiring about his progress on the next volume. "I have not broken ground on it yet; but shall soon do so," Prescott replied, adding, "It must depend on my health, which is good now."[2] Unfortunately, there would be no new edition that would bring closure to the long and eventful reign of the Spanish monarch.

On April 18, 1858, William Prescott, who had maintained a journal for more than 35 years, began his twelfth and final notebook of thoughts and concerns pertaining to his literary pursuits. The historian made just three entries in this journal, the last notation being: "Pepperell, October 28th—Return to town to-morrow. The country is now in its splendid autumn robe, somewhat torn, however, and draggled by the rain. Have been occupied with corrections and additions to my "Mexico." On my return to Boston shall resume my labors on "Philip." and, if my health continues as good as it has been this summer, shall hope to make some progress. But I shall not press matters. Our *villegiatura* has been brightened by the presence of all the children and grandchildren, God bless them! And now we scatter again but not far apart."[3]

In a letter penned on September 14, 1858, to Pascual de Gayangos thanking the Spanish scholar for his recent inquiry about his health, Prescott wrote, "I manage matters with much prudence, and make it a rule, one indeed that I have generally followed, never to sacrifice pleasure to business. But in truth long habit makes me find business—that is literary labor—the greatest pleasure. I suppose this is natural at my time of life."[4]

During the family's stay at Pepperell, Prescott's daughter-in-law recalled a lively incident where the aging William Prescott and Isaac P. Davis, a family friend, were engaged in a good-natured debate as to which of them was more hearing impaired. Susan Prescott proposed that they settle the question of who was more hard of hearing by means of a friendly contest. Susan dangled a large watch on a hook at the end of the room while her husband and Mr. Davis stood at the other end. The two competitors were to slowly walk side by side toward her until one of them could hear the ticking of the watch. With each step taken toward her, William would ask Isaac if he could hear the clock. Each time the answer for both of them was no. When they came within a few paces of Susan, William noticed that the watch was not even working. All enjoyed a good laugh over this incident, including the two hard of hearing rivals.

In a letter to Lady Mary Lyell dated January 10, 1859, Prescott politely declined her invitation for him and Susan to visit London: "As to my wife, a voyage to the moon would not be more chimerical in her eyes than a trip ... across the Atlantic. She will die without ever having got so far as New York." The tone of his letter turned darker with the added line, "Life is so stale when one has been looking at it for more than sixty winters!"[5]

Eternal Rest

William Prescott would soon exhibit telltale signs that his time allowed was rapidly coming to a close. Two weeks before his death, the historian was stricken with an agonizing fever that sapped his strength for nearly a week. Burning fevers alternated with teeth chattering chills to foil Prescott's efforts to carry on with his work. John Kirk, his devoted secretary, continued to read to him, and lively conversations with visiting friends helped to improve his mood and, subsequently, his health.

Just when it appeared that Prescott was on the verge of making a full recovery, the historian was deeply saddened by the news that Mary Dexter, his sister-in-law, had passed away following a long and painful illness. In a letter sent on January 25, 1859, to William Amory Prescott, William informed his son that the family had attended the funeral of his Aunt Mary Dexter. He closed the letter by stating, "The evening of life is coming over those of our generation, and we must be prepared to say farewell to one another."[6] Three days later William Hickling Prescott suffered a fatal apoplectic stroke.

Two days before Prescott's death, the Rev. William H. Milburn, of New York, who also suffered from partial blindness, met with the historian in his library and later recalled that he seemed to move with a "slower and heavier step" and that there was an "occasional thickening of the speech," symptoms which the minister attributed to the paralysis that the author had recently suffered. William's parting words to the Reverend Milburn were, "My greatest delight is the love of my friends and their appreciation of my labors."[7]

Because of inclement weather that had dampened the Friday morning of January 28, 1859, Prescott had to settle for exercising his legs by briskly walking about his room. The secretary John Kirk entertained his employer by reading aloud some riveting passages from *A Journey Due North*, George Augusta Sala's book about life in Russia. One excerpt referred to a previous minister of Russia stationed in Washington, a person alluded to that neither the historian or his secretary could recall the name of. Still having trouble remembering proper names, William walked to the dressing room where his wife was conversing with his sister, Elizabeth Dexter, to inquire if either of them could recall the name of the Russian minister in question. After a brief moment, Susan remembered the name, which surprised him because his wife had never taken an interest in politics. He snapped his fingers to acknowledge the correctness of her answer and let out a chuckle as he turned to leave. As he departed William asked, without expecting a reply, "How come you to remember?"[8] These were the very last words he spoke to his wife.

Prescott returned to his study and then stepped into an adjoining apartment. Shortly thereafter, around a half hour before noon, Mr. Kirk heard him let out a strange sounding moan and rushed over to find his employer unconscious; the historian's labored breathing was accompanied by extremely loud snoring. William was carried to his bedroom shortly before Doctor Jackson, the longtime family friend and physician, was summoned. Several medical attendants were soon at the historian's bedside, one of whom was Doctor Minot, who right away brought news of Prescott's feeble condition to George Ticknor, who, in turn, immediately made his way to the house of his ailing friend. The acclaimed historian never regained consciousness and at approximately half past two in the afternoon William Prescott exhaled his last breath. The suddenness of William's death was a terrible shock to his family, friends, and many admirers.

William Prescott was slated to be buried four days later, but two of his wishes had to be respectfully honored before his body was to be laid to rest. Because of a terrible fear of accidentally being buried alive, the historian left explicit instructions that every precaution should be taken to ensure that such a horrific scenario would never come to pass. Once the doctors had concluded that he was truly dead, a major vein was cut to make sure that death would remain certain. The historian's second request was that his body should have one last opportunity to rest in the study alongside his cherished collection of books. In accordance with Prescott's wish, his body would briefly lie in repose in the very room where he had spent so much of his time studying, reading, contemplating, memorizing, and writing.

Word of Prescott's death had spread so quickly through the city that there was no need to send out announcements for the date and time of his funeral service. The Representatives of the Commonwealth adjourned so that everyone could have the opportunity to attend the service, as did members of the Historical Society. The church was filled to capacity with those who wished to pay their last respects. The ceremony was attended by family, friends, acquaintances, and numerous admirers from near and far. The religious services were performed by the Rev. Rufus Ellis, Prescott's pastor at the First Congregational Church in Boston. Afterwards, William Hickling Prescott was buried in the family tomb at St. Paul's Church, interred alongside his loving mother and father, and little Catherine, the precious four-year-old daughter he had lost so many years ago. All of Boston shared in mourning the loss of one of their city's favorite sons. A special meeting of the Massachusetts Historical Society was held on Tuesday, February 1, 1859, in order that fellow members could pay a farewell tribute to the historian.

After learning of William Prescott's passing, the statesman Charles Sumner wrote to Henry Wadsworth Longfellow: "This death touches me much. Perhaps no man, so much in people's mouths, was ever the subject of so little unkindness. Something of that immunity which he enjoyed in life must be referred to his beautiful nature, in which enmity could not live."[9]

Mr. John Foster Kirk, the historian's last and longest serving secretary, also paid tribute to William Prescott's kindly manner: "No annoyance, great or small, the most painful illness or the most intolerable bore, could disturb his equanimity, or render him in the least degree sullen, or fretful, or discourteous. He was always gay, good-humoured, and manly. He carried his kindness of disposition not only into his public, but into his private, writings. In the hundreds of letters, many of them of the most confidential character, treating freely of other authors and of a great variety of persons, which I wrote at his dictation, not a single unkind or harsh or sneering expression occurs. He was totally free from the jealousy and envy so common among authors, and was always eager in conversation, as in print, to point out the merits of the great contemporary historians whom many men in his position would have looked upon as rivals to be dreaded if not detested."[10]

After learning of William Prescott's death, Robert Carter, another of the historian's dedicated secretaries, expressed a similar respect for the demeanor of his former employer: "Mr. Prescott's cheerfulness and amiability were truly admirable. He had a finely-wrought, sensitive organization; he was high-spirited, courageous, resolute, independent; was free from cant or affectation of any sort.... He was always gay, good humored and manly, most gentle and affectionate to his family, most kind and generous to all around him.... Though not at all diffident, he was singularly modest and unassuming. He had not a particle of arrogance or haughtiness.... Praise did not elate him, nor censure disturb him.... He was totally free from the jealously and envy so common among authors, and was always eager, in conversation, as in print, to point out the merits of the great contemporary historians, whom many men in his position would look upon as rivals."[11]

On March 8, 1859, George Ticknor sent the following mournful note to Pascual de Gayangos:

My dear Don Pascual,
  Since I wrote to you January 5, I have only sent you a newspaper containing the sad, *sad* news of the death of our excellent friend Prescott. Indeed, I have been able to do no more. He died on the 28th of that month of apoplexy—struck down at noon and gone without suffering or the slightest recovery of consciousness at ½ pass II. His death has produced such as was never produced in this country by the death of a man of letters. One proof of it, I forward to you by this mail in the Proceedings of our own Historical Society;—but, there are many others, both in our neighborhood [and] in other parts of the United States.

> He had done nothing at all towards another volume of Philip II; and it is doubtful whether anybody will undertake to go with it. Do you think it will be continued and completed by any body in Spain? He has left the manuscript and printed collections under my particular charge. Indeed I am a trustee for the greater part of his affairs and estate; the fortune he left being considerable for our country and for a man of letters. It amounts to above a million and a half francs. His name, however, is a greater & better inheritance for his children than his fortune.[12]

Following the death of his employer, John Foster Kirk took the time to care for several of the historian's unfinished affairs, which included returning books loaned to him by Don Pascual de Gayangos. George Ticknor also played a role in sending back books that the Spanish scholar had loaned to William Prescott. Kirk would continue to honor the memory of the celebrated historian by editing a 15-volume complete works of William H. Prescott. This revised edition, which included notes the author had hoped to implement when the time came to issue new stereotype plates, was first published in 1873 by J. B. Lippincott & Company. Inspired by the literary efforts of his former employer, John Foster Kirk went on to write a *History of Charles the Bold, Duke of Burgundy*.

Finding himself greatly affected by Prescott's death, George Ticknor sought to assuage his sorrow by writing a memoir of his dear friend. *The Life of William Hickling Prescott*, which was published in 1864, is a superb and insightful biography that serves as a fitting tribute to a scholar who is deservedly recognized as America's first scientific historian.

Chapter Notes

Preface

1. Samuel Eliot, "William H. Prescott," *New England Magazine* IX, no. 4 (December 1893), p. 516.
2. William H. Prescott, *Biographical and Critical Miscellanies* (New York: Fred DeFau & Co., 1912), p. 68.
3. Karl E. Meyer, *Teotihuacan: First City in the Americas* (New York: Newsweek, 1973), p. 119.
4. George Ticknor, *The Life of William Hickling Prescott* (New York: Fred DeFau & Co., 1912), p. 226.
5. Howard F. Cline, C. Harvey Gardiner, and Charles Gibson, *William Hickling Prescott, A Memorial* (Durham: Duke University Press, 1959), p. 15.
6. William H. Prescott, *Biographical and Critical Miscellanies* (New York: Fred DeFau & Co., 1912), p. 125.
7. Stewart L. Udall, *Majestic Journey: Coronado's Inland Empire* (Santa Fe: Museum of New Mexico Press, 1987), p. 138.
8. *Proceedings of the Massachusetts Historical Society in Respect to the Memory of William Hickling Prescott* (Boston: Massachusetts Historical Society, 1859), p. 14.
9. William H. Prescott, *History of the Conquest of Peru* (New York: The Modern Library, 1953), p. 728.
10. Thurston Peck, *William Hickling Prescott* (New York: Greenwood Press, 1969), p. 169.
11. *Ibid.*, p. 127.
12. Emily Morison Beck, ed., *Sailor Historian: The Best of Samuel Eliot Morison* (Boston: Houghton Mifflin, 1977), p. 348.
13. William H. Prescott, *History of the Conquest of Peru* (New York: Modern Library, 1953), p. 728.
14. William H. Prescott, *Biographical and Critical Miscellanies* (New York: Fred DeFau & Co., 1912), p. 64.

Chapter 1

1. William H. Prescott, *History of the Conquest of Peru* (New York: Fred DeFau & Co., 1912), p. 188.
2. Rollo Ogden, *American Men of Letters—William Hickling Prescott* (New York: Houghton Mifflin, 1904), p. 5.
3. George Ticknor, *The Life of William Hickling Prescott* (Boston: Ticknor & Fields, 1864), p. 422.
4. William Prescott, M. D., *The Prescott Memorial: or a Genealogical Memoir of the Prescott Families in America* (Boston: Henry W. Dutton & Son, 1870), pp. 58–59.
5. George Ticknor, *The Life of William Hickling Prescott* (Boston: Ticknor & Fields, 1864), p. 423.
6. William W. Story, ed., *Life and Letters of Joseph Story* (Boston: C. Little & James Brown, 1851), pp. 97–98.
7. C. Harvey Gardiner, *William Hickling Prescott: A Biography* (Austin: University of Texas Press, 1969), p. 13.
8. George Ticknor, *The Life of William Hickling Prescott* (New York: Fred DeFau & Co., 1912), p. 12.
9. George S. Hillard, *Little Journeys to the Homes of American Authors* (New York: G. P. Putnam, 1901), p.105.
10. C. Harvey Gardiner, *William Hickling Prescott: A Biography* (Austin: University of Texas Press, 1969), p. 125.
11. George Ticknor, *The Life of William Hickling Prescott* (Boston: Ticknor & Fields, 1864), p. 13.
12. Rollo Ogden, *American Men of Letters—William Hickling Prescott* (New York: Houghton Mifflin, 1904), p. 20.
13. George Ticknor, *The Life of William Hickling Prescott* (New York: Fred DeFau & Co., 1912), pp. 16–17.
14. *Ibid.*, p. 22.
15. *Ibid.*, p. 23.

Chapter 2

1. Howard F. Cline, C. Harvey Gardiner, and Charles Gibson, eds., *William Hickling Prescott, A Memorial* (Durham: Duke University Press, 1959), p. 170.
2. Helen Thomson, *Murder at Harvard* (Boston: Houghton Mifflin, 1971), p. 29.
3. James Jackson, M.D., *Another Letter to a Young Physician: To Which Are Appended Other Medical Papers* (Boston: Ticknor & Fields, 1861), p. 134.
4. *Ibid.*, pp. 140–141.
5. C. Harvey Gardiner, ed., *The Papers of William Hickling Prescott* (Urbana: University of Illinois Press, 1964), p. 8.
6. George Ticknor, *Life of William Hickling Prescott* (Boston: Ticknor & Fields, 1864) pp. 34–35.
7. *Ibid.*, pp. 38–39.
8. *Ibid.*, p. 40.
9. C. Harvey Gardiner, *William Hickling Prescott: A Biography* (Austin: University of Texas Press, 1969), p. 31.
10. Thurston Peck, *William Hickling Prescott* (New York: Greenwood Press, 1969), p. 40.
11. C. Harvey Gardiner, *William Hickling Prescott: A Biography* (Austin: University of Texas Press, 1969), p. 32.
12. *Ibid.*, p. 34.
13. *Ibid.*
14. *Ibid.*, p. 35.
15. Rollo Ogden, *American Men of Letters—William Hickling Prescott* (New York: Houghton Mifflin, 1904), p. 33.
16. George S. Hillard, *Homes of American Authors* (New York: G. P. Putnam, 1852), pp. 154–155.
17. Rollo Ogden, *American Men of Letters—William Hickling Prescott* (New York: Houghton Mifflin, 1904), pp. 33–34.
18. C. Harvey Gardiner, *William Hickling Prescott: A Biography* (Austin: University of Texas Press, 1969), p. 40.
19. *Ibid.*, p. 41.
20. George S. Hillard, *Life, Letters, and Journals of George Ticknor* (New York: Houghton Mifflin, 1909), p. 317.

Chapter 3

1. Rollo Ogden, *American Men of Letters—William Hickling Prescott* (New York: Houghton Mifflin, 1904), p. 73.
2. Thurston Peck, *William Hickling Prescott* (New York: Greenwood Press, 1969), p. 41.
3. Rollo Ogden, *American Men of Letters—William Hickling Prescott* (New York: Houghton Mifflin, 1904), pp. 61–62.
4. Samuel Eliot, "William H. Prescott," *New England Magazine* IX, no. 4 (December 1893), p. 525.
5. C. Harvey Gardiner, ed., *The Papers of William Hickling Prescott* (Urbana: University of Illinois Press, 1964), p. 30.
6. *Ibid.*, p. 34.
7. Clara Louisa Penney, ed., *Prescott: Unpublished Letters to Gayangos* (New York: Hispanic Society of America, 1927), p. 191.
8. Howard F. Cline, C. Harvey Gardiner, and Charles Gibson, eds., *William Hickling Prescott, A Memorial* (Durham: Duke University Press, 1959), p. 4.
9. William Charvat and Michael Kraus, *William Hickling Prescott* (New York: American Book Company, 1943), p. lxxxix.
10. George Ticknor, *The Life of William Hickling Prescott* (Boston: Ticknor & Fields, 1864), p. 119.
11. C. Harvey Gardiner, *William Hickling Prescott: A Biography* (Austin: University of Texas Press, 1969), p. 66.
12. Thurston Peck, *William Hickling Prescott* (New York: Greenwood Press, 1969), p. 50.
13. *Ibid.*, p. 47.
14. George Ticknor, *Life of William Hickling Prescott* (Boston: Ticknor & Fields, 1864), p. 72.
15. Thurston Peck, *William Hickling Prescott* (New York: Greenwood Press, 1969), p. 48.

Chapter 4

1. C. Harvey Gardiner, ed., *The Papers of William Hickling Prescott* (Urbana: University of Illinois Press, 1964), p. 67.
2. George Ticknor, *The Life of William Hickling Prescott* (Boston: Ticknor & Fields, 1864), p. 70.
3. *Ibid.*, pp. 70–71.
4. *Ibid.*, p. 73.
5. William H. Prescott, *History of the Reign of Ferdinand and Isabella, the Catholic* (New York: Fred DeFau & Co., 1912), page ix.
6. George Ticknor. *The Life of William Hickling Prescott* (New York: Fred DeFau & Co., 1912), pp. 75–76.
7. *Ibid.*, p. 77.
8. *Ibid.*, p. 74.
9. William H. Prescott, *History of the Conquest of Peru* (New York: Modern Library, 1953), p. 729.
10. Rollo Ogden, *American Men of Letters—William Hickling Prescott* (New York: Houghton Mifflin, 1964), p. 80.

11. *Ibid.*, p. 100.
12. C. Harvey Gardiner, ed., *The Papers of William Hickling Prescott* (Urbana: University of Illinois Press, 1964), p. 57.
13. C. Harvey Gardiner, *William Hickling Prescott: A Biography* (Austin: University of Texas Press, 1969), p. 92.
14. *Ibid.*, p. 93.
15. C. Harvey Gardiner, ed., *The Papers of William Hickling Prescott* (Urbana: University of Illinois Press, 1964), pp. 58–59.
16. *Ibid.*, p. 64.
17. Samuel Eliot, "William H. Prescott," *New England Magazine* IX, no. 4 (December 1893), p. 516.
18. George Ticknor, *The Life of William Hickling Prescott* (New York: Fred DeFau & Co., 1912), p. 86.
19. C. Harvey Gardiner, ed., *The Literary Memoranda of William Hickling Prescott* (Norman: University of Oklahoma Press, 1961), p. 109.
20. William Charvat and Michael Kraus, *William Hickling Prescott* (New York: American Book Company, 1943), p. xvii.
21. Roger Wolcott, ed., *The Correspondence of William Hickling Prescott* (Boston: Riverside Press, 1925), p. 3.
22. William H. Prescott, *Biographical and Critical Miscellanies* (New York: Fred DeFau & Co., 1912), p. 44.
23. *Ibid.*, p. 191.
24. C. Harvey Gardiner, ed., *The Literary Memoranda of William Hickling Prescott* (Norman: University of Oklahoma Press, 1961), p. 135.
25. George Ticknor, *The Life of William Hickling Prescott* (Boston: Ticknor & Fields, 1864), p. 205.
26. *Ibid.*, p. 248.
27. *Ibid.*, p. 90.
28. *Ibid.*, p. 91.
29. William Charvat and Michael Kraus, *William Hickling Prescott* (New York: American Book Company, 1943), p. lxxix.
30. C. Harvey Gardiner, *The Literary Memoranda of William Hickling Prescott* (Norman: University of Oklahoma Press, 1961), vol. 1, p. 143.
31. William H. Prescott, *Biographical and Critical Miscellanies* (New York: Fred DeFau & Co., 1912), pp. 42–43.
32. C. Harvey Gardiner, ed., *The Literary Memoranda of William Hickling Prescott* (Norman: University of Oklahoma Press, 1961), vol. 1, p. 149.
33. Rollo Ogden, *American Men of Letters—William Hickling Prescott* (New York: Houghton Mifflin, 1964), p. 80.
34. William Charvat and Michael Kraus, *William Hickling Prescott* (New York: American Book Company, 1943) p. xc.
35. *Ibid.*, p. l.

Chapter 5

1. William H. Prescott, *Biographical and Critical Miscellanies* (New York: Fred DeFau & Co., 1912), p. 201.
2. Rollo Ogden, *American Men of Letters—William Hickling Prescott* (New York: Houghton Mifflin, 1904), pp. 84–85.
3. Thurston Peck, *William Hickling Prescott* (New York: Greenwood Press, 1969), p. 67.
4. Samuel Eliot, "William H. Prescott," *New England Magazine* IX, no. 4 December, 1893), p. 527.
5. George Ticknor, *The Life of William Hickling Prescott* (Boston: Ticknor & Fields, 1864), p. 98.
6. C. Harvey Gardiner, *William Hickling Prescott: A Biography* (Austin: University of Texas Press, 1969), p. 131.
7. Howard F. Cline, C. Harvey Gardiner, and Charles Gibson, eds., *William Hickling Prescott, A Memorial* (Durham: Duke University Press, 1959), p. 6.
8. C. Harvey Gardiner, *Prescott and His Publishers* (Carbondale: Southern Illinois University Press, 1959), p. 19.
9. George Ticknor, *The Life of William Hickling Prescott* (New York: Fred DeFau & Co., 1912), p. 97.
10. C. Harvey Gardiner, *Prescott and His Publishers* (Carbondale: Southern Illinois University Press, 1959), p. 20.
11. George Ticknor, *The Life of William Hickling Prescott* (Boston: Ticknor & Fields, 1864), p. 97.
12. C. Harvey Gardiner, *Prescott and His Publishers* (Carbondale: Southern Illinois University Press, 1959), p. 52.
13. Royal A. Gettman, *A Victorian Publisher: A Study of the Bentley Papers* (Cambridge: Cambridge University Press, 1960), p. 66.
14. Rollo Ogden, *American Men of Letters—William Hickling Prescott* (New York: Houghton Mifflin, 1904), pp. 90–91.
15. Samuel Eliot, "William H. Prescott," *New England Magazine* IX, no. 4 (December 1893), p. 518.
16. Howard F. Cline, C. Harvey Gardiner, and Charles Gibson, eds., *William Hickling Prescott, A Memorial* (Durham: Duke University Press, 1959), p. 130.
17. Victor Wolfgang von Hagen, *Search for the Maya: The Story of Stephens & Cather-*

wood (Westmead, England: Saxon House, 1973), p. 96.
18. Rollo Ogden, *American Men of Letters—William Hickling Prescott* (New York: Houghton Mifflin, 1904), p. 104.
19. *Ibid.*, p. 57.
20. Howard F. Cline, C. Harvey Gardiner, and Charles Gibson, eds., *William Hickling Prescott, A Memorial* (Durham: Duke University Press, 1959), p. 85.
21. Clara Louisa Penney, ed., *Prescott: Unpublished Letters to Gayangos* (New York: Hispanic Society of America, 1927), p. 3.
22. Howard F. Cline, C. Harvey Gardiner, and Charles Gibson, eds., *William Hickling Prescott, A Memorial* (Durham: Duke University Press, 1959), p. 86.
23. *Ibid.*, p. 144.
24. Thurston Peck, *William Hickling Prescott* (New York: Greenwood Press, 1969), p. 128.
25. Howard F. Cline, C. Harvey Gardiner, and Charles Gibson, eds., *William Hickling Prescott, A Memorial* (Durham: Duke University Press, 1959), p. 137.
26. Roger Wolcott, ed., *The Correspondence of William Hickling Prescott* (Boston: Riverside Press, 1925), p. 24.
27. *Ibid.*, p. 25.
28. C. Harvey Gardiner, ed., *The Literary Memoranda of William Hickling Prescott* (Norman: University of Oklahoma Press, 1961), vol. 1, p. 212.

Chapter 6

1. C. Harvey Gardiner, ed., *The Literary Memoranda of William Hickling Prescott* (Norman: University of Oklahoma Press, 1961), vol. 1, p. 67.
2. Thurston Peck, *William Hickling Prescott* (New York: Greenwood Press, 1969), p. 100.
3. Roger Wolcott, ed., *The Correspondence of William Hickling Prescott* (Boston: Riverside Press, 1925), p. 51.
4. Rollo Ogden, *American Men of Letters—William Hickling Prescott* (New York: Houghton Mifflin, 1904), p. 130.
5. Roger Wolcott, ed., *The Correspondence of William Hickling Prescott* (Boston: Riverside Press, 1925), p. 28.
6. Victor Wolfgang von Hagen, *Maya Explorer: John Lloyd Stephens and the Lost Cities of Central America and Yucatan* (San Francisco: Chronicle Books, 1990), p. 190.
7. C. W. Ceram, *The March of Archaeology* (New York: Alfred A. Knopf, 1976), p. 272.
8. C. Harvey Gardiner, *William Hickling Prescott: A Biography* (Austin: University of Texas Press, 1969), p. 155.
9. William H. Prescott, *History of the Conquest of Mexico* (New York: The Modern Library, 1953), p. 4.
10. Rollo Ogden, *American Men of Letters—William Hickling Prescott* (New York: Houghton Mifflin, 1904), p. 133.
11. C. Harvey Gardiner, *William Hickling Prescott: A Biography* (Austin: University of Texas Press, 1969), p. 149.
12. George Ticknor, *The Life of William Hickling Prescott* (Boston: Ticknor & Fields, 1864), p. 156.
13. Rollo Ogden, *American Men of Letters—William Hickling Prescott* (New York: Houghton Mifflin, 1904), p. 116.
14. Thurston Peck, *William Hickling Prescott* (New York: Greenwood Press, 1969), p. 175.
15. Pierre Munroe Irving, *The Life and Letters of Washington Irving* (New York: G. P. Putnam, 1883), vol. 3, p. 133.
16. Rollo Ogden, *American Men of Letters—William Hickling Prescott* (New York: Houghton Mifflin, 1904), p. 134.
17. C. Harvey Gardiner, ed., *The Literary Memoranda of William Hickling Prescott* (Norman: University of Oklahoma Press, 1961), vol. 2, p. 29.
18. William H. Prescott, *History of the Conquest of Mexico* (New York: The Modern Library), pp. 4–5.
19. Thurston Peck, *William Hickling Prescott* (New York: Greenwood Press, 1969), pp. 134–135.
20. George Ticknor, *The Life of William Hickling Prescott* (New York: Fred DeFau & Co., 1912), p. 182.
21. *Ibid.*, p. 184.
22. William H. Prescott, *History of the Conquest of Mexico* (New York: The Modern Library, 1953), p. 694.
23. William H. Prescott, *History of the Conquest of Mexico* (New York: Fred DeFau & Co., 1912), vol. 1, p. 273.
24. C. Harvey Gardiner, *William Hickling Prescott: A Biography* (Austin: University of Texas Press, 1969), p. 189.
25. C. Harvey Gardiner, ed., *William Hickling Prescott: An Annotated Bibliography of Published Works* (Washington, D.C.: Library of Congress, 1958), p. 265.
26. Roger Wolcott, ed., *The Correspondence of William Hickling Prescott* (Boston: Riverside Press, 1925), p. 63.

Chapter 7

1. William H. Prescott, *History of the Conquest of Mexico* (New York: The Modern Library), p. 5.
2. Victor Wolfgang von Hagen, *F. Catherwood, Archt.* (New York: Oxford University Press, 1950), p. 54.
3. Editors of Reader's Digest, *Mysteries of the Ancient Americas: The New World Before Columbus* (Pleasantville, NY: Reader's Digest, 1986), p. 238.
4. C. Harvey Gardiner, ed., *The Papers of William Hickling Prescott* (Urbana: University of Illinois Press, 1964), p. 172.
5. C. Harvey Gardiner, ed., *The Literary Memoranda of William Hickling Prescott* (Norman: University of Oklahoma Press, 1961), vol. 2, p. 93.
6. Victor Wolfgang von Hagen, *Maya Explorer: John Lloyd Stephens and the Lost Cities of Central America and Yucatan* (San Francisco: Chronicle Books, 1990), p. 192.
7. Ibid.
8. Victor Wolfgang von Hagen, *Search for the Maya: The Story of Stephens and Catherwood* (Westmead, England: Saxon House, 1973), p. 223.
9. Roger Wolcott, ed., *The Correspondence of William Hickling Prescott* (Boston: Riverside Press, 1925), p. 240.
10. Victor Wolfgang von Hagen, *Maya Explorer: John Lloyd Stephens and the Lost Cities of Central America and Yucatan* (San Francisco: Chronicle Books, 1990), p. 200.
11. Victor Wolfgang von Hagen, *Search for the Maya: The Story of Stephens and Catherwood* (Westmead, England: Saxon House, 1973), pp. 222–223.
12. Ibid., p. 313.
13. Victor Wolfgang von Hagen, *Maya Explorer: John Lloyd Stephens and the Lost Cities of Central America and Yucatan* (San Francisco: Chronicle Books, 1990), p. 256–257.
14. Ibid. p. 257.
15. Roger Wolcott, ed., *The Correspondence of William Hickling Prescott* (Boston: Riverside Press, 1925), p. 245.
16. Peter Tompkins, *Mysteries of the Mexican Pyramids* (New York: Harper and Row, 1976), p. 125.
17. C. Harvey Gardiner, ed., *The Literary Memoranda of William Hickling Prescott* (Norman: University of Oklahoma Press, 1961), vol. 2, p. 32.
18. George Ticknor, *The Life of William Hickling Prescott* (Boston: Ticknor & Fields, 1864), p. 188.
19. C. Harvey Gardiner, *William Hickling Prescott: A Biography* (Austin: University of Texas Press, 1969), p. 184.
20. C. Harvey Gardiner, ed., *The Papers of William Hickling Prescott* (Urbana: University of Illinois Press, 1964), p. 182.
21. Allan Nevins, ed., *The Diary of Philip Hone 1828–1851* (New York: Dodd, Mead, 1927), p. 597.
22. C. Harvey Gardiner, ed., *The Literary Memoranda of William Hickling Prescott* (Norman: University of Oklahoma Press, 1961), vol. 2, p. 90.
23. Victor Wolfgang von Hagen, *F. Catherwood, Archt.* (New York: Oxford University Press, 1950), p. 160.
24. Ibid., p. 87.
25. Ibid., p. 86.
26. Victor Wolfgang von Hagen, *Search for the Maya: The Story of Stephens and Catherwood* (Westmead, England: Saxon House, 1973), p. 319.
27. Ibid., p. 320.
28. Ibid.
29. George Ticknor. *The Life of William Hickling Prescott* (New York: Fred DeFau & Co., 1912), p. 210.
30. C. Harvey Gardiner, *Prescott and His Publishers* (Carbondale: Southern Illinois University Press, 1959), p. 61.
31. Ibid.
32. Rollo Ogden, *American Men of Letters—William Hickling Prescott* (New York: Houghton Mifflin, 1904), p. 141.
33. Roger Wolcott, ed., *The Correspondence of William Hickling Prescott* (Boston: Riverside Press, 1925), p. 328.
34. C. Harvey Gardiner, ed., *The Literary Memoranda of William Hickling Prescott* (Norman: University of Oklahoma Press, 1961), vol. 2, p. 104.
35. Ibid., vol. 2, p. 113.
36. Pierre Munroe Irving, *The Life and Letters of Washington Irving* (New York: G. P. Putnam, 1883), vol. 3, p. 143.
37. Victor Wolfgang von Hagen, *Maya Explorer: John Lloyd Stephens and the Lost Cities of Central America and Yucatan* (San Francisco: Chronicle Books, 1990), p. 258.
38. Frances Calderón de la Barca, *Life in Mexico* (Garden City: Doubleday, 1954), p. 5.
39. Howard F. Cline, C. Harvey Gardiner, and Charles Gibson, eds., *William Hickling Prescott, A Memorial* (Durham: Duke University Press, 1959), p. 162.
40. Roger Wolcott, ed., *The Correspondence of William Hickling Prescott* (Boston: Riverside Press, 1925), pp. 425–426.
41. C. Harvey Gardiner, *Prescott and His Publishers* (Carbondale: Southern Illinois University Press, 1959), p. 11.

42. William H. Prescott, *History of the Conquest of Mexico* (New York: The Modern Library, 1953), vol. 2, pp. 324–325.
43. George Ticknor, *The Life of William Hickling Prescott* (New York: Fred DeFau & Co., 1912), p. 196.
44. Samuel Eliot, "William H. Prescott," *New England Magazine* IX, no. 4 (December 1893), p. 527.
45. C. Harvey Gardiner, *William Hickling Prescott: A Biography* (Austin: University of Texas Press, 1969), p. 231.
46. Victor Wolfgang von Hagen, *Maya Explorer: John Lloyd Stephens and the Lost Cities of Central America and Yucatan* (San Francisco: Chronicle Books, 1990), p. 270.

Chapter 8

1. George Ticknor, *The Life of William Hickling Prescott* (Boston: Ticknor & Fields, 1864), p. 219.
2. William Charvat and Michael Kraus, *William Hickling Prescott* (New York: American Book Company, 1943), p. lxvii.
3. Roger Wolcott, ed., *The Correspondence of William Hickling Prescott* (Boston: Riverside Press, 1925), p. 513.
4. William Charvat and Michael Kraus, *William Hickling Prescott* (New York: American Book Company, 1943), p. lxxv.
5. George Ticknor, *The Life of William Hickling Prescott* (New York: Fred DeFau & Co., 1912), pp. 216–217.
6. *Ibid.*, p. 217.
7. *Ibid.*, p. 223.
8. C. Harvey Gardiner, ed., *The Literary Memoranda of William Hickling Prescott* (Norman: University of Oklahoma Press, 1961), vol. 2, p. 120.
9. Roger Wolcott, ed., *The Correspondence of William Hickling Prescott* (Boston: Riverside Press, 1925), p. 477.
10. *Ibid.*, p. 479.
11. Victor Wolfgang von Hagen, *Search for the Maya: The Story of Stephens and Catherwood* (Westmead, England: Saxon House, 1973), p. 326.
12. C. Harvey Gardiner, *William Hickling Prescott: A Biography* (Austin: University of Texas Press, 1969), p. 212.
13. Clara Louisa Penney, ed., *Prescott: Unpublished Letters to Gayangos* (New York: Hispanic Society of America, 1927), p. 56.
14. Howard F. Cline, C. Harvey Gardiner, and Charles Gibson, eds., *William Hickling Prescott, A Memorial* (Durham: Duke University Press, 1959), p. 49.
15. Roger Wolcott, ed., *The Correspondence of William Hickling Prescott* (Boston: Riverside Press, 1925), p. 543.
16. C. Harvey Gardiner, *William Hickling Prescott: A Biography* (Austin: University of Texas Press, 1969), p. 215.
17. Roger Wolcott, ed., *The Correspondence of William Hickling Prescott* (Boston: Riverside Press, 1925), p. 481.
18. C. Harvey Gardiner, ed., *The Literary Memoranda of William Hickling Prescott* (Norman: University of Oklahoma Press, 1961), p. 122.
19. Rollo Ogden, *American Men of Letters—William Hickling Prescott* (New York: Houghton Mifflin, 1904), p. 22.
20. George Ticknor, *The Life of William Hickling Prescott* (Boston: Ticknor & Fields, 1864), p. 228.
21. Samuel Eliot, "William H. Prescott," *New England Magazine* IX, no. 4 (December 1893), p. 517.
22. Rollo Ogden, *American Men of Letters—William Hickling Prescott* (New York: Houghton Mifflin, 1904), p. 10.
23. *Ibid.*, vol. 2, p. 141.
24. George Ticknor, *The Life of William Hickling Prescott* (New York: Fred DeFau & Co., 1912), p. 223.
25. C. Harvey Gardiner, *William Hickling Prescott: A Biography* (Austin: University of Texas Press, 1969), p. 222.
26. Rollo Ogden, *American Men of Letters—William Hickling Prescott* (New York: Houghton Mifflin, 1904), p. 66.
27. C. Harvey Gardiner, *Prescott and His Publishers* (Carbondale: Southern Illinois University Press, 1959), p. 74.
28. Rollo Ogden, *American Men of Letters—William Hickling Prescott* (New York: Houghton Mifflin, 1904), p. 66.
29. George S. Hillard, *Little Journeys to the Homes of American Authors* (New York: G. P. Putnam, 1901), p. 86.
30. C. Harvey Gardiner, ed., *The Literary Memoranda of William Hickling Prescott* (Norman: University of Oklahoma Press, 1961), pp. 152–153.
31. *Ibid.*, p. 60.
32. Samuel Eliot, "William H. Prescott," *New England Magazine* IX, no. 4 December 1893), p. 516.
33. George S. Hillard, *Homes of American Authors* (New York: G.P. Putnam, 1852), p. 139.
34. George Ticknor, *The Life of William Hickling Prescott.* (New York: Fred DeFau & Co., 1912), pp. 244–245.
35. Clara Louisa Penney, ed., *Prescott: Unpublished Letters to Gayangos* (New York: Hispanic Society of America, 1927), p. 25.

36. *Ibid.*, p. v.
37. George Ticknor, *The Life of William Hickling Prescott* (Boston: Ticknor & Fields, 1864), p. 435.
38. Roger Wolcott, ed., *The Correspondence of William Hickling Prescott* (Boston: Riverside Press, 1925), p. 560.
39. *Ibid.*, p. 615.
40. George Ticknor, *The Life of William Hickling Prescott* (Boston: Ticknor & Fields, 1864), p. 245.
41. *Ibid.*, p. 241.
42. C. Harvey Gardiner, *William Hickling Prescott: A Biography* (Austin: University of Texas Press, 1969), p. 248.
43. Roger Wolcott, ed., *The Correspondence of William Hickling Prescott* (Boston: Riverside Press, 1925), p. 590.
44. Rollo Ogden, *American Men of Letters—William Hickling Prescott* (New York: Houghton Mifflin, 1904), p. 198.
45. *Ibid.*, p. 199.
46. Emily Morison Beck, ed., *Sailor Historian: The Best of Samuel Eliot Morison* (Boston: Houghton Mifflin, 1977), p. 353.
47. C. Harvey Gardiner, *William Hickling Prescott: A Biography* (Austin: University of Texas Press, 1969), p. 270.
48. George Ticknor, *The Life of William Hickling Prescott* (Boston: Ticknor & Fields, 1864), p. 246.
49. Clara Louisa Penney, ed., *Prescott: Unpublished Letters to Gayangos* (New York: Hispanic Society of America, 1927), p. 62.
50. Thurston Peck, *William Hickling Prescott* (New York: Greenwood Press, 1969), p. 82.
51. Howard F. Cline, C. Harvey Gardiner, and Charles Gibson, ed., *William Hickling Prescott, A Memorial* (Durham: Duke University Press, 1959), p.74.
52. George Ticknor, *The Life of William Hickling Prescott* (New York: Fred DeFau & Co., 1912), p. 261.
53. *Ibid.*, p. 261.
54. William H. Prescott, *History of the Conquest of Mexico* (New York: The Modern Library, 1953), p. 729.
55. Samuel Eliot, "William H. Prescott," *New England Magazine* IX, no. 4 (December 1893), p. 523.

Chapter 9

1. William H. Prescott, *History of the Reign of Philip the Second, King of Spain* (New York: The Modern Library, 1953), p. 183.
2. Samuel Eliot, "William H. Prescott," *New England Magazine* IX, no. 4 (December 1893), pp. 523–524.
3. Rollo Ogden, *American Men of Letters—William Hickling Prescott* (New York: Houghton Mifflin, 1904), p. 218.
4. C. Harvey Gardiner, wd., *The Papers of William Hickling Prescott* (Urbana: University of Illinois Press, 1964), p. 248.
5. Rollo Ogden, *American Men of Letters—William Hickling Prescott* (New York: Houghton Mifflin, 1904), p. 72.
6. Clara Louisa Penney, ed., *George Ticknor Letters to Pascual de Gayangos* (New York: Hispanic Society of America, 1927), p. 546.
7. Rollo Ogden, *American Men of Letters—William Hickling Prescott* (New York: Houghton Mifflin, 1904), p. 83.
8. Clara Louisa Penney, ed., *George Ticknor Letters to Pascual de Gayangos* (New York: Hispanic Society of America, 1927), p. 542.
9. William H. Prescott, *History of the Reign of Philip the Second, King of Spain* (New York: Fred DeFau & Co., 1912), p. iv.
10. C. Harvey Gardiner, *William Hickling Prescott: A Biography* (Austin: University of Texas Press, 1969), p. 280.
11. William Charvat and Michael Kraus, *William Hickling Prescott* (New York: American Book Company, 1943), p. cii.
12. *Ibid.*, p. cviii.
13. C. Harvey Gardiner, *William Hickling Prescott: A Biography* (Austin: University of Texas Press, 1969), p. 288.
14. *Ibid.*
15. Helen Thomson, *Murder at Harvard* (Boston: Houghton Mifflin, 1971), p. 69.
16. C. Harvey Gardiner, ed., *The Papers of William Hickling Prescott* (Urbana: University of Illinois Press, 1964), pp. 279–280.
17. *Ibid.*, p. 280.
18. C. Harvey Gardiner, *William Hickling Prescott: A Biography* (Austin: University of Texas Press, 1969), p. 297.
19. Helen Thomson, *Murder at Harvard* (Boston: Houghton Mifflin, 1971), p. viii.
20. George Ticknor, *The Life of William Hickling Prescott* (Boston: Ticknor & Fields, 1864), p. 277.
21. Rollo Ogden, *American Men of Letters—William Hickling Prescott* (New York: Houghton Mifflin, 1904), pp. 161–162.
22. *Ibid.*, 165.
23. Thurston Peck, *William Hickling Prescott* (New York: Greenwood Press, 1969), p. 105.
24. Rollo Ogden, *American Men of Letters—William Hickling Prescott* (New York: Houghton Mifflin, 1904), p. 166.

25. C. Harvey Gardiner, *Prescott and His Publishers* (Carbondale: Southern Illinois University Press, 1959), pp. 273–274.
26. Thurston Peck, *William Hickling Prescott* (New York: Greenwood Press, 1969), p. 107.
27. *Ibid.*
28. C. Harvey Gardiner, ed., *The Literary Memoranda of William Hickling Prescott* (Norman: University of Oklahoma Press, 1960), vol. 2, p. 196.
29. George Ticknor, *The Life of William Hickling Prescott* (New York: Fred DeFau & Co., 1912), p. 297.
30. Thurston Peck, *William Hickling Prescott* (New York: Greenwood Press, 1969), p. 111.
31. C. Harvey Gardiner, *William Hickling Prescott: A Biography* (Austin: University of Texas Press, 1969), p. 311.
32. George Ticknor, *The Life of William Hickling Prescott* (New York: Fred DeFau & Co., 1912), p. 315.
33. William Charvat and Michael Kraus, *William Hickling Prescott* (New York: American Book Company, 1943), p. cxiv.
34. C. Harvey Gardiner, *William Hickling Prescott: A Biography* (Austin: University of Texas Press, 1969), p. 318.
35. C. Harvey Gardiner, *Prescott and His Publishers* (Carbondale: Southern Illinois University Press, 1959), p. 271.
36. Rollo Ogden, *American Men of Letters—William Hickling Prescott* (New York: Houghton Mifflin, 1904), p. 12.
37. George Ticknor, *The Life of William Hickling Prescott* (Boston: Ticknor & Fields, 1864), p. 358.
38. C. Harvey Gardiner, *Prescott and His Publishers* (Carbondale: Southern Illinois University Press, 1959), p. 120.
39. C. Harvey Gardiner, ed., *The Literary Memoranda of William Hickling Prescott* (Norman: University of Oklahoma Press, 1961), vol. 2, p. 214.
40. *Ibid.*, p. 216.
41. C. Harvey Gardiner, *Prescott and His Publishers* (Carbondale: Southern Illinois University Press, 1959), p. 31.
42. Rollo Ogden, *American Men of Letters—William Hickling Prescott* (New York: Houghton Mifflin, 1904), p. 221.
43. *Ibid.* pp. 223–224.
44. Clara Louisa Penney, ed., *George Ticknor Letters to Pascual de Gayangos* (New York: Hispanic Society of America, 1927), p. 268.
45. C. Harvey Gardiner, ed., *The Papers of William Hickling Prescott* (Urbana: University of Illinois Press, 1964), p. 359.
46. *Ibid.*, p. 323.
47. Rollo Ogden, *American Men of Letters—William Hickling Prescott* (New York: Houghton Mifflin, 1904), p. 209.
48. C. Harvey Gardiner, *Prescott and His Publishers* (Carbondale: Southern Illinois University Press, 1959), p. 96.

Chapter 10

1. C. Harvey Gardiner, ed., *The Literary Memoranda of William Hickling Prescott* (Norman: University of Oklahoma Press, 1961), vol. 2, p. 163.
2. George Ticknor, *The Life of William Hickling Prescott* (New York: Fred DeFau & Co., 1912), p. 385.
3. Clara Louisa Penney, ed., *Prescott: Unpublished Letters to Gayangos* (New York: Hispanic Society of America, 1927), p. 58.
4. *Ibid.*, pp. 116–117.
5. C. Harvey Gardiner, *Prescott and His Publishers* (Carbondale: Southern Illinois University Press, 1959), p. 97.
6. George Ticknor, *The Life of William Hickling Prescott* (Boston: Ticknor & Fields, 1864), p. 379.
7. C. Harvey Gardiner, *Prescott and His Publishers* (Carbondale: Southern Illinois University Press, 1959), p. 224.
8. Samuel Eliot, "William H. Prescott," *New England Magazine* IX, no. 4 (December 1893), p. 516.
9. C. Harvey Gardiner, *William Hickling Prescott: A Biography* (Austin: University of Texas Press, 1969), p. 341.
10. Victor Wolfgang von Hagen, *Maya Explorer: John Lloyd Stephens and the Lost Cities of Central America and Yucatan* (San Francisco: Chronicle Books, 1990), p. 193.
11. George Ticknor, *Papers discussing the comparative merits of Prescott's and Wilson's Histories, pro and con., as laid before the Massachusetts Historical Society* (Boston: Massachusetts Historical Society, 1861), p. 2.
12. *Ibid.*, p. 4.
13. Howard F. Cline, C. Harvey Gardiner, and Charles Gibson, eds., *William Hickling Prescott, A Memorial* (Durham: Duke University Press, 1959), pp. 12–13.
14. George Ticknor, *The Life of William Hickling Prescott* (New York: Fred DeFau & Co., 1912), p. 396.
15. James Jackson, M.D., *Another Letter to a Young Physician: To Which Are Appended Other Medical Papers* (Boston: Ticknor & Fields, 1861), p. 150.
16. Rollo Ogden, *American Men of Let-*

ters—*William Hickling Prescott* (New York: Houghton Mifflin, 1904), pp. 230–231.

17. George Ticknor, *The Life of William Hickling Prescott* (Boston: Ticknor & Fields, 1864), p. 2.

Chapter 11

1. C. Harvey Gardiner, ed., *The Literary Memoranda of William Hickling Prescott* (Norman: University of Oklahoma Press, 1961), vol. 2, p. 150.

2. C. Harvey Gardiner, *William Hickling Prescott: A Biography* (Austin: University of Texas Press, 1969), p. 351.

3. George Ticknor, *The Life of William Hickling Prescott* (New York: Fred DeFau & Co., 1912), p. 400.

4. Clara Louisa Penney, ed., *Prescott: Unpublished Letters to Gayangos* (New York: Hispanic Society of America, 1927), pp. 140–141.

5. C. Harvey Gardiner, *William Hickling Prescott: A Biography* (Austin: University of Texas Press, 1969), p. 351.

6. C. Harvey Gardiner, ed., *The Papers of William Hickling Prescott* (Urbana: University of Illinois Press, 1964), p. 401.

7. George Ticknor, *The Life of William Hickling Prescott* (Boston: Ticknor & Fields, 1864), p. 443.

8. Samuel Eliot, "William H. Prescott," *New England Magazine* IX, no. 4 (December 1893), p. 525.

9. Rollo Ogden, *American Men of Letters—William Hickling Prescott* (New York: Houghton Mifflin, 1904), p. 200.

10. Thurston Peck, *William Hickling Prescott* (New York: Greenwood Press, 1969), p. 87.

11. Emily Morison Beck, ed., *Sailor Historian: The Best of Samuel Eliot Morison* (Boston: Houghton Mifflin, 1977), p. 352.

12. Clara Louisa Penney, ed., *George Ticknor Letters to Pascual de Gayangos* (New York: Hispanic Society of America, 1927), pp. 287–288.

Bibliography

Aguilar-Moreno, Manuel. *Life in the Aztec World.* New York: Oxford University Press, 2006.
Bacon, Edwin M. *Rambles Around Old Boston.* Boston: Little, Brown, 1914.
Beck, Emily Morison, ed. *Sailor Historian: The Best of Samuel Eliot Morison.* Boston: Houghton Mifflin, 1977.
Bernand, Carmen. *The Incas: People of the Sun.* London: Harry N. Abrams, 1994.
Boubon, Fabio. *The Lost Cities of the Mayas: The Life, Art, and Discoveries of Frederick Catherwood.* Vercelli, Italy: Edizioni White Star, 1999.
Calderón de la Barca, Frances. *Life in Mexico.* Garden City: Doubleday, 1954.
Ceram, C.W. *Gods, Graves, and Scholars.* New York: Alfred A. Knopf, 1967
_____. *The March of Archaeology.* New York: Alfred A. Knopf, 1976.
Charvat, William, and Michael Kraus. *William Hickling Prescott.* New York: American Book Company, 1943.
Cline, Howard F., C. Harvey Gardiner, and Charles Gibson, eds. *William Hickling Prescott, A Memorial.* Durham: Duke University Press, 1959.
The Correspondence of William Hickling Prescott. Transcribed and edited by Roger Wolcott. Boston: Riverside Press, 1925.
Eliot, Samuel. "William H. Prescott." *New England Magazine* IX, no. 4 (December 1893), 515–529.
Fagen, Brian M. *The Adventure of Archaeology.* Washington, D.C.: National Geographic Society, 1985.
_____. *The Aztecs.* New York: W.H. Freeman and Company, 1984.
_____. *Kingdoms of Gold, Kingdoms of Jade. The Americas Before Columbus.* London: Thames and Hudson, 1991.

Gardiner, Harvey C. *Prescott and His Publishers.* Carbondale: Southern Illinois University Press, 1959.
_____. *William Hickling Prescott: A Biography.* Austin: University of Texas Press, 1969.
_____. *William Hickling Prescott: An Annotated Bibliography of Published Works.* Washington, D.C.: Library of Congress, 1959.
Gardiner, C. Harvey, ed. *The Literary Memoranda of William Hickling Prescott.* Norman: University of Oklahoma Press, 1961.
_____, ed. *The Papers of William Hickling Prescott.* Urbana: University of Illinois Press, 1964.
Gettman, Royal A. *A Victorian Publisher: A Study of the Bentley Papers.* Cambridge: Cambridge University Press, 1960.
Hagen, Victor Wolfgang von. *The Ancient Sun Kingdoms of the Americas.* Cleveland: World, 1961.
_____. *The Aztec: Man and Tribe.* New York: The New American Library, 1961.
_____. *Frederick Catherwood, archt.* New York: Oxford University Press, 1950.
_____. *Maya Explorer: John Lloyd Stephens and the Lost Cities of Central America and Yucatan.* San Francisco: Chronicle Books, 1990.
_____. *Search for the Maya: The Story of Stephens and Catherwood.* Westmead, England: Saxon House, 1973.
Hillard, George S. *Homes of American Authors.* New York: G.P. Putnam, 1852.
_____. *Life, Letters, and Journals of George Ticknor.* New York: Houghton Mifflin, 1909.
_____. *Little Journeys to the Homes of*

American Authors. New York: G. P. Putnam, 1901.

Innes, Hammond. *The Conquistadors.* New York: Alfred A. Knopf, 1969.

Irving, Pierre Munroe. *The Life and Letters of Washington Irving, Vol III.* New York: G. P. Putnam, 1883.

Jackson, James. *Another Letter to a Young Physician: To Which Are Appended Other Medical Papers.* Boston: Ticknor & Fields, 1861.

Meyer, Karl E. *Teotihuacán: First City in the Americas.* New York: News Week Book Division, 1973.

Morison, Samuel Eliot. *William Hickling Prescott 1796–1859.* Boston: Massachusetts Historical Society, 1958.

National Geographic, editors of. *Lost Empires: Living Tribes.* Washington, D.C.: National Geographic Society, 1982.

Nevins, Allan, ed. *The Diary of Philip Hone 1828–1851.* New York: Dodd, Mead, 1927.

The New Encyclopædia Britannica. 23 vols. Chicago: Encyclopædia Britannica, 1972.

_____. 29 vols. Chicago: Encyclopædia Britannica, 1990.

Ogden, Rollo. *American Men of Letters—William Hickling Prescott.* New York: Houghton Mifflin, 1904.

The Oxford Encyclopedia of Mesoamerican Cultures. Davíd Carrasco, editor in chief. New York: Oxford University Press, 2001.

Peck, Thurston. *William Hickling Prescott.* New York: Greenwood Press, 1969.

Penney, Clara Louisa, ed. *George Ticknor Letters to Pascual de Gayangos.* New York: Hispanic Society of America, 1927.

_____, ed. *Prescott: Unpublished Letters to Gayangos.* New York: Hispanic Society of America, 1927.

Prescott, William H. *Biographical and Critical Miscellanies.* New York: Fred De Fau & Co., 1912.

_____. *History of the Conquest of Mexico.* New York: The Modern Library, 1953.

_____. *History of the Conquest of Mexico.* New York: Fred DeFau & Co., 1912.

_____. *History of the Conquest of Peru.* New York: The Modern Library, 1953.

_____. *History of the Reign of the Emperor Charles the Fifth.* New York: Fred DeFau & Co., 1912.

_____. *History of the Reign of Ferdinand and Isabella, the Catholic.* New York: Fred DeFau & Co., 1912.

_____. *History of the Reign of Philip the Second, King of Spain.* New York: Fred DeFau & Co., 1912.

Prescott, M. D., William. *The Prescott Memorial: or a Genealogical Memoir of the Prescott Families in America.* Boston: Henry W. Dutton & Son, 1870.

Proceedings of the Massachusetts Historical Society in Respect to The Memory of William H. Prescott. Boston: Massachusetts Historical Society, 1859.

Reader's Digest, editors of. *Mysteries of the Ancient Americas: The New World Before Columbus.* Pleasantville, NY: Reader's Digest, 1986.

Story, William W. *The Life and Letters of Joseph Story.* London: John Chapman, 1851.

Ticknor, George. *The Life of William Hickling Prescott.* New York: Fred DeFau & Co., 1912.

_____. *The Life of William Hickling Prescott.* Cambridge: Cambridge University Press, 1864.

_____. *Papers discussing the comparative merits of Prescott's and Wilson's Histories, pro and con., as laid before the Massachusetts Historical Society.* Boston: Massachusetts Historical Society, 1861.

Tompkins, Peter. *Mysteries of the Mexican Pyramids.* New York: Harper & Row, 1976.

Thomson, Helen. *Murder at Harvard.* Boston: Houghton Mifflin, 1971.

Udall, Stewart L. *Majestic Journey: Coronado's Inland Empire.* Santa Fe: Museum of New Mexico Press, 1987.

Index

Abbotsford 193
Abbott, Lawrence 208
Acosta, José de 117, 155
Adams, John 41
Adams, John Quincy 26, 41, 74, 149, 188
Adams, Sir William 40, 41, 44, 48, 133
Adirondack 151
Aiken, Lucy 84
Alamán, Don Lucas 109, 218
Albany 152, 171
Albert, Prince 137, 190, 195
Alison, Archibald 189
Allen, Dr. John 100
Amadis de Gaula 25, 26, 63, 145
American Ethnological Society 134, 135
American Stationers' Company 95, 96, 97, 103
Ames, Joseph 149
Amory, Thomas Coffin 26, 55
Amory, William 26, 55, 79, 91, 170, 188, 216
Amsterdam 193
The Antiquities of Mexico 7, 109, 110, 111, 117
Antwerp 193
Appleton, William 162, 186
Argyll, Duke of 195
Ascham, Roger 59
Ashburton, Lord 188
Aspinwall, Col. Thomas 41, 90, 91, 92, 93, 120, 140, 141, 159, 171, 201
Atlantic Monthly 10, 213
Atwater, Caleb 135
Auburn 151, 152
Aurelius, Marcus 69
Austria 179
Azores 3, 21, 35, 36, 37, 42, 51, 150, 151, 182, 186

Babington, Lord Thomas 189
Baltimore 73, 74, 75
Bancroft, George 88, 92, 96, 149, 160, 167, 168, 188
Barante, Amable 84

Barbados 13
Barcia, Andrés Gonzalez 110
Baring Brothers & Company 80, 202
Barings Bank 107
Bartlett, John R. 135, 136
Belgium 178, 192, 193, 195
Belize 125
Bentley, Richard 93, 95, 99, 102, 120, 140, 141, 159, 160, 171, 188, 191, 192, 196, 197, 200, 202, 204, 206, 217
Berlin 153
Biographical and Critical Miscellanies (Critical and Historical Essays) (Prescott) 7, 159, 160, 161
Boccaccio, Giovanni 61
Bologna 45
Boston 1, 3, 5, 16, 23, 25, 38, 45, 47, 49, 50, 60, 73, 74, 75, 76, 77, 96, 109, 121, 128, 129, 133, 134, 138, 149, 150, 152, 164, 167, 168, 180, 182, 184, 187, 188, 219, 221
Boston Asylum for Indigent Boys 61
Boston Athenaeum 11, 25, 26, 61, 75, 95, 110, 139
Boturini, Lorenzo 111
Bouterwek, Friedrich 63
Bowditch, Nathaniel 20
Breed's Hill *see* Bunker Hill
Brevoort, Henry 134
Bridgeman, Laura Dewey 86
British Museum 42, 108, 178
Brooks, Preston 167
Brooks, Van Wyck 6
Brown, Charles Brockden 87, 88, 160
Browne, Sir Thomas 59
Brummell, Beau 123
Brussels 192, 193
Buckingham Palace 190
Buffalo 152
Bulfinch, Thomas 28, 197
Bullock, William 117, 25, 55, 117
Bulwer, Sir Henry 188
Bunker Hill 1, 18, 19, 24, 121
Bustamante, Carlos de 109

237

238 INDEX

Butler, Andrew P. 167
Butler, Joseph 78
Byron, Lord 123

Cabot, Samuel 128, 129, 130
Calderón de la Barca, Angel 103, 104, 109, 120, 121, 124, 128, 180
Calderón de la Barca, Fanny 7, 101, 109, 110, 122, 124, 127, 143, 144, 156, 160, 166, 168
Calhoun John C. 73
Camaldoli, Count 108
Camargo, Diego 117
Cambridge 49, 182, 183, 185
Canada 87, 151, 152
Carey, Henry 134
Carlisle, Lord 190, 195
Carroll, Charles 74
Carter, Robert (secretary) 172, 175, 181, 222
Carvajal, Luis del Mármol 80
Casas, Bartolomé de las 118, 210, 211
Castle Howard 195, 196
Catherwood, Frederick 11, 124, 125, 126, 128, 129, 135, 136, 137, 138, 143, 146, 152, 153, 210, 211
Catskills 151, 171
Cervantes, Miguel de 63, 160
Charles V 46, 65, 106, 193, 205, 206, 207, 208
Chichen Itza 129
Cicero 59, 69
Circourt, Count Adolphe de 99, 108
Clavijero, Francisco Xavier 111
Clay, Henry 74, 94
Clemencin, Don Diego 84
Club 54, 59, 70, 84, 88, 91, 95
Cogolludo, Lopez de 128
Cogswell, Joseph G. 113, 145
Collins, Dr. John 34
Columbus, Christopher 88, 113, 114, 116
Compans, Henro Ternaux 108, 177
Conde, José Antonio 69, 85
Cooper, Sir Astley 40
Cooper, James Fenimore 41, 91
Copán 126
Copp's Hill 18, 187
Cortés, Hernán 100, 106, 107, 109, 113, 115, 116, 118, 130, 132, 134, 141, 143, 144, 145, 146, 147, 172, 177, 203, 210, 211, 212
Crossed Swords 70, 164
Cuba 127

Dabney, Charles 182
Dane, Nathan 19
Dante, Alighieri 61
Dartmouth College 25
Dexter, Franklin 2, 28, 53, 56, 61, 158, 185, 212
Dexter, Mary 220

Dexter, Samuel 56
Diaz del Castillo, Bernal 113, 115, 117, 118, 211, 212
Dickens, Charles 86, 94, 140, 141, 144
Dickinson (printer) 90, 96
Disraeli, Benjamin 189
Drake, Daniel 135
Dunham, Samuel Astley 176

Eberty, Dr. H. 142
Edgeworth, Maria 72, 94
Edinburgh Review 76, 99, 100, 144, 147
Egypt 123, 124, 125
Eliot, Samuel 56, 197
Elliott, Dr. Samuel Mackenzie 133, 134, 167, 168
Ellis, Rev. Rufus 221
England 9, 13, 21, 24, 35, 38, 39, 48, 68, 71, 90, 91, 101, 136, 147, 172, 188, 189, 195, 203
English, James Lloyd (secretary) 70, 71, 77, 81
Ercilla, Alonso de 66
Everett, Alexander 67
Everett, Edward 47, 59, 67, 131, 137, 141, 144, 160, 179, 187, 188, 206

Fare, Dr. Richard 40
Farrar, John 28
Fauriel, Charles 99
Fay, Theodore Sedgwick 153
Female Asylum 53, 61
Ferdinand, King of Spain 66, 67, 68, 69, 72, 79, 81, 84, 85, 88, 90, 97, 101, 108, 164, 203
Fernandez, Diego 155
Ferreras, Juan de 69
Fisher, Dr. John Dix 85
Florence 45, 46, 47, 191, 204
Folsom, Charles 2, 28, 95, 139, 171, 202, 203, 216
Folsom, Wells, & Thurston of Cambridge 95, 96, 103, 171
Ford, Richard 102, 190, 192, 217
France 9, 44, 45, 47, 48, 68, 74, 79, 101, 125, 134, 180
Franklin, Benjamin 19, 91, 120
French Institute 44, 149, 150
Friedrichstahl, Emanuel von 128
Frisbie, Levi 27, 28

Gallatin, Albert 44, 134, 135, 155, 210
Gallaudet, Rev. Thomas Hopkins 86
Gama, Antonio Leon y 111
Gamboa, Pedro Sarmiento de 155
Gardiner, Rev. John S. 24, 57
Gardiner, William 2, 24, 25, 29, 31, 32, 38, 51, 53, 67, 92, 98, 158, 216
Gayangos, Pascual de 100, 101, 102, 107, 108, 109, 120, 141, 146, 153, 156, 164,

165, 169, 176, 177, 178, 179, 192, 193, 203, 206, 219, 222, 223
Genoa 45, 47
George III 42
George IV 41
Germany 9, 47, 68, 94, 125, 147
Gibbon, Edward 78
Gladstone, William 189
Gloucester 49
Gonzalez, Tomás 104
Gotha 153, 179
Gray, John Chipman 44, 45, 46, 47, 48
Greece 125, 128
Greenough, Richard S. 149
Greenwood, Francis William Pitt 28, 98
Griffen, George 134
Groton 15, 16, 17
Guatemala 123, 126, 211, 212

Hallam, Henry 69, 84, 94, 141, 189, 192
Halleck, Fitz-Greene 41, 91
Hamilton, John C. 134
Harper Brothers 136, 138, 139, 140, 142, 159, 160, 171, 200, 201
Harvard 1, 2, 3, 16, 19, 23, 27, 28, 32, 33, 41, 45, 47, 53, 62, 67, 70, 81, 88, 90, 91, 95, 98, 107, 128, 133, 134, 149, 150, 156, 181, 182, 183, 186, 187, 196, 198
Hawthorne, Nathaniel 20, 87, 180
Herodotus 83, 118
Herrera, Antonio de 113, 117, 118
Hickling, Amelia (aunt of William Hickling) 37, 38
Hickling, Harriet (aunt of William Hickling) 37, 38, 182, 186, 187
Hickling, Thomas (maternal grandfather of William Hickling) 3, 21, 35, 36, 37, 38, 39
Higginson, Mehitable 22
Hilliard, Gray & Company 95
Historical Society of Massachusetts 164
History of the Conquest of Mexico (Prescott) 7, 11, 95, 106, 115, 120, 126, 130, 137, 139, 140, 141, 142, 143, 145, 153, 157, 170, 171, 177, 218
History of the Conquest of Peru (Prescott) 7, 11, 106, 152, 153, 155, 156, 159, 163, 166, 168, 169, 170, 171, 172
History of the Reign of Charles the Fifth (Prescott) 207, 208
History of the Reign of Ferdinand and Isabella, the Catholic (Prescott) 6, 9, 29, 68, 82, 85, 88, 89, 90, 91, 95, 96, 97, 98, 99, 100, 101, 102, 103, 104, 105, 106, 113, 114, 119, 120, 136, 137, 138, 139, 140, 141, 142, 161, 169, 190, 191, 198, 201, 203, 207
History of the Reign of Philip the Second, King of Spain (Prescott) 4, 8, 174, 179, 180, 185, 199, 200, 202, 203, 204, 205, 207, 208, 213, 216, 217, 218

Holland, Lady 141
Holland, Lord 100
Honduras 211
Hone, Philip 134
Howe, Samuel Gridley 85, 86, 119
Hudson Valley 87, 151, 171
Humboldt, Alexander von 110, 112, 117, 123, 131, 135, 142, 146, 147, 150, 153, 158, 159, 179, 205
Hume, David 78

Irving, Pierre 114, 115
Irving, Washington 12, 41, 43, 85, 91, 99, 102, 113, 114, 115, 116, 131, 133, 137, 143, 155, 160, 164, 170, 171, 188
Isabella, Queen of Spain 66, 67, 68, 69, 72, 79, 81, 84, 85, 88, 90, 96, 98, 99, 108, 164, 203
Italy 45, 48, 68, 125, 134
Ixtlilxochitl, Fernando de Alva 111, 117

Jackson, Dr. James 30, 34, 35, 133, 166, 209, 213, 214, 215, 221
Jamaica Plain 52, 119

King Philip's War 15
Kingsborough, Lord (Edward King) 7, 109, 110, 111, 117, 122, 123, 128, 136
Kirk, John Foster (secretary) 175, 188, 192, 200, 202, 211, 219, 220, 222, 223
Kirkland, Rev. John Thornton 27
Knapp, Jacob 21, 22
Koch, Christoph Wilhelm 69

Lafayette, Marquis de 45
Lake Champlain 87
Lake George 87
Lake Ontario 87
Lancaster 14, 15
Landsdowne, Lord 195
Larryoya, Pedro Sabau y 104
Lawrence, Abbott 189, 198
Lawrence, James 189, 198, 216
Lembke, Friedrich Wilhelm 106, 108, 177, 178
Linzee, Hannah (mother of Susan Prescott) 55, 56, 79
Linzee, Capt. John (grandfather of Susan Prescott) 55, 164
Little, Brown & Company 103, 119, 137, 138, 139, 140, 144
Littlefield, Ephraim 183, 184, 186
Liverpool 49, 76, 188, 189, 196
Livy 46, 59, 83
London 15, 21, 40, 41, 42, 44, 48, 49, 74, 76, 80, 91, 107, 120, 125, 133, 137, 140, 143, 176, 177, 178, 189, 192, 193, 202, 217
London Tower 41, 138
Longfellow, Henry Wadsworth 91, 145, 167, 221

Longman & Company 93, 141
Lunt, George (secretary) 67
Lyell, Sir Charles 94, 189, 199
Lyell, Lady Mary 173, 189, 190, 205, 219

Mabley, Abbé Gabriel Bonnot de 83
Madison, James 79
Madrid 6, 68, 69, 70, 79, 101, 104, 106, 107, 120, 142, 177, 178
Mahon, Lady 190
Mandeville, Sir John 118
Mariana, Juan de 66
Massachusetts 1, 36, 79, 90, 168, 201
Massachusetts Historical Society 11, 120, 176, 211, 221, 222
Mason, John Y. 167
McCandlish, Mr. (secretary) 49
McKeon, Rev. Joseph 28
Metcalf, Keith, & Nichols 139, 202
Mexico 6, 7, 9, 10, 83, 101, 107, 108, 109, 110, 111, 112, 113, 116, 117, 118, 123, 124, 125, 126, 128, 129, 131, 135, 142, 143, 144, 145, 146, 155, 156, 166, 172, 177, 209, 210, 212
Middleton, Arthur 2, 27, 28, 104, 106, 107, 108, 177
Middleton, Conyers 78
Mignet, François M. 178
Mignot, Abbé 69
Milan 45, 46
Milburn, Rev. William H. 220
Milman, Henry Hart 94, 144, 189
Milton, John 49, 59, 71
Molière 61, 105, 106, 160
Montesinos, Fernando de 155
Montezuma 115, 132, 134
Montreal 87
Morgan, Lewis Henry 212
Morison, Samuel Eliot 9, 10, 197
Morpeth, Lord 141, 180
Morris, Gouveneur 91
Morton, Dr. Samuel 135
Motley, John Lothrop 170, 171, 204
Motolinia, Fray Toribio de Benavente 111, 117
Mount Monadnock 27, 77, 170
Mount Vernon 74
Muñoz, Juan Bautista 107, 111, 153
Murray, John 92, 141, 176, 192

Napier, Macvey 99
Naples 46, 47
Napoleon 123, 124
Navarette, Martin Fernández de 99, 108, 120, 150
New Hampshire 15, 27, 86
New York City 73, 74, 103, 104, 121, 126, 126, 128, 129, 131, 133, 134, 142, 149, 166, 167, 171, 188, 196, 219, 220
New York Historical Society 120, 135, 136

Newton, Sir Isaac 49
Niagara Falls 87, 151, 152, 153, 197
Nissitssit, River 27
noctograph 5, 6, 43, 44, 58, 60, 71, 72, 73, 74, 82, 84, 169, 176
North American Review 5, 12, 48, 52, 53, 59, 60, 62, 85, 91, 98, 105, 107, 159, 160, 187, 203, 212

Otis, Edward B. (secretary) 149, 164
Oviedo, Gonzalo Fernández de Oviedo 118
Oxford 49, 191

Palenque 122, 123, 124, 126
Paris 44, 45, 107, 122, 123, 124, 177, 178, 192
Parker, Hamilton (secretary) 67, 70
Parkman, Elizabeth 181, 184
Parkman, Francis 196, 197
Parkman, Dr. George 11, 181, 182, 183, 184, 185, 186, 187, 196
Parsons, Theophilus 53, 56, 209
Peck, Harry Thurston 10, 11
Perkins School for the Blind 85, 86, 87, 118
Peru 7, 10, 83, 152, 153, 155, 156, 173
Petrarch, Francesco 47, 61
Philadelphia 142, 166
Philip II, King of Spain 105, 106, 173, 176, 177, 178, 179, 193, 200, 203, 206, 215, 216
Phillips, Sir Thomas 141, 178
Phillips, Sampson & Company 201, 206, 208, 213, 217
Pickering, John 92, 98, 135, 176
Pickering, Timothy 20
Pizarro, Francisco 100, 148, 153, 154, 203
Plato 69
Pliny 46
Poe, Edgar Allan 87
Poinsett, Joel Roberts 110
Polk, James K. 167, 188
Ponce, Don Vargas y 107, 111
Ponte, Signor Lorenzo de Ponte 60
Pope Pius VII 46
Porcellian Club 28, 53
Portugal 68
Prescott, Abigail (grandmother of William Hickling) 19, 26, 61
Prescott, Augusta Peabody Josephine (daughter-in-law) 198, 216, 219
Prescott, Benjamin (son of Jonas) 15
Prescott, Catherine (Kitty—daughter of William Hickling) 62, 75, 77, 78, 221
Prescott, Catherine Elizabeth (sister of William Hickling) 21, 28, 51, 52, 55, 220
Prescott, Catherine Greene Hickling (mother of William Hickling) 3, 21, 22, 23, 26, 32, 35, 39, 42, 50, 53, 55, 61, 104, 121, 150, 157, 162, 175, 182, 183, 185, 186, 198, 221

Prescott, Edward Goldsborough (brother of William Hickling) 21, 24, 51, 65, 87, 150, 151
Prescott, Elizabeth (daughter of William Hickling) 75, 151, 171, 187, 198
Prescott, James (son of Benjamin) 15, 16
Prescott, John (first emigrant of the family) 13, 14, 15
Prescott, Jonas (son of John and Mary) 15
Prescott, Mary (wife of John) 13, 14, 15
Prescott, Oliver (oldest son of Oliver) 16, 18
Prescott, Oliver (youngest son of Benjamin) 16
Prescott, Susan (wife of William Hickling) 26, 55, 56, 57, 62, 67, 70, 72, 75, 133, 162, 164, 167, 175, 186, 188, 198, 205, 213, 219, 220
Prescott, William (father of William Hickling) 1, 3, 19, 20, 21, 22, 23, 24, 26, 32, 35, 50, 51, 52, 53, 55, 59, 60, 61, 67, 70, 75, 76, 79, 88, 89, 97, 121, 142, 150, 157, 158, 161, 162, 164, 165, 221
Prescott, Col. William (grandfather of William Hickling) 1, 16, 17, 18, 19, 55, 70, 121, 162
Prescott, William Amory (son of William Hickling) 79, 151, 171, 187, 216, 220
Prescott, William Gardiner (son of William Hickling) 67, 134, 151, 156, 157, 184, 188, 192, 195, 198, 216
Prescott, William Hickling: academic and literary awards 120, 121, 149, 173, 176, 191, 197, 208; apoplexy 213, 214, 222; Azores 3, 35–39; Belgium 192; Boston 23, 26, 30, 33, 50, 56, 61, 70, 90, 104, 157, 161, 162, 163, 165, 175, 202; Canada 87, 151–152; England 3, 39–44, 48–49, 188–192, 193–196; essays 8, 12, 48, 59, 60, 62, 85, 86, 144, 159; France 3, 44–45, 47–48, 192; horse riding 52, 71, 72, 82, 104, 119, 162, 170, 175; Italy 3, 45–47; journal entries 5, 57, 58, 59, 60, 61, 65, 66, 68, 69, 71, 73, 78, 82, 83, 84, 85, 87, 89, 102, 104, 106, 111, 112, 115, 116, 118, 119, 124, 131, 133, 141, 142, 148, 149, 151, 156, 157, 159, 160, 162, 163, 165, 168, 169, 174, 175, 176, 177, 187, 199, 200, 201, 202, 215, 218; letter to Arthur Middleton 108; letter to Catherine Elizabeth Prescott (sister) 37; letter to Charles Folsom 203; letter to Charles Sumner 167; letter to Frederick Catherwood 153; letter to Friedrich Wilhelm Lembke 106; letter to George Ellis 70; letter to George Routledge 218; letter to Israel Putnam 162; letter to Jared Sparks 92; letter to Lord Morpeth 180; letter to Obadiah Rich 80; letter to Phillips, Sampson& Company 208; letter to Theophilus Parsons 56; letter to Tomás Gonzalez 104; letter to William Amory Prescott 220; letters to Angel Calderón de la Barca 128, 180; letters to Catherine Greene Hickling Prescott (mother) 41, 43, 44, 45; letters to Edward Everett 131, 136, 160; letters to Fanny Calderon de la Barca 122, 168; letters to father 28, 39, 41, 43, 44, 45; letters to George Bancroft 63, 88, 168; letters to George Ticknor 63, 162, 191, 208; letters to John Lloyd Stephens 126, 127, 130; letters to Lady Mary Lyell 173, 205, 219; letters to Pascual de Gayangos 100, 120, 146, 153, 156, 164, 165, 169, 176, 206, 219; letters to Richard Bentley 140, 191, 196, 200, 204, 207; letters to Susan Prescott 74, 75, 167, 190, 192, 193, 195; letters to William Gardiner Prescott 184, 185; Lynn Bay 199, 201; Nahant 75, 76, 77, 87, 104, 152, 153, 157, 168, 171, 197, 199, 201; Netherlands 192; New York City 131, 133–134, 149, 167, 171; New York (upstate) 87, 151–152, 171, 197; Pepperell 16, 19, 21, 26, 27, 74, 76, 77, 104, 141, 157, 162, 169, 197, 202, 218, 219; powers of recall 1, 4, 6, 24, 31, 71, 81, 82, 84, 137, 215; rheumatism 3, 4, 34, 35, 36, 39, 40, 51, 52, 67, 72, 76, 151, 152, 200, 209; Salem 20, 23, 215; Scotland 193–196; vision impairment 2, 3, 4, 30, 31, 34, 35, 36, 37, 38, 39, 40, 44, 47, 48, 52, 67, 68, 70, 76, 81, 88, 116, 117, 120, 133, 139, 167, 168, 172, 173, 174, 175, 187, 215; walks 38, 72, 77, 82, 162, 199, 220; Washington D.C. 73–75, 166–167, 187–188

Quarterly Review 76, 102, 144, 156, 192
Quebec 87, 121

Ramirez, Don José F. 218
Ranke, Leopold von 176, 179
Raumer, Friedrich von 99, 142, 150
Rich, James 79, 106, 110, 141
Rich, Obadiah 79, 80, 91, 106, 107, 110, 114
Robertson, William 8, 69, 107, 108, 115, 126, 127, 155, 176, 205, 206, 207, 208, 210
Robinson, Dr. Edward 135
Rochester 151, 152, 209
Rogers, Samuel 141, 189
Rome 45, 46, 47, 55, 65
Roscoe, William 84
Routledge, George 207, 217, 218
Royal Academy of History in Madrid 107, 108, 120
Russell, Lord John 188

Sahagun, Bernardino de 111, 117
Saint Lawrence River 87

Saint Michael's island *see* Azores
Saint Paul's Church 158, 198, 221
Saint Peter's Basilica 46
Salem 1, 6, 20, 21, 22, 23, 45, 92, 151, 180, 215
Sarmiento, Don Juan 152
Schenectady 152
Schoolcraft, Henry R. 135
Scotland 38, 48
Scott, Sir Walter 8, 38, 63, 72, 76, 160, 164, 189, 193, 194
Scott, Gen. Winfield 177
Sears, David 53, 162
Seville 74, 101, 107
Shaw, Robert Gould 182, 183, 184
Sibley, John Langdon 95, 96
Simancas 104, 105, 106, 178, 206
Simonds, Henry (secretary) 88
Sismondi, Jean Charles Leonard de 63, 100
Smith, Sydney 99
Sohier, Edward 185, 186
Solís, Don Antonio de 63, 66, 107, 113
Southey, Robert 89, 93
Spain 1, 3, 4, 9, 10, 66, 68, 71, 74, 79, 100, 104, 106, 109, 114, 124, 131, 143, 171, 178, 180, 192, 193, 203
Spanish Academy 111
Sparks, Jared 53, 76, 87, 88, 91, 92, 93, 95, 96, 98, 149, 186, 196
Spooner, William Jones 28
Staël, Madame de 48
Stephens, John Lloyd 11, 41, 117, 124, 125, 126, 127, 128, 129, 130, 135, 136, 137, 138, 143, 146, 147, 152, 153, 210, 211
stereotype 92, 95, 103, 138, 139, 140, 171, 201, 202, 216, 223
Stirling, William 190, 192, 206
Story, Joseph 23
Stowe, Harriet Beecher 197
Sturgis, Russell 202
Sumner, Charles 114, 166, 167, 168, 221
Sumner, George 114
Sydney, Sir Philip 59

Tacitus 59, 83
Taylor, Zachary 188
Temple, Harry 189
Tenochtitlán 109, 110, 116, 146, 210
Teotihuacan 110, 112, 131
Thackery, William Makepeace 164
Thierry, Augustin 80, 84, 100
Thoreau, Henry David 10
Thucydides 6, 83
Ticknor, George 2, 3, 11, 25, 26, 32, 47, 48, 56, 62, 63, 64, 73, 74, 75, 80, 90, 91, 95, 99, 100, 105, 106, 135, 139, 142, 160, 161, 162, 167, 176, 179, 191, 196, 203, 206, 208, 211, 214, 216, 221, 222, 223
Torquemada, Juan de 111, 117
Trentham Hall 194, 195
Tukey, Marshal Francis 182, 184
Tytler, Patrick Fraser 100, 141

Uxmal 126

van Buren, Martin 73, 110
Vaughn, Charles Richard 74
Vega, Garcilaso de la 152, 155
Venice 45
Verona 46
Vesuvius 47
Victoria, Queen 93, 137, 190, 195
Voltaire 69, 84, 115

Wainwright, the Rev. Jonathan 2, 28, 131, 133, 134
Waldeck, Jean Frédéric Maximilien 122, 123, 124, 127
Walker, Rev. James 9
Ward, Henry George 117
Ware, Arthur 28
Ware, George Frederick (secretary) 130, 172
Ware, Henry 27
Ware, John 2, 28
Washington, George 19, 74, 91, 133
Washington, D.C. 73, 166, 167, 187, 188
Watson, Robert 29, 69, 176
Webster, Daniel 73, 75, 100, 180, 185, 200
Webster, Prof. John 11, 181, 182, 183, 184, 185, 186, 187
Webster, Nathan 52, 58, 157, 188, 216
Wellesley, Arthur (Duke of Wellington) 190
West, Benjamin 42
West Point 171
Westminster Abbey 41, 42
Wilkinson, Sir John 135
Wilmer, Lambert 211, 212
Wilson, Robert Anderson 209, 210, 211, 212
Windsor Castle 41, 101
Withington, George R.M. 67
Wolf, Dr. Ferdinand 179
Wyeth, Jonas 183

Yucatan 122, 124, 126, 128, 129, 210, 211

Zuazo, Alonso de 117

www.ingramcontent.com/pod-product-compliance
Lightning Source LLC
Chambersburg PA
CBHW051219300426
44116CB00006B/632